HISTORIC CORPUS CHRISTI
A Sesquicentennial History

By Vivienne Heines

A publication of the Corpus Christi Chamber of Commerce

Historical Publishing Network

A division of Lammert Incorporated

San Antonio, Texas

ACKNOWLEDGMENTS

My efforts to research, write and illustrate the fascinating history of Corpus Christi would have been far more difficult without the assistance and support of the following people and institutions:

The Corpus Christi Chamber of Commerce, in particular Pam Arredondo, membership director, and Tom Niskala, president and CEO; Texas A&M University-Corpus Christi's Mary and Jeff Bell Library, especially Dr. Thomas H. Kreneck, head of the Special Collections & Archives Department, and staff members Grace Charles and Cecilia Venable; the resources of the local history room at the downtown branch of the Corpus Christi Public Library; and finally, the encouragement of my family, including my husband Andy, two sons, Zachary and Aaron, and daughter Tessa.

Thank you for making this book possible.

Vivienne Heines
Corpus Christi, Texas
September 2002

First Edition

Copyright © 2002 Historical Publishing Network

All rights reserved. No part of this book may be reproduced in any form or by any means, electronic or mechanical, including photocopying, without permission in writing from the publisher. All inquiries should be addressed to Historical Publishing Network, 8491 Leslie Road, San Antonio, Texas, 78254. Phone (210) 688-9006.

ISBN: 1-893619-29-X
Library of Congress Card Catalog Number: 2002112705

Historic Corpus Christi: An Sesquicentennial History

author:	Vivienne Heines
contributing writers for	
"sharing the heritage":	Scott Williams
	Marie Beth Jones

Historical Publishing Network

president:	Ron Lammert
vice president:	Barry Black
project representatives:	Roger Smith
	Pat Steele
	Rob Steidle
director of operations:	Charles A. Newton, III
administration:	Angela Lake
	Donna Mata
	Dee Steidle
graphic production:	Colin Hart

✧

Participants at an early twentieth century Mexican American wedding pose solemnly for the photographer. This photo is part of a collection from Rafael and Virginia C. Galvan, who were among the city's most prominent Hispanic citizens.

COURTESY OF THE RAFAEL SR., AND VIRGINIA REYES GALVAN FAMILY PAPERS, SPECIAL COLLECTIONS AND ARCHIVES, MARY AND JEFF BELL LIBRARY, TEXAS A&M UNIVERSITY-CORPUS CHRISTI.

CONTENTS

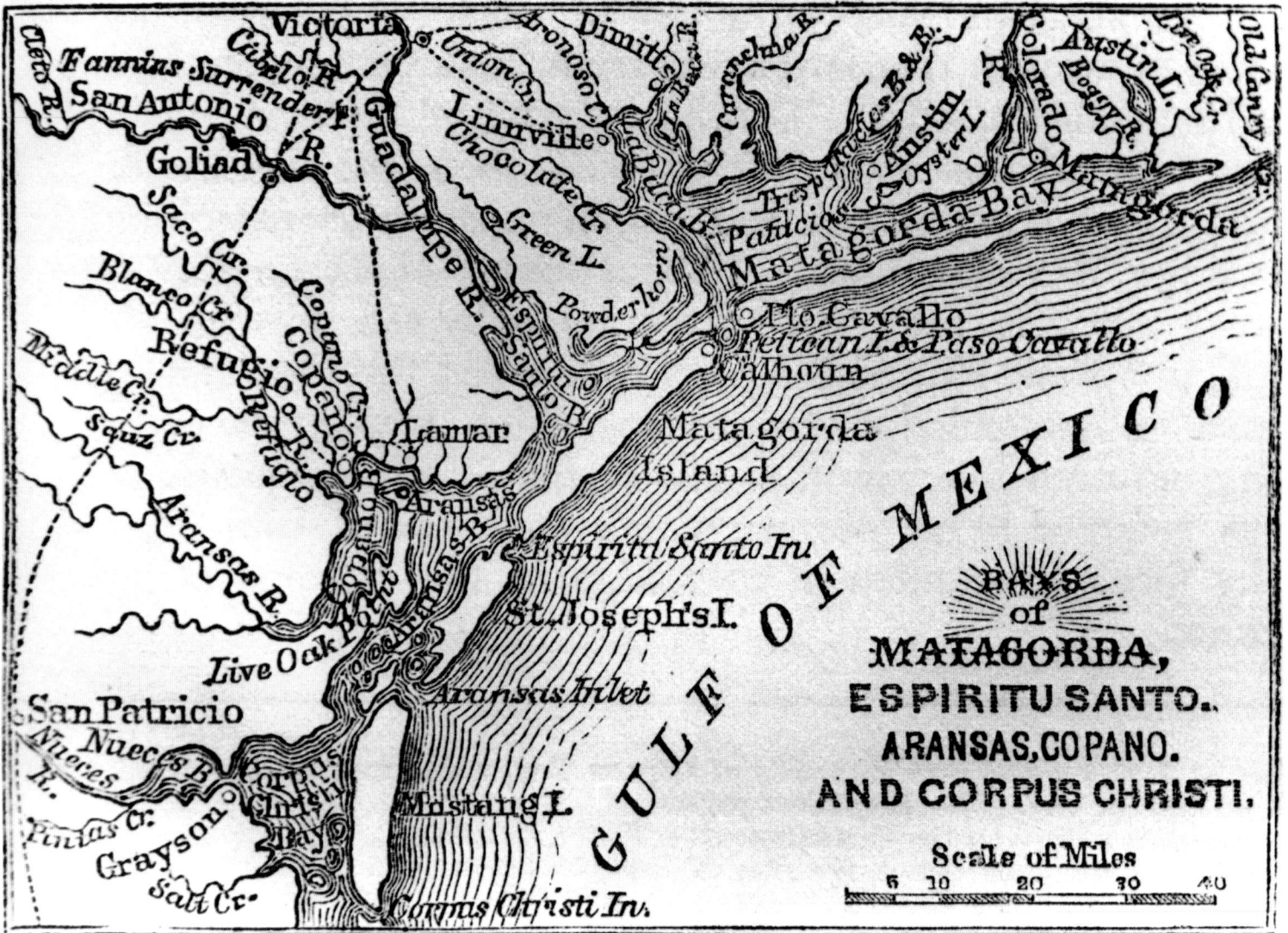

BAYS
of
MATAGORDA,
ESPIRITU SANTO.
ARANSAS, COPANO.
AND CORPUS CHRISTI.

Scale of Miles
5   10   20   30   40

Taming the Wilderness:
Explorers, Pirates, and Promoters

"Stories and legends abound. Tales of pirate gold buried near Corpus Christi Pass and the mouth of the Nueces flourish, and old Spanish coins have been found on the beaches of Padre Island. The basis of most of these legends, however, seems to be as tenuous as gossamer thread."
— from *City by the Sea: A History of Corpus Christi, Texas, 1519-1875*, by Eugenia Reynolds Briscoe.

Close your eyes and imagine, if you can, the Gulf coastline without cars, buildings, streets or streetlights. The thick landscape is dominated by mesquite and pecan trees, thick grasses and the silhouette of a raccoon or jackrabbit. The air is heavy, warm and humid, the distant sound of wind and waves whispers through day and night, and the sandy soil crunches beneath your feet. Herds of wild mustang and game, including buffalo, roam freely in the distance. Suddenly, you see a tall, majestic-looking man in the distance—muscular, fierce-looking and imposing.

The man is from the Karankawa Indian tribe, believed to be the earliest human residents of the Corpus Christi region. These Indians are known as much for their stature as for their much-debated ferocity. One author described them as the "cannibals of the coast," for their most memorable legacy today, alas, is their reported penchant for eating their enemies.

It is a most fearsome and romanticized historical vision of what is today believed to be an eminently respectable Native American coastal tribe. And like many legends, there may be some basis in truth. Some historians speculate that the tribe may have engaged in ritualistic cannibalism. Other historians point out they may have picked up the practice from the Europeans, who came to the area later and, in starving desperation, partook of the flesh of one of their dead settlers.

The Karankawas were the dominant Indian tribe in the Corpus Christi area. Other tribes that lived in the region included the Tonkawas, Comanches and Lipan-Apaches. The Karankawas' name means dog lovers, which refers to the fact that they kept canines. They were hunters who fed on buffalo meat, deer and bear, geese, ducks and turkey, as well as fish, berries, and nuts.

The Tonkawas were a tribe that lived near Corpus Christi in the early 1840s and were known for their superb horsemanship. The Comanches, the most well-known of the tribes in this area, were renowned for their boldness and courage. The Lipan-Apaches were nomadic hunters, who mostly pursued buffalo and deer.

These native tribes did not fare well when the Europeans arrived. Missionary efforts were often unsuccessful. Historians have noted that the Karankawas were among the first Texas Indians to greet the Franciscan missionaries to the region, but were not interested in being Christianized. They remained in conflict with the settlers to the region for decades, which likely discouraged the establishment of the Spanish mission system in the Corpus Christi Bay area.

Of the native tribes, the Karankawas probably survived the longest; they are believed to have existed on the coastline until 1858, when their tribe was exterminated in an attack by settlers after more than three centuries of conflict.

Clearly, the early environment in this coastal region was less than welcoming. New arrivals to the shoreline found there were both advantages and drawbacks to settling on the curving, half-moon shores of the Corpus Christi Bay. There was the heat, the humidity, the abundant wildlife, the rich grasslands, and the relative isolation—plus the isolation of the region and the menacing presence of hostile Indians, cannibalistic or not.

Still, they came—in search of new lands, wealth, and a passage through the continental land mass. Local historical legend attributes the discovery of Corpus Christi Bay to Spanish explorer Alonso Álvarez de Piñeda in 1519. Many believe that he was likely the first European to see Corpus Christi Bay.

✧

This reproduction of an 1840s map of the Texas coastal area shows Corpus Christi Bay and the Nueces River.

His arrival on these shores predated the Pilgrims landing at Plymouth Rock or the founding of Jamestown colony by a full century.

De Piñeda was inspired by tales of exploration and riches brought home by previous explorers, such as Hernán Cortés, who landed in Mexico and returned with tales of Aztec treasures. De Piñeda's ship traveled along the Gulf of Mexico shoreline, making frequent stops and charting all the waterways. According to tradition, he arrived at these waters on the Roman Catholic feast day of Corpus Christi, whence the name derives.

Other historians believe that the bulky Spanish galleons under de Pineda's command could not have crossed the sandbars that prevented entrance into Corpus Christi Bay at that time. Some credit Amerigo Vespucci, who sailed along the South Texas Coast in 1498, with the distinction of being the first European to sight the bay.

Other early arrivals included Álvar Nuñez Cabeza de Vaca, who was among a group of Spaniards shipwrecked on the Texas coast and captured by the Indian tribes. De Vaca and his fellow prisoners lived with the Indians for six years, finally escaping near Corpus Christi and later writing of his travails in such detail that modern historians have been able to identify the Corpus Christi region. Some historians believe that de Vaca was the first to

Left: Spanish explorer Alvar Nuñez Cabeza de Vaca's ship was wrecked along the Texas coast, and his crew captured by Indians. De Vaca and his men later managed to escape their captors near Corpus Christi.

Below: The writing on this slab of rock bears the name of Alonso Alvarez de Piñeda, a Spanish explorer who commanded an expedition along the Gulf of Mexico coastline in 1519. He and his men were the first to map the region, and he is also credited as one of the first Europeans to see Corpus Christi Bay.

enter the bay, particularly from his descriptions of seeing what he called the "Bay of Espiritu Santo" (possible Corpus Christi Bay) and what may have been the mouth of the Nueces River. The area was also possibly visited by Rene-Robert Cavelier, Sieur de la Salle, in 1683, who reportedly saw a 'Riviere d'or," or River of Gold, which could have been the Nueces River.

In those early days, the area was thick with native trees including the huisache, oak, mesquite, retama, pecan and Chinese tallow. There were many snakes, some poisonous, such as the rattlesnake and water moccasin, as well as lizards, turtles, frogs and toads. Birds were in abundance, including geese, ducks, sparrow, mockingbirds, roadrunners, and seagulls.

The region surrounding the city, Nueces County, was named by another Spanish explorer, Alonzo de León. The name "Nueces" means "nuts," and refers to the "Río de los Nueces" that de Leon described when he came to the area and found a river with an abundance of pecan trees on its banks.

It wasn't until 1746, however, that the first settlement was attempted in Corpus Christi. Don José de Escandón of Spain received a commission to settle the Gulf Coast region between Tampico, Mexico, and the San Antonio River. Escandón's assignment was conquer and colonize the area—before the French explorers could lay claim to it.

When his men reported that the Nueces River area was fertile, Escandón attempted to bring a band of settlers to what is Corpus Christi today. But a drought intervened and the settlers never made it to the original area and the bay "shaped like a horseshoe."

The first known official use of the name "Corpus Christi" for the area was in 1766, when it was printed on a Spanish map. The first permanent residents of the region were likely the Mexican ranchers, who migrated from the Rio Grande area with their herds and *vaqueros*.

In the 18th century, other settlements began to grow in the region. Among the most notable was Rancho Santa Petronila, a ranch owned by Blas María de la Garza Falcón and established in the 1760s south of Corpus Christi. By 1766, Falcón was reported to have "a goodly number of people, a stock of cattle, sheep and goats, and cornfields" at his ranch. During this time period, the Spanish government, in an effort to encourage colonization, was generous with land grants. Although one per family was granted, often several members of the same family would apply and receive adjoining grants, creating large tracts of land.

The entire Padre Island was granted to Padre Nicolás Ballí and his nephew Juan Ballí. Padre Ballí was a Catholic priest from Spain who sought a haven on the 112-mile long barrier island that was known by early navigators as "Isla Blanca" (White Island) for its white sand beach. The island became known as Isla del Padre, and the name was later simplified to the present-day Padre Island.

Padre Ballí established residence and constructed a mission on the island in the late 1700s. He had with him about 47 followers, as well as his nephew. He received the title to the island from King Charles VI of Spain in 1800. After Mexico obtained its independence from Spain in 1821, Padre Ballí and his nephew applied to the Mexican government for confirmation of their land grant, which was received in 1829. The family stayed on the island until 1884, when they were driven off by a severe storm.

The following description of the granting of Padre Island to Rafael Solís, brother-in-law of Padre Ballí, in 1828, gives insight into the formal legal procedures of the time. The alcalde, or mayor, of the village of Matamoros accompanied Solís to the property and, in the presence of witnesses, officially granted the title to him. "I the judge in the name of the free and sovereign state of Tamaulipas and in the presence of those cited above and of the others who were there present, took the aforesaid Rafael Solís by the hand, led him across the land, he took some earth and scattered it, he picked up a stick, he tore up the grass, he took some water and sprinkled the earth and performed other acts of possession and said in a loud voice: Gentlemen, all of you present are my witness that I have taken possession in conformity with law without opposition from a third party that may claim a better right."

Smugglers also came to these lush, semitropical shores, in part because of Spain's policy of forbidding trade with foreigners. That created a brisk smuggling market, and settlers could buy or trade for tobacco, sugar, and firearms on the shores of Corpus Christi Bay.

The region came under Mexican control as the district of Tampaulipas, when Mexico won its independence from Spain in 1821. Despite the Texas Revolution in 1836, the region remained technically a part of the district of Tampaulipas for another decade. As the area began to see settlements, a new type of visitor came to the shore. The legendary pirate Jean Lafitte is rumored to have passed through Corpus Christi Bay several times and some believe that he left a fortune in pirate's gold and treasure near the Corpus Christi Pass. The treasure has never been found, but old Spanish coins have been found on Padre Island.

Adventure, both real and legendary, are plentiful from the early days of the 258-mile waterfront border to Nueces County. Some of the stories seem destined to remain myths, such as the rumored existence of a silver mine within two days drive of the city. Other tales, of piratical derring-do and attack from hostile Indian tribes, are as factual as they are colorful.

Settlers were often in fear of hostile Indian attack from the Karankawa tribe as well as invading Comanches. It was a precarious existence for settlers to the coastal colony, but it was also the beginning of growth for this port on the horseshoe-shaped bay.

✧

Left: Spanish explorer Alonso Álvarez de Piñeda, who is credited with giving Corpus Christi its name, is immortalized in this eight-foot statue located at the Plaza de Piñeda, 2500 Agnes Street. Local legend has it that de Piñeda was the first European to arrive at Corpus Christi Bay.

Below: Padre Nicholas Ballí was a Catholic priest who established a home and church in the 1700s on what is known today as Padre Island.

THE NAPLES OF THE GULF

"It appears that Corpus Christi will grow into something grand, as a major military depot
is soon to arrive and a month ago Col. Kinney announced great festivities,
like horse racing and bullfights, for next May."
— November 2, 1851, letter from Maria Von Blucher to her parents in Germany, from Maria Von Blucher's
Corpus Christi: Letters from the South Texas Frontier, 1849-1879.

The earliest colonists to the Corpus Christi area were a hardy bunch, undeterred by the omnipresent threat of hostile Indians and the inhospitable climate and soil. Still, the first efforts to colonize the region were less than successful. The threat of Indian raids undoubtedly deterred many would-be settlers from the area, and land grants were sought for the area below the Rio Grande instead of along the Nueces River.

After several failed attempts, the first colony was established by two Irish merchants, James McGloin and John McMullen. In 1828, the two men obtained an *empresario* contract to establish a settlement of 200 families near the Nueces River. They set up San Patricio Colony, located about 25 miles northwest of what is now the city of Corpus Christi. As *empresarios*, the two merchants received a contract from the Mexican government to colonize an area in exchange for land.

The first 58 families arrived in October 1829, settling near the old mission of Our Lady of Refuge, Despite the difficulties in the wilderness, the colonists survived and established San Patricio de Hibernia a year later. Crops began to thrive, and the Irish settlers enjoyed the bounty of the wild game and fish. A Mexican census in 1834 reported that there were approximately 600 settlers in the San Patricio colony. The short period of peace was shattered during the war for Texas Independence, when the San Patricians joined the Texan cause and even fought at the Alamo.

Smuggling remained the main draw for many of those who came to the area. Spain had forbidden trade with foreigners, a ban that was maintained by Mexico. The result was a black market, where smugglers offered goods at prices lower than the Spanish-Texas prices. Tobacco, sugar and weapons were traded for silver and gold on the beach at Corpus Christi Bay. The smugglers' vessels were also well-suited to the bay, since their shallow draft allowed them to cross the sandbars near the mouth of the Nueces and anchor offshore the site of the present city of Corpus Christi.

It was trading that drew one of the most significant figures in Corpus Christi's history to the region. That was Henry L. Kinney, who arrived in either 1838 or 1839 with William P. Aubrey to establish a trading post overlooking the Corpus Christi Bay. This adventurer and entrepreneur established a *rancho* on the Corpus Christi Bay that was, for at least a decade following the Texas Revolution, the first Anglo-American settlement west of the Nueces River.

Kinney, described as both fearless and unscrupulous, would prove to be a key figure in the development of the city. The son of a Pennsylvania attorney, he was known for his magnetic personality as well as his astute ability as a trader. He was also famed for his courage in fighting the marauding Indian tribes and for his skilled horsemanship. One of his main contributions to the city was that he promoted it tirelessly to early settlers, helping to increase its population. He also was quick to envision its value to the state, touting Corpus Christi as an advantageous base for military operations in the property dispute between the United States and Mexico.

Kinney advertised Corpus Christi as "the Naples of the Gulf" in England, Germany and Ireland, describing the area as a beautiful horseshoe-shaped bay with the world's richest soil. The land was indeed inexpensive—Kinney had purchased more than 44,000 acres in 1842 for 16 cents an acre.

His efforts drew many settlers to the area who played vital roles in helping to shape the community's future. Among these were Felix A. von Blucher, a German immigrant who came to the frontier town of Corpus Christi with his wife Maria in 1849. Blucher, who became the county's first surveyor, made many early maps of the region that serve today as invaluable historical records.

✧

On November 15, 1849, the von Bluchers purchased eight acres for $1,000 and built this cottage, into which Maria von Blucher moved the rosewood piano she had brought with her from Germany.

COURTESY OF THE CHARLES F. H. VON BLUCHER FAMILY PAPERS, SPECIAL COLLECTIONS AND ARCHIVES, MARY AND JEFF BELL LIBRARY, TEXAS A&M UNIVERSITY-CORPUS CHRISTI.

His work as a surveyor was continued after his death in 1879 by his son, Charles, and later his grandson, Conrad Blucher. The historical documents are today housed at the Conrad Blucher Surveying Center at Texas A&M University-Corpus Christi.

Kinney seems to have had a remarkable ability to maintain good relations with the Mexican authorities, as well as with the Texas political leaders in Austin. At one point, President Lamar appointed Kinney as special agent "to cultivate friendly negotiations between the Americans on the border and the Mexicans." Despite being arrested several times by both Mexican and Texan authorities, Kinney always managed to survive and even thrive.

During this time period, both Texas and Mexico claimed the land which included the settlement of Corpus Christi. Mexican authorities

threatened to go to war if the United States annexed Texas—which the United States did, in 1845, when Texas became the 28th state. Then-President James Knox Polk ordered General Zachary Taylor to take an army to the frontier in case of war. Kinney encouraged officials to recommend Corpus Christi as the base for operations against Mexico.

The little community, with only about 100 residents, became the first on the Texas mainland to fly the Stars and Stripes on July 31, 1845, when the U.S. Army landed on Corpus Christi Beach. General Taylor, who brought 4,000 troops to the city, set up headquarters about half a block north of where the Texas State Aquarium sits today. The cantonment was named Fort Marcy, in honor of William L. Marcy, U.S. Secretary of War, and the troops were known officially as the Army of Occupation.

The military's arrival caused an explosion in the small town's population, from about 100 to several thousand. The number of so-called "grog shops," as the saloons were termed, multiplied almost overnight, from two to more than 200. Equally rapid growth occurred in the number of tradesmen, merchants, and brothels. The army stayed in Corpus Christi about seven and a half months, engaging in hunting, horseracing, and learning to deal with the heat and varmints, particularly rattlesnakes. In one day,

the soldiers reportedly killed 114 snakes in and around the camp.

The fledgling town became deserted as the soldiers headed south to Brownsville, where their arrival was seen as an act of aggression by Mexico, which sent troops across the Rio Grande. On May 13, 1846, Congress declared war against Mexico.

That same year, the Texas Legislature authorized the formation of Nueces County. A year later, the town was officially named Corpus Christi and received its first post office. It remained small, a hamlet of only about 300 people. Mexico's claim to the land was formally relinquished on February 2, 1848, under the Treaty of Guadalupe Hidalgo. It wasn't until 1852 that Corpus Christi was officially incorporated, however.

Kinney, who had grown wealthy from his business dealings and trading, decided to launch a campaign to lure settlers to the region. In 1848, he advertised the town in the nation's leading newspapers as well as in Europe.

In 1850, there were 689 residents in 151 dwellings, without any schools or churches. To promote the town and draw more settlers, businessman Kinney decided to host the Lone Star Fair, even importing a carnival from New Orleans. Although the fair was not as successful as he had hoped, the area did continue its steady growth. By 1853, one year after Corpus Christi was incorporated, the population had grown to approximately 1,000. Churches were built, as was a courthouse and a jail; the town seemed on its way to prosperity.

✧

Left: Felix and Maria von Blucher came to Corpus Christi from Germany in 1849, fleeing political troubles in their homeland, and became leaders of the community. Felix von Blucher was the county's first surveyor and Maria was the first librarian.

COURTESY OF THE CHARLES F. H. VON BLUCHER FAMILY PAPERS, SPECIAL COLLECTIONS AND ARCHIVES, MARY AND JEFF BELL LIBRARY, TEXAS A&M UNIVERSITY-CORPUS CHRISTI.

Below: As the community grew, so did the need for city services such as this fire department from the 1870s.

COURTESY OF THE CORPUS CHRISTI CHAMBER OF COMMERCE

Then, in 1854, a yellow fever epidemic arrived in the form of a fruit vessel. Customers bought oranges, bananas, limes, lemons, mangoes and pineapples—and nearly every household became infected with the plague. Although reports at the time blamed "contaminated fruit," modern medical experts believe that the illness is transmitted by infected mosquitoes, which were likely concealed among the tropical fruit. An estimated one-fourth of the residents died, which was a huge setback for the growth of the community.

Kinney's efforts gradually diminished as he grew older and less interested in entrepreneurship. Finally, during a trip to Matamoros to recoup his fortunes, he was shot while visiting a former lover in 1862. Other community leaders emerged, carrying on his goals of city growth and promoting the economic and trade advantages of Corpus Christi.

The port continued to increase its traffic in many different supplies, such as beef, cattle and hides. In the summer of 1860, the Corpus Christi Ship Channel Co. was established to dredge a deeper channel between the municipal docks and Aransas Pass—a task that, if it succeeded, would ensure Corpus Christi's lasting significance as a coastal port.

But the campaign was interrupted by the Civil War. Corpus Christi residents dressed in the gray of the Confederacy and steeled themselves for a naval attack, since they were on a bay accessible from the Gulf of Mexico. Texas' secession from the Union came on March 2, 1861, a move which was heartily supported by the delegates from Corpus Christi. Some leading citizens, including Kinney, opposed secession, and others even went so far as to join the northern cause. However, when the issue came to a vote before the citizens of Corpus Christi on February 23, 1862, the majority favored secession by a vote of 142 to 42.

The first impact of the war was a federal blockade of the Gulf Coast area, which meant supply shortages for the approximately 1,300 residents. The community's reputation as a trade route, if an illicit one, continued unabated. A wagon road, known as the Cotton Road, about 10 miles west of Corpus Christi, ran through the Banquete area and was used by Confederate states trading cotton with Mexico. The route provided an important way of circumventing the blockade of trade along the coastline.

There were several skirmishes in Corpus Christi, and one local legend insists that dud cannonballs had been emptied of gunpowder and filled with bourbon whiskey—supposedly to relieve the Union sailors' tedious nights on duty. The primary hardship for citizens was the increasing food shortages. By Christmas 1872, hunger was so fierce that the local newspaper reported on the commotion when desperate residents discovered a few old turkeys that had escaped being cooked for a holiday meal. Two attempts to occupy the city were successfully resisted, but the city finally fell to the Federal troops in 1874.

The war's end brought Union occupation to the city, where residents suffered somewhat from deprivations and indignities of the occupying troops. However, support for the Confederacy had eroded during the hardships of the blockade, and many Union officers found sympathizers here.

The next decade was a difficult one for Corpus Christi, as it declined economically. Efforts to acquire a deep-water channel for the city had been disbanded during the war, and the port could host only shallow-draft vessels, which diminished its ability to attract larger ocean-going vessels.

❖

A funeral cortege winds its way down an unpaved Waco Street during the 1890s.

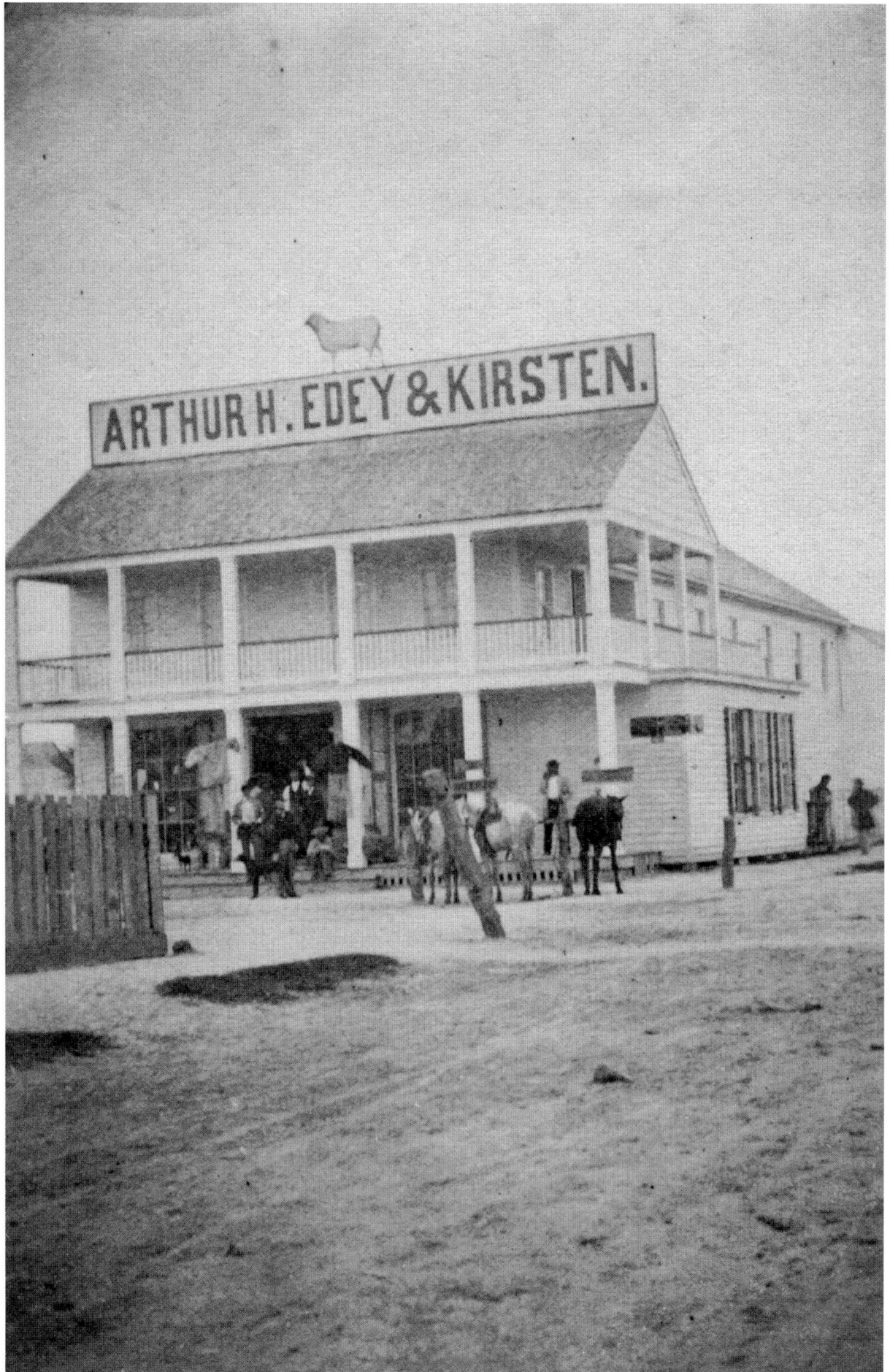

SHEEP, CATTLE AND COMMERCE

"I am willing to take a good many chances, but I certainly would not live on a stock ranch west of the Nueces .... My position in command of a company of troops I do not consider half so hazardous as that of those living on the ranches."
— Captain L.H. McNally, chief of Texas Rangers, speaking to a legislative committee about the problems of cattle rustling and bandits in the area of the Nueces River Valley during the mid 1870s.

In April 1870, Texas was restored to the Union, an event which seems to have been accepted with equanimity by most Corpus Christi residents. Overall, the Reconstruction was reportedly less arduous on the community than in other places, at least in part because many Union soldiers had come to establish their homes here and married into local families.

However, many complained bitterly about the presence of the Union soldiers, particularly the African-Americans, who were stationed in Corpus Christi. Some residents reported that they were regularly subjected to humiliation and insults from the federal troops, and that the soldiers would walk into a residence unannounced and demand that they be served food or coffee.

Nonetheless, the next decade was a violent one for the community, as the "gentry of the bush"—a term used by area residents to refer to cattle rustlers, renegades and bandits—thrived and murders were abundant. It is estimated that more than a million head of cattle were stolen and more than 2,000 ranchers and workers were murdered. The blame for the troubles was placed on bandits from Mexico, Union renegades, unemployed Confederate soldiers and citizen posses with little regard for the law.

Highway robberies, murders, kidnapping and cattle raids were the order of the day throughout the county. One resident remarked that four or five murders a week was a commonplace occurrence, an era of lawlessness that continued until 1875 when the Texas Rangers stepped in and one of the most infamous Mexican bandits, Juan N. Cortina, was arrested.

The violence culminated with the Nuecestown raid in 1875, when a large band of Mexicans came to Corpus Christi and set up a roadblock near the city, robbing and kidnapping travelers. Many prominent citizens were waylaid, mothers fled with their children, and captives were tortured. The bandits came to the city and raided a store, hung a servant, and beat other captives before fleeing at the impending arrival of an armed volunteer force. The resulting retaliation against many Mexicans, including innocent settlers, was equally savage, providing an ugly chapter in the city's history.

Sheep became the cash crop of the decade, as Corpus Christi became a thriving wool market between 1870 and 1880. Previously, most ranchers had preferred to raise cattle because they required less care. But as the price of wool rose, many area ranchers turned to sheep. The community enjoyed a thriving wagon and oxcart trade in wool, hides and skins.

Sheep ranchers in Nueces County in 1870 produced more wool than the combined total of the five lower counties on the Rio Grande River. For many years, Nueces County was the state's leader in the number of sheep—an enterprise that continued until ranchers became convinced that cattle and sheep could not inhabit the same pastures, and the cattle gradually edged the sheep out. The demise of the sheep industry was also aided by a plague that hit the region, killing nearly all the sheep.

In the 1870s, the city of 3,5000 residents was thriving and commerce was bustling. Thirty-five businesses, located mostly on Chaparral between Schatzel and Lawrence Streets, operated below the bluff and 15 smaller companies on the bluff itself. Hundreds of bales of cotton were shipped from city warehouses to Galveston via Morgan Line steamers, which held a monopoly of the Texas Coastal trade.

The men who came home to the Corpus Christi area after the Civil War found many changes. Among them were the vast herds of unbranded cattle roaming the plains of South Texas, all the way south to

Right: Postcards such as these, depicting a Corpus Christi boathouse and natatorium, were popular in the city's early days.

COURTESY OF THE DAN KILGORE HISTORIC PICTURE POSTCARD COLLECTION, SPECIAL COLLECTIONS AND ARCHIVES, MARY AND JEFF BELL LIBRARY, TEXAS A&M UNIVERSITY-CORPUS CHRISTI.

Below: Organizations, like this Sociedad Concordia Mexican-American Women, provided social and philanthropic outlets for women at the turn of the century.

COURTESY OF THE RAFAEL SR., AND VIRGINIA REYES GALVAN FAMILY PAPERS, SPECIAL COLLECTIONS AND ARCHIVES, MARY AND JEFF BELL LIBRARY, TEXAS A&M UNIVERSITY-CORPUS CHRISTI.

Opposite: Promoters touted the health benefits and cooling breezes to attract early bathers to Corpus Christi. The pleasure boat Japonica is in the background.

COURTESY OF THE DAN KILGORE HISTORIC PICTURE POSTCARD COLLECTION, SPECIAL COLLECTIONS AND ARCHIVES, MARY AND JEFF BELL LIBRARY, TEXAS A&M UNIVERSITY-CORPUS CHRISTI.

the Rio Grande. Noted Texas historian J. Frank Dobie estimates that there were close to six million cattle in Texas at the end of the Civil War.

Many of these cattle had been raided from ranch owners, who did not yet fence their lands. It soon became clear to many ranchers that the profits to be had were from driving the herds of longhorn cattle to the north. Massive cattle drives, bringing thousands of animals from Texas to the railheads in Kansas, were

organized and a rancher's worth was determined by the number of cattle he owned. The new enterprise brought prosperity to the region and created the first cattle barons.

Among them were the founders of the King Ranch, which was to become one of the world's most vast working cattle ranches. In 1852, riverboat captain Richard King came to

Natatorium and North Beach.   CORPUS CHRISTI, Texas.

Right: North Beach, which is now called
Corpus Christi Beach, hosted many forms
of entertainment for early tourists, including
this waterfront dance hall, fishing pier and
bathhouse.

COURTESY OF THE DAN KILGORE HISTORIC PICTURE
POSTCARD COLLECTION, SPECIAL COLLECTIONS AND
ARCHIVES, MARY AND JEFF BELL LIBRARY, TEXAS A&M
UNIVERSITY-CORPUS CHRISTI.

Below: In 1886, the San Antonio and
Aransas Pass Railroad began operations in
Corpus Christi. This postcard depicting the
passenger depot is from 1919.

COURTESY OF THE DAN KILGORE HISTORIC PICTURE
POSTCARD COLLECTION, SPECIAL COLLECTIONS AND
ARCHIVES, MARY AND JEFF BELL LIBRARY, TEXAS A&M
UNIVERSITY-CORPUS CHRISTI.

Corpus Christi for the Lone Star Fair organized by Kinney. King joined with businessman Gordon "Legs" Lewis to establish a ranch on the Santa Gertrudis Creek, an oasis of clear, sweet water in the middle of the Wild Horse Desert south of Corpus Christi. This was the inception of what would become King's 825,000-acre cattle empire in South Texas, and what is recognized today as the birth of the modern ranching industry.

The two men purchased a 15,500-acre Mexican land grant, and King headed south to hire employees for his ranchland. He rode into Mexico, where he encountered a drought-stricken village and invited all the villagers to return to Texas with him, where they would be given work and cared for. The unique result of his invitation is *los kinenos*, literally "King's men," who came to live and work on the ranch. These *vaqueros* were utterly devoted to King, raising

S. A. & A. P. Passenger Depot,
Corpus Christi, Tex.

AT THE COTTON GIN

TEXAS, THE LONE STAR STATE

✧

Above: The Texas Mexican Railroad was the first railroad in Corpus Christi, and it opened up the growing city to both trade and culture.

COURTESY OF THE CORPUS CHRISTI PUBLIC LIBRARY, CENTRAL BRANCH, LOCAL HISTORY ROOM.

Left: Cotton gins were commonplace in the late 19th century, when Corpus Christi was a key shipping point for crops such as cotton and for cattle headed up east.

COURTESY OF THE DAN KILGORE HISTORIC PICTURE POSTCARD COLLECTION, SPECIAL COLLECTIONS AND ARCHIVES, MARY AND JEFF BELL LIBRARY, TEXAS A&M UNIVERSITY-CORPUS CHRISTI.

Below: Although sheep were the cash crop of the 1870s, the next decade saw the rise of the cattle industry. This Santa Gertrudis bull is from the King Ranch.

COURTESY OF THE CORPUS CHRISTI PUBLIC LIBRARY, CENTRAL BRANCH, LOCAL HISTORY ROOM.

their families on the ranch and sending their children to King Ranch schools, then training their sons and grandsons as successors on the ranch. Even today, there are fifth and sixth-generation kinenos working on the King Ranch.

The partnership between King and Lewis was short-lived. Lewis was later killed by a jealous husband, but King continued his ranch with partner Mifflin Kenedy and then branched out to create his own empire. As rustling continued, both men realized they needed to fence their pastures. Kenedy was the first to do so, building a 36-mile long fence on his Laureles Ranch in 1869. King did the same soon afterward at Santa Gertrudis.

To sell their cattle up north, ranchers such as King organized huge cattle drives, sending thousands of cattle on the trails northward. During one drive, the King Ranch reportedly sent 17,000 cattle up the Chisholm Trail. Although cattle drives, with their romantic images of the rugged cowboy existence, became a popular symbol of the Wild West, they were actually a brief phenomenon, lasting only about 20 years. It is estimated that more than five million cattle moved up the trails between Texas and the midwest in the 1860s and the 1880s. The drives began after the Civil War ended and were ended by the advent of the railroads, which made such arduous trips unnecessary.

The growth of the cattle industry led directly to the development of further commerce for Corpus Christi—ranchers needed railroads and shipping barges to transport their stock to market. The city's increasingly important role as a hub for trade continued.

Misfortune, however, arrived in the form of a yellow fever epidemic, both in 1854 and then again in 1867. Nearly a third of the community's 1,000 citizens died as the epidemic raged throughout the town, leaving others so ill they could barely bury the dead. The editor of the *Daily Ranchero* in Brownsville warned that Corpus Christi, and the other coastal towns, needed to insist upon quarantine measures to prevent spread of the plague:

The fearful epidemic prevailing at Corpus Christi proves conclusively that that place is just as subject to yellow fever as any other place on the coast.... Corpus Christi is naturally the healthiest place on the coast, but her reputation and prestige has gone through neglect to enforce non-intercourse with infected ports," according to the newspaper.

In the meantime, city leaders continued to work toward the establishment of a deeper ship channel. In 1871, citizens approved a $25,000 bond issue to dredge the channel deeper. In 1874 a channel through Corpus Christi Bay was dredged to a depth of eight feet, deep enough to allow steamships to dock at Corpus Christi. This move, which allowed direct access to the Morgan Lines steamship routes, helped to ensure the community's future economic growth.

In 1876, the first railroad was built, the Corpus Christi, San Diego and Rio Grande Narrow Gauge Railroad. The railroad, nicknamed the "Manana Express," was completed in 1881. It served to connect the city's port with Texas communities in the south, as well as border cities including Laredo and into northern Mexico. This route was eventually renamed the Texas-Mexican Railroad.

There were other improvements, as the coastal city began the process of becoming a more civilized and disciplined community. With so much livestock roaming the streets that it hindered trade, city fathers were forced to pass ordinances that limited the number of milk cows an individual owner could keep within the city limits; to require animal owners to clean the stalls of horses, cows, hogs and other domestic animals before 8 a.m. daily; and to remove the dead carcasses of animals from city streets.

By 1871, there were weekly stagecoaches between Corpus Christi and the Rio Grande City, and better mail delivery from New Orleans. By 1880, the city's population had grown to 3,257, despite the ravages of war, unrest and several bouts of yellow fever.

By the end of the century, Corpus Christi had became a key shipping point for Texas cattle moving to eastern markets, and for crops, including cotton, which was first shipped from Corpus Christi in 1883. In 1886, another railroad, the San Antonio and Aransas Pass, was constructed.

The arrival of the railroads put an end to the lucrative cart trade with Mexico, but they also opened up the city for expanded commerce and tourism.

✧

*Lozano General Merchandise, which sold
everything from souvenirs to dry goods,
was among dozens of shops and businesses
that lined the unpaved roads in the late
19th century.*

COURTESY OF THE DAN KILGORE HISTORIC PICTURE
POSTCARD COLLECTION, SPECIAL COLLECTIONS AND
ARCHIVES, MARY AND JEFF BELL LIBRARY, TEXAS A&M
UNIVERSITY-CORPUS CHRISTI.

CREATION OF A CITY STRUCTURE

"The spring of 1913 found the little city of Corpus Christi an ill-lighted, poorly served,
sandy and run-down tourist resort.... It had but a few miles of sidewalk paving to aid its citizens
or guests in getting about when the worn-out and decrepit streetcars refused to run."
— from an *American City Magazine* article published in October 1916

From its humble beginnings as a frontier trading post, the community had a long way to go to become the sophisticated and cosmopolitan city we see today. Originally known as Kinney's Trading Post, or Kinney's Ranch, for its founder, Henry Lawrence Kinney, its first residents were frontiersmen and smugglers, hardly the sort to worry about developing amenities.

The community's fortunes changed in July 1845, when American soldiers under General Zachary Taylor's command established camp here to prepare for war with Mexico. Taylor's army stayed in the community until March 1846, when it decamped for the Rio Grande Valley to enforce it as the southern U.S. border.

The soldiers' presence—and newspaper articles about their stay here and plans to wage war with Mexico—helped spread the community's name and location to residents across the nation. In 1847, the community was officially named Corpus Christi because "a more definite postmark for letters was needed." Five years later, on September 9, 1852, the city incorporated, and residents elected a city council and mayor. The first mayor was Benjamin F. Neal, who was elected in 1852 and served until 1855.

The first law enacted in the fledgling city of Corpus Christi pertained to the subjects that most engaged the early settlers—wild livestock. That original ordinance, adopted on January 15, 1879, made it illegal to allow hogs and goats to run loose.

The first city charter was adopted in 1876, establishing the city's principles, functions, and governmental organization. Also in the late 1800s, a water system was created, a fire department established, and the first hospital built.

Among the many families that had begun to settle in the city were Felix von Blucher and his young bride, Maria, a German beauty and musician who had studied under Franz Liszt. Felix was equally accomplished with a degree in civil engineering, law and languages, of which he spoke six. Upon her arrival, Maria wrote to her parents, "I thought to find nothing but a miserable den with wretched huts, instead of it I see already from the ship the pleasantest houses glittering, built partly on the seaside or on the height."

The Bluchers purchased eight acres for $1,000, an area that later became known as Blucherville as other family members built homes on the property. One of their sons, George, bought the first automobile in Corpus Christi in 1901. The auto, purchased directly from Mr. Olds, had a tiller instead of a steering wheel, cost $650, and arrived packed in a box like a piano.

As the 20th century began, tourists began to be attracted to the city, drawn by its cool breezes, beachfront resorts and reportedly healthy climate. In 1905, the city's first authentic Chamber of Commerce, known as the Corpus Christi Commercial Club, was organized; it was later renamed the Corpus Christi Commercial Association. There were piers built along the bayfront, and businesses offered activities such as dancing, dining, drinking, fishing, and entertainment. So many saloons were built that in 1915 the city council relegated them to only the east side of the street so ladies could walk the other side without being offended.

An examination of the city in the year 1908 reveals that there were about 8,000 residents, 300 telephones, and electricity, but no paved streets. The city had four newspapers, an ice-making factory, two cotton gins, four dentists, five lumber yards, and three banks. Visitors to the city spent their time at an amusement park on North Beach known as Epworth by the Sea.

In 1909, the city opened the La Retama Library and the Corpus Christi Country Club. State lawmakers created the Corpus Christi Independent School District. On October 22, 1909, the city

❖

Horse-drawn wagons haul pipes for the first fresh-water artesian well on the Santa Gertrudis Ranch in 1938.

had one of its most prominent visitors, when President William Howard Taft came to the area to visit his half-brother's ranch nearby. Thousands of city residents came to hear the president speak from the foot of the bluff on Mesquite Street.

In 1910, progress in the form of electric-powered streetcars replaced the horse-drawn carriages on the city's streets. A year later, the first causeway was built across the Nueces Bay, which created a more direct route to the northern bay area. Street lights were installed in 1912.

The city's elegant Nueces Hotel opened in 1913, and invited guests paid $5 a plate to attend the opening banquet. The hotel later sheltered many residents during the 1919 hurricane and was the site of many business and social events until it was torn down in 1971 to make room for La Quinta Royale.

In 1914, when La Retama Club had the funds for a paid librarian, Maria von Blucher

became the first to fill the position. Two years later, citizens hotly debated the issue of the day—prohibition. Those who favored prohibition included most of the community's women, who, even though they could not vote, exerted tremendous influence on the men. Prohibition passed by 218 votes, and Corpus Christi did not again have legal drinking until 1933.

Electricity had arrived, but not with the unfettered access that we enjoy today. In 1916, you could ride in an electric streetcar through the streets of Corpus Christi. In Corpus Christi (population 9,000) and other large cities that had a light plant, you could also read by the light of an electric bulb until 10 or 11 o'clock at night, when the light plant would normally shut down.

The light plant also was shut down during the daylight hours, except for Tuesday. Since the electric appliance that people were most likely to own was an iron, the light plant

✧

The Nueces Hotel, built in 1913, offered well-to-do tourists a spectacular view of the bayfront as well as downtown Corpus Christi. It also served as a haven for residents during the 1919 hurricane.

NUECES HOTEL,
CORPUS CHRISTI, TEXAS.

Top: Electric streetcars, which came to the city in 1910, quickly became the favored mode of public transportation, replacing the horse-drawn carriages.

COURTESY OF THE CORPUS CHRISTI PUBLIC LIBRARY, CENTRAL BRANCH, LOCAL HISTORY ROOM.

Middle: Three clerks stand ready to wait on customers in this 1920s butcher shop in Corpus Christi.

COURTESY OF THE CORPUS CHRISTI CHAMBER OF COMMERCE.

Bottom: Among the most prominent visitor to the city during the early 20th century was President Taft, who came to visit his half-brother's ranch in nearby Gregory in 1909.

COURTESY OF THE DAN KILGORE HISTORIC PICTURE POSTCARD COLLECTION, SPECIAL COLLECTIONS AND ARCHIVES, MARY AND JEFF BELL LIBRARY, TEXAS A&M UNIVERSITY-CORPUS CHRISTI.

President Taft and Party, on the Taft Ranch, Gregory, Texas.   4564

Right: Port Aransas was famed for its sport fishing. Anglers who visited the area included President Franklin Delano Roosevelt, shown here fishing for tarpon in 1937.

COURTESY OF THE CORPUS CHRISTI PUBLIC LIBRARY, CENTRAL BRANCH, LOCAL HISTORY ROOM.

Below: Patriotic organizations such as this local chapter of the Order of the Sons of America were popular in the 1920s.

COURTESY OF THE CORPUS CHRISTI CHAMBER OF COMMERCE

Newlywed Rafael Galvan, the first
Mexican-American police officer in Corpus
Christi, poses for the camera with his bride,
Virginia Reyes.

COURTESY OF THE RAFAEL, SR., AND VIRGINIA REYES
GALVAN FAMILY PAPERS, SPECIAL COLLECTIONS AND
ARCHIVES, MARY AND JEFF BELL LIBRARY, TEXAS A&M
UNIVERSITY-CORPUS CHRISTI.

offered electricity for a few hours each
Tuesday so that the ironing could be done.
And although housewives were talking about
newfangled appliances like electric refrigerators, ranges, washing machines and clocks,
they were not found yet in most homes.

A hurricane came through on August 18,
1916, causing heavy damage to the causeway
and destroying the railroad trestle. There were
sixteen lives lost to the storm. This may have
lulled many residents into a false sense of security when a much more devastating storm hit
the city three years later.

In 1917, when the United States entered
World War I, the Navy and later the Army
occupied the Beach Hotel, which became
the Breakers.

By the summer of 1919, there were
approximately 20,000 residents—and few of
them showed concern at the approaching

hurricane. The resulting devastation was enormous, with more than 600 lives lost and hundreds of homes washed away. It also, however, lent impetus to the growing demand for a protected port and a seawall. Among the groups who were instrumental in the push for an intracoastal canal and deepwater harbor was the Corpus Christi Commercial Association, which was renamed the Corpus Christi Chamber of Commerce in 1924.

The opening of the Port of Corpus Christi, on September 14, 1926, is regarded as the dawning of the modern era. Chamber directors helped to raise $50,000 to pay for the opening festivities. In 1934, construction began on what would become one of the most striking aspects of downtown landscape, the seawall. Designed by sculptor Gutzon Borghum, who also designed Mount Rushmore, the seawall is a 14-foot staircase descending to the Corpus Christi Bay. A bond election in 1939 was required to complete the $2.5-million project, which provides storm protection for downtown.

Throughout its development, leaders have emerged whose vision and commitment helped shape the community's appearance and energy.

The causeway construction was the start of a municipal improvement program spear-

headed by Mayor Roy Miller, who was elected in 1913. The 29-year-old Miller was adamant about the need for a deep-water port, but he also took issue with the town's disreputable appearance. His administration provided the city's first paved streets, completing 12 miles of roadway. Under his leadership, the city also installed 26 miles of sanitary and storm sewers; created a $300,000 water system; and organized a paid fire department.

Another significant community leader during this era was Walter Elmer Pope, an attorney and state representative. Born in 1879, he moved to Corpus Christi in 1908 and, in 1917, sponsored a bill calling for remission of ad valorem taxes to finance construction of the city's seawall. In 1919, he sponsored a similar bill to help pay for the construction of the Port of Corpus Christi and donated land for the first turning basin.

Pope also introduced bills which provided for the construction of a highway to the Rio Grande Valley and the purchase of 90,000 acres of land on Padre Island for use as public parks. He was instrumental in the establishment of Texas A&I University in Kingsville, and worked on the building of a causeway to Padre Island, along with various bayfront improvement projects in Corpus Christi.

❖

Four Corpus Christi lawmen display confiscated liquor. The city banned liquor in 1916, and the prohibition lasted until 1933.

COURTESY OF THE CORPUS CHRISTI PUBLIC LIBRARY, CENTRAL BRANCH, LOCAL HISTORY ROOM.

✧

Above: A row of young tap dancers prepares for a performance at the Wright Dance Studio in February 1935.

COURTESY OF THE CORPUS CHRISTI PUBLIC LIBRARY, CENTRAL BRANCH, LOCAL HISTORY ROOM.

Left: Duke Ellington was among well-known musicians who made appearances at the Galvan Ballroom during its heyday.

COURTESY OF THE RAFAEL, SR., AND VIRGINIA REYES GALVAN FAMILY PAPERS, SPECIAL COLLECTIONS AND ARCHIVES, MARY AND JEFF BELL LIBRARY, TEXAS A&M UNIVERSITY-CORPUS CHRISTI.

Right: The city's first library opened in
1909, as the community's growth led to the
development of many educational and
cultural amenities.

COURTESY OF THE CORPUS CHRISTI PUBLIC LIBRARY,
CENTRAL BRANCH, LOCAL HISTORY ROOM.

Opposite: Dr. Hector P. Garcia founded the
American G.I. Forum in Corpus Christi in
1948. The organization became a leading
force in the struggle for Mexican-American
civil rights.

COURTESY OF THE DR. HECTOR P. GARCIA PAPERS,
SPECIAL COLLECTIONS AND ARCHIVES, MARY AND JEFF
BELL LIBRARY, TEXAS A&M UNIVERSITY-CORPUS CHRISTI.

Other events testified to the growing significance of this coastal community. Famed aviator Charles Lindberg visited Corpus Christi in his plane, *Spirit of St. Louis*, in 1927. The city also became the home of a major civil rights movement, as the birthplace of the League of United Latin American Citizens in 1929. With Ben Garza as the head, the group had its first convention in Corpus Christi and has since grown to national significance.

In 1937, President Franklin Delano Roosevelt came to the area to fish for tarpon, for which the community of nearby Port Aransas was well-known. He stayed in the historic Tarpon Inn, a two-story hotel which today displays a fish scale autographed by the president.

Other prominent community leaders were Rafael and Virginia Reyes Galvan Sr., whose former residence has been restored and is now located in the city's historic Heritage Park. Businessman, civic leader, a founder of LULAC, and the city's first Mexican-American policeman, Rafael Galvan, Sr. (1887-1966) was instrumental in a variety of civic affairs. Among his many endeavors, in 1949 he constructed and opened the Galvan Ballroom, which became a focal point of social life for residents of Corpus Christi and its environs. The Galvans produced several children, including Ralph, Jr., Eddie, and Robert, all of whom became accomplished musicians and had an impact on the musical development of their region.

Another groundbreaking Hispanic organization that had its start in Corpus Christi in the mid 1900s was the American G.I. Forum, founded by civil rights leader and physician Dr. Hector P. Garcia.

Garcia, who lived between 1914 and 1996, is considered today one of the nation's most historically significant Mexican-American leaders. A World War II veteran, he established his general medicine practice in Corpus Christi in 1946 and became aware of the discrimination that Mexican Americans faced in Texas society. To address those problems and the difficulties faced by Hispanic war veterans, he founded the American G.I. Forum in 1948. The organization was committed to education as a key to advancement.

Garcia and his new organization gained national attention during the case of Private Felix Longoria. A funeral home owner in Three Rivers refused to allow the use of his chapel for a wake for Longoria, who had been killed in the Philippines during World War II and was brought back to the United States for reburial. Garcia was able to bring the matter to the attention of then-Congressman Lyndon B. Johnson, who arranged for Longoria to be buried at Arlington National Cemetery and attended his funeral in 1949.

In less than a century, Corpus Christi had been transformed from a frontier post to a modern community. Several events that occurred during that transformation, including the establishment of a deep-water port and the arrival of the Navy, merit a more detailed discussion for their impact on the civic landscape.

THIRD ANNUAL
AMERICAN G. I. FORUM
NATIONAL CONVENTION

LEADERSHIP
AND
EDUCATION

LEADERSHIP
AND
EDUCATION

DR. HECTOR P. GARCIA
"Founder"

WHITMAN HOTEL

830 North Main   Pueblo, Colo.

JUNE 22-23-24
1956

COMMERCE E[...]

THEKLA [...] BEAUMONT

REALIZING THE DREAM
OF A DEEP-WATER PORT

"Siren whistles blow, flags and handkerchiefs wave; thousands thunder their cheers; a few old timers deeply stirred shed tears of emotion. It is a moment that all have waited for, worked for; the credit goes to no single man; a moment rather that belongs to the persistence, and faith of generations of pioneers. The Port of Corpus Christi, baby port of the nation, is opened to the commerce of the world."

— description of the port's opening on September 14, 1926 in *Texas Seaport: The Story of the Growth of Corpus Christi and the Coastal Bend Area* by Coleman Campbell.

It was a goal that had been envisioned by many of Corpus Christi's earliest leaders—the creation of a deep-water port, to open up the shipping commerce so vital in maintaining the community's significance as one of the nation's leading ports. By the early 20th century, city leaders and developers

Port. Corpus Christi

#23.

focused their energies on the goal of deepening the shipping channel and obtaining a deep-water port designation from the federal government. They knew that such a designation would further solidify the city's stance as a premier shipping point for goods moving through the region and headed north. A deep-water port—which meant federal government assistance for dredging and maintenance— would ensure the city's prosperity and continued growth.

In January 1919, a $600,000 bond issue was passed for the construction of a breakwater along the bayfront. But it wasn't until September 1919, when the city's most devastating hurricane washed away thousands of dollars in property and more than 600 lives, that the project gained a true sense of urgency. A request was made by city leaders for a federally funded 21-mile ship channel at Corpus Christi, a move opposed by residents in nearby Aransas Pass and Rockport, who wanted the deep-water port to be built in the North Bay area. The federal government, however, declined to help with a channel in any of the communities unless the area could be protected from storm damage.

Texas lawmakers instead passed a bill allowing the city of Corpus Christi to use property taxes from six surrounding counties for the next 25 years to fund the construction of a seawall and breakwater. The proposal had widespread support, because the construction was seen as an

✧

The Bascule Bridge had to be raised as ships entered the Port of Corpus Christi when it first opened in 1926. Traffic congestion later forced the replacement of the Bascule Bridge with the present-day Harbor Bridge.

COURTESY OF THE SPECIAL COLLECTIONS AND ARCHIVES, MARY AND JEFF BELL LIBRARY, TEXAS A&M UNIVERSITY-CORPUS CHRISTI.

CHAPTER V

3 5

BATHING BEAUTIES AT PORT CELEBRATION CORPUS CHRISTI - 9-14-26.

#10.

✧

A parade through downtown of beauty contestants was part of the festivities marking the opening of the Port of Corpus Christi on September 14, 1926.

COURTESY OF THE SPECIAL COLLECTIONS AND ARCHIVES, MARY AND JEFF BELL LIBRARY, TEXAS A&M UNIVERSITY-CORPUS CHRISTI.

economic boost to the entire region, not just Corpus Christi. The proposal was conditional upon the federal government designation Corpus Christi as a deep-water port.

In 1920, Congress agreed to authorize a U.S. Army Corps of Engineers study on the feasibility of a deep-water port and the possibility of locating such a port at one of the following locations: Corpus Christi, Aransas Pass, Rockport and Port Aransas. In Corpus Christi's favor was its geography and the railroads—the other three towns were lower and had been devastated by storm tides in previous hurricanes. Corpus Christi had a bluff of 39 to 40 feet, and it was served by three railroads. Aransas Pass and Rockport were served by only one railroad, and Port Aransas had none.

Finally, in 1922, the federal government picked Corpus Christi as the site for its deep-water port, and, on January 16, 1925, dredge boats began digging the channel while harbor facilities were built with local and state funds. The Port of Corpus Christi opened on September 14, 1926, and Corpus Christi was

on its way to becoming a major center for the oil refining and petrochemical industries.

It was a major achievement, the realization of a longstanding community goal that had required the effort of many in the community, including the Chamber of Commerce. The opening was one of the biggest parties the city had ever seen. There was a military parade, complete with flag-waving and whistle-blowing, down Mesquite Street, a visit from the governor and the arrival of USS *Borie*, which steamed through the Bascule Bridge to officially open the port. A 25-foot deep channel had been dug from the Gulf of Mexico through Aransas Pass and across 21 miles of the Corpus Christi Bay.

The event was eagerly touted by area developers, as evidenced by an old prospectus soliciting buyers for a new subdivision, Del Mar Addition, in 1926. "It is no exaggeration to say that the location is not excelled on the seacoasts of America. This tract of land had been withheld from the public who had waited and wished for it for years, but had

Ocean Drive, Corpus Christi, Texas

never dared to hope that it would be improved, developed and restricted in the most approved manner of the larger cities…. The land was laid out in the most modern way, the streets excavated, curbs built, palms and other gorgeous semi-tropical trees and shrubs planted, water, natural gas, and sewers going in behind every lot, boulevarding and

DESTROYERS IN HARBOR
PORT CELEBRATION - CORPUS CHRISTI - 9-14-26.

#13.

HATFIELD 231

JOHN D. EDWARDS 216

"WHERE TEXAS MEETS THE SE[A]

THE PORT OF

CORPUS CHRISTI

AUGUST. 24. 1927.

❖

The Port of Corpus Christi - "Where Texas Meets the Sea" — drew trade from national and international destinations. This scene includes S.S. West Cressey of Seattle; S.S. Cody of Philadelphia; S.S. Point Sur of San Francisco; M.S. Cape of Good Hope of Glasgow; S.S. Leersum of Amsterdam; and S.S. West Tacook of Portland, Oregon.

parking going on, paving begun, and many prominent people on the waiting list ready to buy sites and begin the erection of handsome homes as soon as the property is opened," according to the developers, Wright, Dinn and Allison.

The port's opening was, in many ways, the beginning of a new chapter in the city's history. The economy was no longer based on agriculture but on a sophisticated transportation and manufacturing complex. In the port's early days, the main export was cotton. Nueces County and the surrounding area led the state in cotton production.

Business was so brisk that the port's original four loading docks had to be expanded, and an additional two docks were built with bond funds approved in 1928. In 1930, the ship channel was deepened from 25 to 30 feet. In 1941, the seawall was completed.

In the meantime, the city's oil and gas fields had just begun to be discovered. On September 6, 1913, a test well blew itself out at White Point, on the north shore of Corpus Christi Bay in San Patricio County. The well destroyed itself, but another test was launched. Started in 1914, the well was completed with an estimated production volume of 10 million cubic feet of gas per day. The event was considered enormously significant for the development of the Corpus Christi region.

"What experts consider the biggest strike of gas in the world was made a few miles from this city Friday afternoon …. The roar is such that drillers working at close range were forced to stuff cotton into their ear drums. Visitors, of whom there were hundreds, could not get within 200 yards of the well in safety….," according to a January 2, 1916, newspaper article in the *San Antonio Light*.

Those who went to see the gas escaping from the big well reported that you could hear the roar for 15 miles. With most Texas cities manufacturing gas for domestic and industrial fuel, officials hoped to harness the natural gas—but weren't able to do so for several years.

The discovery of oil fields in the region went hand-in-hand with the development of the port, as oil docks were needed to ship oil. Soon, wildcatters were bringing in wells throughout the region, in Duval, Webb, Jim Hogg and Zapata Counties. Closer to home, the Saxet Company brought in Nueces County's first producing gas well on December 22, 1923, with John Dunn Number One.

By 1927, Humble Oil and Refining Company had built a refinery south of Ingleside. In 1930, oil was discovered at Saxet Field and more refineries were built.

Beginning in the early 1930s, the Corpus Christi area became a major oil-producing area. In 1935, the county claimed 60 oil wells in two oil fields. By 1937, the county had 894 wells in 15 fields. At one time, there were an estimated 3,760 oil wells within a 125-mile radius of the Port of Corpus Christi.

Within a decade, the city's population more than doubled, from 27,742 in 1930 to 57,301 in 1940.

The oil companies required loading docks and facilities, and soon refineries and other heavy industries began to be established along the ship channel. The first major industry to locate in

✧

Two workers wait to unload cotton bales at the Port compress on August 20, 1927. The Texas cotton crop was so large that one county produced 170,000 bales per year.

COURTESY OF THE CORPUS CHRISTI PUBLIC LIBRARY, CENTRAL BRANCH, LOCAL HISTORY ROOM.

✧

*Above: A tugboat leads two ships to their
moorings at the Port of Corpus Christi
in the 1940s.*

COURTESY OF THE CORPUS CHRISTI PUBLIC LIBRARY,
CENTRAL BRANCH, LOCAL HISTORY ROOM.

*Right: Local businessmen welcome the
arrival of the first banana boat, the
Dorothy Duke from Bermuda, at the Port
of Corpus Christi on February 4, 1939.*

COURTESY OF THE CORPUS CHRISTI PUBLIC LIBRARY,
CENTRAL BRANCH, LOCAL HISTORY ROOM.

*Opposite, top: The smoke from an oil well
blowout in 1938 blackens the skies near
Corpus Christi.*

COURTESY OF THE CORPUS CHRISTI PUBLIC LIBRARY,
CENTRAL BRANCH, LOCAL HISTORY ROOM.

*Opposite, bottom: Workers and spectators
watch the sight of a raging oil well fire near
Corpus Christi in 1937.*

COURTESY OF THE DAN KILGORE HISTORIC PICTURE
POSTCARD COLLECTION, SPECIAL COLLECTIONS AND
ARCHIVES, MARY AND JEFF BELL LIBRARY, TEXAS A&M
UNIVERSITY-CORPUS CHRISTI.

Corpus Christi was Southern Alkali Corporation, a subsidiary of Pittsburgh Plate Glass Co. The company needed a mile-and-a-half extension to the channel, which was built by the Board of Navigation and Canal Commissioners, and is now known as the Industrial Canal.

In 1934, the Taylor Refining Company located along the port, and the primary product being moved through the port began a gradual shift, from cotton to petroleum. Other refineries to locate in the area included Taylor Refinery, Pontiac Refinery, Sinclair Refinery and American Smelting and Refining Co.

Agricultural production also underwent a change, as the Coastal Bend area became known for its production of grain sorghum products. In 1947, to take advantage of that market, the Corpus Products Refining Company located its plant in Corpus Christi. The company produced sugar, syrups and starches from grain. The port also built a grain elevator that opened in 1953 and was enlarged in 1959 and again in 1961.

Interestingly, the original Bascule Bridge—which was lowered and raised when ships approached the entrance of the Port—had become a problem. Ship and automobile traffic had increased, resulting in constant bottlenecks waiting to cross the bridge. The Bascule Bridge was eventually replaced with the Harbor Bridge, which was completed in 1959. The Harbor Bridge, leading to Portland, Rockport, and Aransas Pass, is a high-rise bridge that provides a spectacular view of the harbor today for motorists entering the city from its northern borders.

Today, the Port of Corpus Christi owns over 21,000 acres of land, of which approximately 16,000 acres is submerged land. It also has eight cargo docks, and eleven oil docks

Right: In 1930, Southern Alkali Corporation became the first major industry to locate in Corpus Christi.

COURTESY OF THE DAN KILGORE HISTORIC PICTURE POSTCARD COLLECTION, SPECIAL COLLECTIONS AND ARCHIVES, MARY AND JEFF BELL LIBRARY, TEXAS A&M UNIVERSITY-CORPUS CHRISTI.

Below: The Palace Theater in downtown Corpus Christi was showing the action film, Bullets or Ballots starring Edward G. Robinson, Joan Blondell and Humphrey Bogart on June 28, 1938.

COURTESY OF THE CORPUS CHRISTI PUBLIC LIBRARY, CENTRAL BRANCH, LOCAL HISTORY ROOM.

This aerial view of the Port of Corpus Christi shows the industrial section of the city as well as the Harbor Bridge leading to downtown.

COURTESY OF THE CORPUS CHRISTI CHAMBER OF COMMERCE.

worth millions of dollars. In 2000, a renovation effort produced a 100,000-square-foot refrigerated warehouse. The warehouse targets import and export markets from the United States, Mexico, Central and South America, Europe, Africa, Russia, Australia, and New Zealand.

One of the newest additions is the Congressman Solomon P. Ortiz International Center, a massive conference and banquet facility used to host large events. With five meeting rooms and a 16,000-square-foot banquet hall, the facility can accommodate groups from ten to two thousand. The Ortiz Center is also located under the Corpus Christi Harbor Bridge, offering a view of the harbor and ship channel. Ultimately, the facility is intended as a cruise terminal for passengers embarking on trips to Mexico and the Caribbean.

The Port and Port Industries are a major economic force in Corpus Christi. Together they provide about 40,000 jobs and generate more than $1 billion in salaries and approximately $150 million in taxes.

A number of new initiatives are in place as the Port prepares for the future. One is the Joe Fulton International Trade Corridor, an 11.5-mile road and seven-mile rail project that will connect U.S. Highway 181 and Interstate 37.

The Fulton corridor will improve access to industry and generate more international trade. Construction on the $42 million project could begin 2003, with completion in 2006. Other initiatives include the deepening and widening of the Corpus Christi Ship Channel. Once complete, the Port of Corpus Christi will boast a channel depth of fifty-two feet, thus becoming the deepest port in Texas. With a strategic military seaport designation, the Port of Corpus Christi is beginning to handle a significant amount of military cargo. The Port has plans to develop a layberth facility that would accommodate military vessels during peacetime and at the same time provide quick access to international waters in the event of a deployment. Perhaps, one of the Port's most ambitious and impactful projects is the development of a major container terminal, known as La Quinta Trade Gateway.

With an uncongested forty-five foot channel and access to major rail lines and highways, the Port continues its efforts to expand and strengthen its operations in Corpus Christi. Decades after the City's founders realized the need for a deepwater port, the result is more than they could have envisioned. Yet their foresight and persistence helped to provide impetus for what the Port has become today.

A CALL TO ARMS

"In a comparatively short time, approximately 17,000 acres of the rich agriculture land of Southwest Texas, as well as the sandy stretches of beaches and brush lands outside of Corpus Christi, have been transformed into the world's largest Naval Air Training Center. "The Main Station of the Naval Air Training Center occupies a site on Corpus Christi Bay.... it is a vast cluster of Hangars, Barracks, Assembly, Repair Shops and Administration Buildings, over which swarms of buzzing little Trainer Planes, PBY Flying Boats, Patrol Bombers and Fighter Planes drone from morning and far into the night."

— from U.S. Navy-produced postcard booklet about the newly opened base, 1941

✧

During World War II, many women were hired for jobs that had traditionally been occupied by men.

The military has always played a significant role in the fortunes of the city, beginning with General Taylor's troop encampment in 1845. However, it wasn't until 1941, when the Navy turned its attention to this quiet bayfront community, that its fortunes and the military's would become permanently entwined.

In 1914, the Navy had established its flight school in Pensacola, and the growing interest in naval aviation coincided with the nation's participation in World War I. But it wasn't until the latter part of the 1930s that Congress appropriated adequate funding for the construction of new bases with planes, equipment, and flight training facilities. In its search for a flight training base, the Navy appointed a board to study possible locations.

Lobbying efforts by Texas Congresssman Richard M. Kleberg to locate a new naval air station in the largest city in his congressional district brought Navy surveyors to South Texas in 1938 to consider the sleepy fishing village of Corpus Christi, with its population of 60,000. They found what they were seeking in the sandy flatlands southeast of the city, where there were only snakes and fishing shacks. Among the area's advantages were a moderate year-round climate, waterfront location, plentiful airspace for novice pilots, and abundant available acreage for runways, barracks, hangars, and roads. In addition, there was locally available aviation fuel, flat terrain, and suitable soil for runway construction. And with an air station at Corpus Christi as well as Pensacola, the Navy intended for the Gulf coast to be the safest continental U.S. shoreline.

A site was chosen on a peninsula in the Gulf of Mexico, south of Corpus Christi, in an area known as Flour Bluff. President Franklin D. Roosevelt signed the bill approving $25 million in funds for construction of the base in June 1940. It was an action which would eventually transform the community, providing an influx of money and people that would have a huge impact on the quiet tourist community.

Construction began on June 13, 1940, and the $53 million-base was dedicated by the secretary of the Navy on March 12, 1941. The original plans had called for the facility's completion in three years. However, the commissioning took place only nine months after groundbreaking, with 70 percent of the project complete, spurred by escalating world tensions. On January 14, 1941, the project reached a peak employment of 9,348 employees and had a weekly payroll of $305,125. Eight miles of 100-pair telephone cables for a permanent telephone system were laid in 10 days, and a 20-mile-long railroad was completed in 35 days.

Dubbed "University of the Air," the Corpus Christi base was the largest naval training station in the world at the time. It was used to train aviation cadets as pilots, navigators, aerologists, gunners, and radio operators. The first student aviators arrived March 20, 1941 and graduated November 1. By the end of the year, the base was graduating 300 pilots a month. That increased to 600 per month after the attack on Pearl Harbor.

The total station covered some 20,000 acres in three counties. To augment the training, six auxiliary air stations were built in the South Texas region to support the mission and provide additional landing fields. Four auxiliary stations were constructed in Flour Bluff including Rodd, Cabaniss, Cuddihy, and Waldron, as well as two self-contained air stations, Naval Auxiliary Air Station Kingsville

✧

Below: Soldiers in Corpus Christi practice marching drills beside a row of tents in 1940.

COURTESY OF THE CORPUS CHRISTI PUBLIC LIBRARY, CENTRAL BRANCH, LOCAL HISTORY ROOM.

Opposite: Officers conduct a personnel inspection of an OS2U squadron on the Naval Air Station Corpus Christi flight line. The unit's Vought OS2U Kingfisher aircraft are parked in the background, with canvas covers over the engines and canopies.

COURTESY OF THE NAVAL INSTITUTE PHOTO COLLECTION

in adjacent Kleberg County and Naval Auxiliary Air Station Chase Field in Bee County.

More than 35,000 naval aviators graduated from the base during the war. At the time, Corpus Christi was the only primary, basic, and advanced training base in the nation.

By 1945, there were 997 hangars and other buildings, and the cost had exceeded $100 million. Infrastructure to support the military base included a 980-foot rail and highway bridge and a 400-foot trestle bridge over Oso Bay; a 16-inch cast iron water pipes laid from Corpus Christi to Flour Bluff; and a permanent 11-mile military highway.

Among the many pilots who trained at Corpus Christi are former President George W. Bush Sr., game show host Bob Barker, and astronaut John Glenn. Ted Williams, the Boston Red Sox star hitter, was a physical fitness instructor at Corpus Christi after he received his wings. Hollywood film star Tyrone Power received flight training there as well.

The military's arrival not only provided a huge economic boost for the community, it also changed it from a quiet tourist town into a major city. Entrepreneurs rushed to meet the needs of the new arrivals with hotels, restaurants, stores and entertainment. Many prominent figures came to the city, including President Franklin D. Roosevelt, Rear Admiral Chester W. Nimitz, and heads of state such as King Ibn Saud of Saudi Arabia. Celebrity entertainers also arrived to entertain the recruits, including Bob Hope, Frank Sinatra, Louis Armstrong, Ginger Rogers, Rita Hayworth, and Katharine Hepburn.

By 1944 more than 20,000 civilians worked at the base, with another 20,000 employed at satellite fields. The city's population almost doubled between 1940 and 1950, rising from 57,301 to 108,287.

By 1950, the base was training naval aviators in the advanced stages of flight training, including flying multi-engine land and sea planes. Other Navy facilities operating at the base were the United States Naval Hospital, the United States Naval School of All-Weather Flight, the Fleet Logistic Air Wing, Acceptance, Test and

Transfer Unit, and the headquarters for the Corpus Christi Naval Reserve Training Center.

The end of World War II meant a decrease in the need for pilots. As a result, the services at Corpus Christi were cut back. Both auxiliary stations at Kingsville and Beeville were deactivated for several years. In 1948, the Naval Air Advanced Training Command transferred to Corpus Christi from Jacksonville, Florida, when the Navy decided to use the South Texas complex as headquarters for its air training command and for teaching jet training for advanced students. The Navy's flight demonstration team, the Blue Angels, were headquartered in Corpus Christi from 1949 to 1955, when they moved to Pensacola, Florida.

The Kingsville base, which had been leased to the Texas College of Arts and Industries, was reactivated in 1951 during the Korean Conflict. The base, which had been a temporary facility, was rehabilitated to a permanent status, and new buildings were constructed. Kingsville's fields were rebuilt to handle the requirements of the Navy's jet aircraft.

❖

A flight instructor orients naval aviation cadets to the layout and flight restrictions of the Corpus Christi vicinity in 1942, using a large map painted on the apron.

Kingsville, along with the auxiliary field in Beeville, was to be used for training advanced flight students who would go on to fly the Navy's fighter jets and bombers.

On June 30, 1959, the Navy shut down a major repair and assembly facility, used to maintain the seaplanes and carrier-based air-craft for teaching pilots, which had employed

❖

Above: Navy WAVES participate in emergency training drills at Naval Air Station Corpus Christi in September 1942.

Left: A Corpus Christi shop window promotes the sale of war bonds by appealing to the sense of wartime patriotism with this graphic illustration of a mannequin, blindfolded and shackled, versus the Statue of Liberty.

✧

A young sailor stands beside a recruiting poster at the Corpus Christi post office in this 1941 photo.

COURTESY OF THE CORPUS CHRISTI PUBLIC LIBRARY, CENTRAL BRANCH, LOCAL HISTORY ROOM.

conducts joint training for students from other service branches, including the Marine Corps, Air Force, and Coast Guard.

Three training squadrons, overseen by Training Air Wing Four, teach students the various stages of flight training. Approximately 400 students graduate annually. The base is also home to a naval mine warfare helicopter squadron; Mine Warfare Command; the U.S. Coast Guard; the Corpus Christi Army Depot; U.S. Customs; and the U.S. Naval Hospital.

One of the Navy's auxiliary training bases, Chase Field in Bee County, closed permanently in 1991 by order of the Base Closure and Realignment Commission. However, the Kingsville base continues to train advanced flight students from the Navy as well as the Marine Corps to fly high-tech combat jets. The Kingsville's bases two training squadrons teach students to fly jets, to engage in air-to-air combat, to drop bombs, and to land on the Navy's principal warships, aircraft carriers.

In addition to training naval aviators, the Corpus Christi area soon was to become the site of another Navy mission. In 1985, the Navy chose the city of Ingleside across Corpus Christi Bay as the home port for the battleship USS *Wisconsin*. However, Coastal Bend military installations were threatened by federal budget cuts, and the USS *Wisconsin* was decommissioned in 1991 after the Persian Gulf War. Instead, the newly built naval base was chosen to serve as the center of the Navy's expanded mine warfare fleet. In 1992, the Atlantic Fleet designated Naval Station Ingleside as its mine warfare command headquarters.

The base was officially dedicated on July 6, 1992, and the first mine countermeasures ship, USS *Scout*, arrived in June 1992. The ship has the distinction of being the first U.S. Navy ship homeported in Texas since World War II.

Navy officials have since consolidated the mine warfare ships, aircraft, divers, and training schools at Ingleside, which has brought more than 3,000 Navy personnel and 25 mine countermeasures ships to the base. The Navy's first command and control ship, USS *Inchon*, was located here as well, until its decommissioning in the summer of 2002.

Tenant commands on the base include the Regional Support Group, which provides main-

3,000 civilians. The Army took over the facility in 1961, converting it to the Army Aeronautical Depot Maintenance Center. Originally used to repair fixed- and rotary-wing aircraft, the depot phased out the fixed-wing repairs in 1967 because of increased demand for helicopter service.

By 1968, the depot annually repaired more than 400 helicopters. In 1974, its name was changed to Corpus Christi Army Depot. Now the Army's largest helicopter repair depot, it now employs 2,772 civilians, who work on rotary wing aircraft from all branches of the military.

Since the 1960s, the Corpus Christi base has continued to train pilots for its multi-engine land and sea planes, including students from many foreign countries. It also

✧

Above: This aerial photograph of Naval Air Station Corpus Christi shows the training planes on the flight line, as well as tenant commands such as the Corpus Christi Army Depot with "Fly Army" written on the building wall.

COURTESY OF THE U.S. NAVY

Left: Naval aviators fill out paperwork during flight jacket issue at Naval Air Station Corpus Christi in 1946.

COURTESY OF THE CORPUS CHRISTI PUBLIC LIBRARY, CENTRAL BRANCH, LOCAL HISTORY ROOM.

Right: Sailors stand at attention before the main building during a flag raising ceremony at Naval Air Station Corpus Christi.

COURTESY OF THE CORPUS CHRISTI PUBLIC LIBRARY, CENTRAL BRANCH, LOCAL HISTORY ROOM.

Below: The aircraft carrier USS Lexington served in World War II, then was used to train naval aviation students, and then was decommissioned to become a museum in Corpus Christi Bay.

COURTESY OF THE U.S. NAVY

Opposite, top: The Blue Angels "Fat Albert" takes off during an airshow at Naval Air Station Corpus Christi.

COURTESY OF THE U.S. NAVY

Opposite, bottom, left: A T-45 Goshawk training jet flies over the King Ranch near Kingsville during a flight. The Kingsville base provides advanced flight training for naval aviation students.

COURTESY OF THE U.S. NAVY

tenance and training for the ships at Ingleside; Mine Countermeasures Squadrons One and Two, deployable squadrons sent to mine warfare ships overseas; Shore Intermediate Maintenance Activity, which makes special and advanced ship repairs; and a branch medical and dental clinic.

In all, there are approximately 11,000 military and civilian employees at the Navy's facilities in South Texas. A local task force, with community leaders from throughout the region, works to protect area installations from any future base closures.

✧

Below: Flight simulators that use computer-generated images are used to train advanced flight students at Naval Air Station Kingsville.
COURTESY OF THE U.S. NAVY.

THE WINDS OF CHANGE

" Lying there awake I began to think of the family. Brother and I had always shared a room and had sometimes shared the same bed. I wondered where his body lay. Then Papa and Mama, were they washed up on some brushy shore or were they at the bottom of the muddy bay? For the first time since my whimpering and sobbing was calmed by Aunt Doshie, tears were filling my eyes. I eased out of bed and felt my way to where I knew (my older sister) Esther lay. I crawled into her bed and as she sat up, threw my arms about her. I am sure that those were her first tears to be shed over our loss. "

— personal account of surviving the 1919 hurricane in Corpus Christi, from Theodore A. Fuller's autobiography, *When the Century and I Were Young.* Fuller, who was 10, lost his mother, aunt and big brother in the storm.

The aftermath of Hurricane Celia, which struck Corpus Christi in 1970, included dozens of boats that were wrecked in the harbor. COURTESY OF AMERICAN ELECTRIC POWER.

The steady bayfront breezes that grace and cool the Corpus Christi area have their dark side. These winds can turn brutal, especially when coupled with the force of nature known as a hurricane—a storm that has been known to wreak havoc upon the coastal communities that line the Gulf of Mexico.

One such storm occurred here in 1919, known simply and appropriately as the Great Storm of 1919. It was a storm which decimated every home within a block of the bayfront, leaving an estimated 600 people dead. Although there was some warning about the potential dangers of the coming hurricane, the community was largely complacent because it had escaped mostly unscathed during a 1916 storm, when people were evacuated and only 16 lives were lost. By contrast, people refused to leave when evacuations were attempted before the 1919 storm—and with dreadful effect.

However, the tragedy also played a dramatic role in deciding the community's future. Corpus Christi residents were united in their efforts to petition the federal government for the construction of a protected harbor and a channel. Those efforts, in turn, led to the beautiful waterfront vista along the Corpus Christi Bay that draws so many visitors today. The seawall along the city's bayfront was completed in 1941.

Historians believe that there were a number of notable storms that likely came ashore in the eighteenth and nineteenth centuries. One such hurricane, in 1791, reportedly killed 50,000 cattle owned by José de le Garza Falcón at the Santa Petronilla Ranch south of the Nueces River. Other storm-related losses were also recorded during a storm that came to the area in 1837.

In 1874, the eye of a major hurricane hit the city and the community suffered major property damage, although no lives were lost. Six years later, in 1880, a storm that hit Matamoros, Mexico, caused an eight-foot tidal wave in Corpus Christi. In 1916, the tide rose nine feet and destroyed many piers and waterfront structures—although a timely evacuation of low-lying areas prevented major loss of life.

The 1919 hurricane remains the community's most destructive in terms of loss of life. This hurricane continues to hold the record as the city's most devastating. Hurricane tracking was in its infancy at the time, depending mostly on eyewitness sightings.

A review of the storm of 1919 offers an intimate glimpse into the life of Corpus Christi during that era. The storm, which formed near the Windward Islands in the Atlantic Ocean, arrived at the Florida Keys on September 8 and 9 and then blew into the Gulf of Mexico.

The traditional storm warning flags were raised along the coast of Texas and the U.S. Weather Bureau cautioned about the magnitude of the hurricane. However, most residents remained calm, since they had been through a hurricane three years earlier. The storm flags came down on a Saturday and people found that the fishing was extraordinarily good, with schools surfacing near the shore—a sign that something was amiss.

The rain began on Saturday night and continued through Sunday morning. The Weather Bureau forecast rain, but no immediate danger and the storm flags went back up. As the wind increased on Sunday afternoon, low-lying areas began flooding rapidly. Sixteen-foot seas were approaching the shore.

PAVILION HOTEL & PIER, CORPUS CHRISTI, TEX.

Right: Early tourists to Corpus Christi might have stayed at the Pavilion Hotel & Pier, which was built in the Corpus Christi Bay. The hotel was destroyed in the 1919 hurricane.

Below: Much of downtown was destroyed during the 1919 hurricane, and the city had to be placed under martial law during cleanup efforts.

Left: This early view of the city shows the electric trolley tracks and the proximity of homes and buildings to the waterfront. When the 1919 hurricane hit, all the buildings within a block of the bayfront were destroyed.
COURTESY OF THE CORPUS CHRISTI CHAMBER OF COMMERCE.

Below: Workers clear rubble from the streetcar barn in the wake of the 1919 hurricane.
COURTESY OF THE CORPUS CHRISTI PUBLIC LIBRARY, CENTRAL BRANCH, LOCAL HISTORY ROOM.

The eye of the storm crossed land 25 miles south of the city, with 110 mph winds and a 16-foot wall of water, flooding all of the city's North Beach and washing hundreds of people out to sea.

Those who lived through the storm told horrifying tales of watching relatives washed away and of floating for hours, bleeding and battered, in the raging flood waters. One woman was rescued by her collie. A man saw his wife and seven children drown. Survivors washed up on the beach the next day, with their clothing stripped away by the wind and water.

The city was without electricity, trolleys and water, and had to be placed under martial law. Everyone in town was drafted to help with cleanup and rescue efforts, and relief organizations from all over the state sent volunteer workers, food, mattresses, clothes, and coffins.

The courthouse was turned into a morgue, and the local newspaper ran descriptions of the bodies which had not been identified, such as: "Unidentified white girl, 14 or 15, wearing a Wall of Troy ring on the fourth finger of the left hand."

It was a devastating time for Corpus Christi, probably the most monumental setback of its existence since its precarious inception. Then-Texas Governor William P. Hobby penned a declaration of encouragement to the community on November 26, 1919, reminding them that they would be able to overcome the adversity of the horrific storm:

To the People of Corpus Christi: Emerging triumphant from the severest test of your endurance, you face a future that may be made alluring by lofty vision and by the strength of your will molded into a monument of lasting greatness. With a steadfastness of heroic courage, the persistency of indefatigable labor, the pride of home and family, the ambition of forward-looking Americans animating the lives and purpose of your citizenship, you cannot fail. These qualities I know you possess. They shall electrify the endeavors of the ensuing years and burn away the barrier to your progress.

Some historians believe that these regularly occurring storms, including a series that came

through in the 1960s, 1970s and 1980s, are a sort of brutal urban renewal program that serve as Mother Nature's way of wrecking substandard buildings and rejuvenating the coastal waters.

"Hurricanes have a revitalizing effect on the environment by flushing out bays and estuaries and stirring up unhealthy deposits of silt. They are harsh and cruel. They kill, maim and destroy. Yet they weed out the old and give the city a bright new face. For good or for bad, they have made Corpus Christi the 'Sparking City by the Sea,'" wrote historian Bill Walraven in his book, *Gift of the Wind*.

During the 1960s, several hurricanes came through the city, including Hurricane Carla in 1961, which brought beachfront flooding, and Beulah in 1967, which destroyed 178 dwellings.

Then there was Hurricane Celia, one of Texas' most devastating storms. Celia, which hit Corpus Christi on August 3, 1970, is considered the most destructive storm in the city's history. Because of modern weather forecasting and better building laws, there were fewer lives lost—only eleven—than in 1919. But the storm was extremely powerful, with wind gusts of up to 180 mph.

✧

Thousands of acres of ranch and farm land were flooded during Hurricane Beulah, which slammed into Corpus Christi on September 24, 1967.

COURTESY OF THE CORPUS CHRISTI PUBLIC LIBRARY, CENTRAL BRANCH, LOCAL HISTORY ROOM.

A sailor struggles against the wind in the marina as Hurricane Celia approaches. The 1970 hurricane ripped through Corpus Christi with 180-mile per hour winds.

Guardsmen patrolled the city to keep looters from emptying the damaged homes and businesses. It took nearly a year for the city to recover from the devastation.

In 1980, Allen destroyed 210 buildings, and did heavy damage to boats, piers and marinas on Corpus Christi Beach. More recently, tropical storm Charley hit the city in 1998 with 60 mph winds, very heavy rain, and flooding. Inland, there were 14 deaths due to the flooding. A year later, the city was spared the wrath of Hurricane Bret, a 125-mph storm which came ashore 50 miles to the south of Corpus Christi.

Statistically, the Corpus Christi area seems to receive a hurricane every four years or so, although sometimes those storms merely brush the region. Interestingly, September seems to be the month that historically brings the most devastating hurricanes to the Texas coastline. The hurricane season begins on June 1 and ends November 30, but the worst storms have traditionally arrived in August and September. Meteorologists believe that is the time when summer's heat brings warmth to the surface of the Atlantic Ocean, which creates storms along an area from the African coast to the western Gulf of Mexico.

Galveston was the site of the nation's worst on September 8, 1900, which left an estimated 6,000 people dead. Corpus Christi's deadliest hurricane, the Great Storm of 1919, occurred on September 14. Farther along the coast, the port city of Indianola was nearly wiped out by a hurricane that hit on September 16, 1875. Smaller storms that also wreaked devastation on the Gulf Coast during September include an unnamed hurricane that hit Brownsville on September 5, 1933; Hurricane Carla came ashore near Port Lavaca on September 11, 1961; and Beulah pounded Corpus Christi on September 20, 1967.

On average, there are 100 of these weather disturbances formed per year, with only a few transforming into tropical storms and even fewer into hurricanes.

However, thanks to improved weather forecasting, public alert systems, and evolving evacuation plans, today's hurricanes rarely cause as many fatalities as the storms of generations past.

Celia ripped through the city, leaving half a billion dollars in wind damage and power outages that lasted up to two weeks. but resulted in only 11 deaths. Its impact was somewhat of a surprise, because it had originally been predicted to be a moderate hurricane, with 90 mph winds, and many residents chose to stay in their homes. However, as it approached the Coastal Bend, the storm doubled in size in less than three hours and the wind gusts hit more than 180 mph. The tides were recorded at 12 feet at Aransas Pass, and six inches of rain fell. By the time Celia had passed through the region, it had destroyed a total of 8,950 homes.

Thousands of people were left homeless and slept in Red Cross shelters. Mobile field kitchens were used to feed them. National

✦

When the 1919 hurricane hit Corpus
Christi, its 110 mph winds and 16-foot seas
destroyed dozens of buildings and killed
approximately 600 people. Much of the
devastation was on Corpus Christi Beach, as
shown here.

COURTESY OF THE SPECIAL COLLECTIONS AND ARCHIVES,
MARY AND JEFF BELL LIBRARY, TEXAS A&M UNIVERSITY-
CORPUS CHRISTI.

CHAPTER VII

61

THE TEXAS RIVIERA COMES OF AGE

"Winds prevent the possibility of the accumulation of noxious vapors or disease germs,
and furnish a perpetual supply of the purest air from the ocean."
— from an 1886 tourism advertisement for Corpus Christi

Throughout its history, Corpus Christi has enjoyed a reputation as a resort community, attracting tourists early on with its sparkling coastline, moderate climate, and cooling breezes. Fishing piers, bathing houses, and shorefront carnivals were popular as early as the late 1800s, drawing a steady but small number of visitors to the region.

A favorite entertainment for early visitors was the "bathing beauty contest," held regularly at local hotels. One of the more enduring such contests was known as Splash Days, which began in 1917 as a beauty contest and picnic to kick off the summer tourist season. Splash Days evolved into the Buccaneer Days Celebration, which was first held in 1938 and continues today. The event's theme is the capture of the city by pirates, who then stage a parade to show off their spoils. Even today, the mayor is forced to "walk the plank" as part of opening ceremonies; other events include parades, a rodeo, dances, sporting events, and carnival.

However, until the 1980s, there was little in the way of large-scale entertainment or facilities designed solely for tourism. Corpus Christi's traditional economic base had always been in trade, agriculture, and industry; the military became a part of that economic base in the 1940s. The city's petrochemical complex was developed around the deep water port and the oil and gas industry.

For several decades after World War II, the city continued to grow both in population and industry. Several refineries located in the city, and Celanese Corp. of America established its plant in Bishop, about 34 miles from Corpus Christi. By 1951, there were six refineries in Corpus Christi, with a few others located in nearby towns. Twenty-four natural gas plants were located within a 50-mile radius of Corpus Christi, with a capacity of 2.2 million gallons per day.

The oil and gas industry in the area amounted to 2.5 billion barrels, about 8 percent of the total reserves in the nation. The natural gas reserves, approximately 30 trillion cubic feet, were one-sixth of the nation's reserves. Nueces County alone had 36 oil fields, 1,400 oil wells and approximately 400 gas wells.

In 1950, a four-mile causeway linking Corpus Christi with the 120-mile long Padre Island beach, known at first as the Padre Island Causeway but later renamed the John F. Kennedy Causeway, was opened. The construction of churches, schools and new residential developments continued steadily. Several important hospitals were established in the 1950s, including Spohn Hospital (today's Christus Spohn Health Care System) and Driscoll Foundation Children's Hospital.

In 1959, the Harbor Bridge that spans the Corpus Christi Ship Channel was completed, putting an end to the traffic delays that had been caused by the raising and lowering of the old Bascule Bridge. The next year saw the dedication of Corpus Christi International Airport.

In 1962, President Kennedy authorized the purchase of 80.5 miles of Padre Island for a national seashore, four years after legislators introduced the first bill calling for its creation. In Corpus Christi, the era saw the development of a number of cultural amenities, including museums and the Harbor Playhouse. By 1970, the city's population had reached 204,525.

A new convention center opened in 1981, and the construction of the 140-mile Interstate 37 was finished, connecting Corpus Christi with San Antonio. Another important event occurred in 1982, when city leaders dedicated the Choke Canyon Reservoir northwest of the city, a $112-million project intended to create a more reliable water source for residents and also to provide recreational opportunities.

But the 1980s also brought major changes for the region, as the oil and gas industry began its downturn. By 1986, crude oil prices declined 38 percent. City and community leaders realized the urgent need for economic diversity.

❖

A 1942 carnival on North Beach, now known as Corpus Christi Beach, offered rides, entertainment and refreshments for tourists.

Although tourism had always played a role in the city's fortunes, it wasn't until 1982 that the community leaders devoted significant resources and effort to promoting Corpus Christi as a travel destination. More than 200 buildings on Corpus Christi Beach had been destroyed by Hurricane Allen in 1980, and city officials prepared a variety of economic incentives to attract large-scale construction.

As a result, a host of tourist attractions was developed for the bayfront area and beyond, including the Texas State Aquarium and Lexington Museum on the Bay on Corpus Christi Beach; the Bayfront Arts and Science Park and the Watergarden, and the Art Center of Corpus Christi along the downtown bayfront.

The decade also saw a debate over development of another land mass in the Corpus Christi Marina. City planners wanted to create a shopping area and other tourist attractions in the marina, but many citizens opposed the plan. In 1986, the Army Corps of Engineers denied a permit for the project, which put an end to the plans.

In 1985, residents approved a ½-cent sales tax to fund a regional bus service. One year later, a new $4 million Corpus Christi Public Library opened. Other improvements includ-

ed a new six-story City Hall and, at the Bayfront Arts and Science Park, the $2.38 million Watergarden, a dancing water sculpture that serves as the park's centerpiece.

The Watergarden, designed by Robert Zion, was donated to the city by Edwin and Patsy Singer in 1988. It is flanked on two sides by museums, the Corpus Christi Museum of Science and History and the Art Museum of South Texas. The Museum of Science and History, dedicated on October 6, 1968, was the first building in the Arts and Sciences Park, but was soon followed by the Art Museum of South Texas. Created at the urging of local teachers and prominent business leaders, the museum collects and preserves natural and cultural history objects with emphasis on South Texas. It is also the marine archeology repository for Texas.

In 1993, the museum acquired the Ships of Christopher Columbus, $6.5 million reproductions of the vessels used by Columbus on his voyage to the New World. The ships were built by the government of Spain to commemorate the quincentenary of Columbus' voyage. In 2001, museum attendance was 72,342, mostly out-of-town visitors. Schoolchildren are admitted free, accounting

❖

Appreciative spectators crowd the balcony at the Breakers Hotel during a bathing beauty competition on June 9, 1937. Such contests were common during the early 20th century.

for more than 22,000 of the annual visitors.

On the other side of the Watergarden is the Art Museum of South Texas, designed by internationally famed architect Philip Johnson and completed in 1972. The white concrete-and-plaster building, located at the north end of downtown's Shoreline Boulevard, is a work of art in itself—in addition to serving as the city's primary facility for fine art.

Consisting of three levels, approximately 12,000 of the building's 30,000 square feet belong to galleries. The lowest level, located at sea level, contains classrooms, studios, a library, and storage and work areas. The next level, the main entrance, faces the Bayfront Arts and Science Park and is equipped with galleries, a gift shop, an auditorium, and interactive kids' playroom. A 60-foot catwalk runs above the main level and leads to a sky-lit gallery on the 3rd level. The floor-to-ceiling windows offer a spectacular view of Corpus Christi Bay as well as the Harbor Bridge.

Another attraction near the Arts and Sciences Park is a collection of historic homes that have been renovated and opened to the public. Heritage Park, opened by the city in 1977, contains nine historic homes that have been moved from their original sites and refurbished by various non-profit organizations.

Corpus Christi battled several cities for the official state aquarium designation and finally acquired it. The Texas State Aquarium, which opened in 1990, is considered the city's most popular tourist attraction, with more than five million visitors since its opening. Of the 25 accredited aquariums in the nation, the Texas State Aquarium ranks 15th in the number of visitors—500,000—per year. The 43,000-square foot facility features 3,500 animals in 40 different habitats. The largest tank is the Islands of Steel habitat, a replica of an offshore oil and gas platform that is 132,000 gallons with a 35-foot viewing window. In the fall of 2001, the Aquarium began construction on its newest

✧

Above: Families and cars gathered along Padre Island National Seashore in July 1951.

COURTESY OF THE CORPUS CHRISTI PUBLIC LIBRARY, CENTRAL BRANCH, LOCAL HISTORY ROOM

Opposite, top: The Tommy Dorsey Orchestra, with Doc Severenson on trumpet, Buddy Rich on drums and Charlie Shavers on trumpet, played at the Galvan Ballroom during the annual Buccaneer Days festival on March 30, 1949.

COURTESY OF THE RAFAEL, SR., AND VIRGINIA REYES GALVAN FAMILY PAPERS, SPECIAL COLLECTIONS AND ARCHIVES, MARY AND JEFF BELL LIBRARY, TEXAS A&M UNIVERSITY-CORPUS CHRISTI.

Opposite, bottom: Four hunters pose with a bountiful assortment of game after a successful hunting trip. Hunting has always been a popular pastime for visitors to Corpus Christi.

COURTESY OF THE CORPUS CHRISTI PUBLIC LIBRARY, CENTRAL BRANCH, LOCAL HISTORY ROOM

exhibit, Dolphin Bay, a lagoon that will house Atlantic bottlenose dolphins.

Likewise, competition to provide a permanent home for the World War II-era *Lexington* aircraft carrier was fierce. Nicknamed the Blue Ghost by the Japanese because it repeatedly defied reports that it had gone down during World War II, the *Lexington* downed more than 1,000 enemy planes, sank 300,000 tons of Japanese shipping, and damaged another 600,000 tons.

Because of Corpus Christi's long history with the Navy and naval aviation in particular, the Corpus Christi Area Economic Development Commission formed a task force of community leaders, known as Landing Force 16, to bring the ship—nicknamed the Blue Ghost—to the city. With an active fundraising campaign and strong community support, the Corpus Christi City Council

endorsed a $3 million dollar bond sale to finance the project.

In August 1991, Landing Force 16 presented Corpus Christi's proposal to Secretary of the Navy Lawrence Garrett, III and the city was awarded the *Lexington*. Today, the decommissioned aircraft carrier-turned-museum sits in the Corpus Christi Bay and draws thousands of visitors per year. The museum also hosts a number of educational events and camps.

Across town, another tourist attraction was opened in 1988, the Corpus Christi Botanical Gardens. This 180-acre site along Oso Creek offers colorful, exotic floral exhibits blended with nature tourism and eco-education. Among the exhibits are the Orchid Exhibit House, Plumeria collection, Hibiscus Garden, Sensory Garden, Rose Garden, Arid Garden, and a Water Garden. There is also a shaded Bird and Butterfly Trail through the native habitat, a

Right: Sport fishing in Port Aransas has always been a draw for visitors, with many opting to take charter boat trips.

Below: A sailboat glides across the Corpus Christi Bayfront in front of the seawall and the Bayfront Plaza and Convention Center. The Harbor Bridge is in the background.

Above: The Watergarden, shown here with
the Art Museum of South Texas in the
background, was built in 1988.

COURTESY OF THE CORPUS CHRISTI
CHAMBER OF COMMERCE

Left: Visitors and residents alike enjoy
renting aqua cycles, a sort of water bicycle,
for traversing the bayfront.

COURTESY OF THE CORPUS CHRISTI
CHAMBER OF COMMERCE

CHAPTER VIII

69

Wetlands Boardwalk, and a Birding Tower and Palapa Grande located on Gator Lake. The site is listed as one of the state's premier birding sites, on the Great Texas Coastal Birding Trail. The Visitors Center includes a gift shop and gallery.

By 1990, the city's population had grown to 257,453. The mainstay of the city's eco- nomic base was tourism, the port, and the military. In 1992, developers opened the Corpus Christi Greyhound Racetrack, one of seven in Texas under legislation that permits parimutuel betting on dog races.

The attention of the international music world came to Corpus Christi on March 31,

1995, when young Tejano singer Selena Quintanilla-Perez was murdered at a Corpus Christi motel by the founder of her fan club. Thousands of tourists annually visit the memorial statue in her honor located along the bayfront and pay their respects at her gravesite. City leaders also renamed the city's auditorium in her honor.

In 1997 the city began work on the Gateway Project that was designed to add a parkway and landscaping to the city's entrance. The first phase created a six-acre greenbelt from the old Nueces County Courthouse to Shoreline Boulevard, where a new $22 million federal courthouse was completed in 2001. Although future development is still being debated by the City Council, plans call for merging the divided lanes of Shoreline Boulevard to create a bayfront park adjacent to the seawall.

Today, Corpus Christi is the state's second most popular vacation destination, with more than five million visitors per year. Nestled behind the barrier islands of Mustang and Padre, Corpus Christi is the gateway to Padre Island National Seashore, a short and pleasant drive from downtown.

Tourist brochures highlight the natural recreation opportunities, emphasizing that the Corpus Christi region shares the same latitude as Tampa, Florida, giving it a similar semitropical climate. The proximity of the Gulf of Mexico means that the temperate climate can be found all year.

Those early promoters who touted the area's healthful breezes couldn't have envisioned the tourist attractions of today. Nonetheless, their instincts about the community's destiny as a vacation site have proved correct.

✦

Businesses and hotels located along the downtown waterfront sparkle at dusk.

COURTESY OF THE CORPUS CHRISTI CHAMBER OF COMMERCE.

LOOKING TOWARD THE FUTURE

"Residents of Corpus Christi obviously love their bay. Why else would they put a large picture window in their art museum so visitors could pause from looking at man-made art and look out at the natural beauty of the bay? Why else build a marina close enough to the downtown office buildings so boat owners can walk down and relax with a sail at the end of the day?"
— from Robert Rafferty's book, *Texas Coast and the Rio Grande Valley*, Texas Monthly Guidebooks.

The coastline discovered by Spanish explorers of centuries past is today a modern and gleaming waterfront community. Known for its recreational opportunities, the city of Corpus Christi is one of the state's most popular tourist destinations. Each year more than 5 million visitors come to the city, known as the "Sparking City by the Sea." On the 150th anniversary of its founding, it is an entirely modern city yet it still retains much of the flavor that drew the earliest settlers to these coastal shores.

Corpus Christi, with a population of 275,000, is the largest city on the Texas coast and the sixth largest port in the nation. Major industries include petrochemical, tourism, healthcare, retail, education, shipping, agriculture, and the military. It serves as a regional hub for marketing, packaging, processing, and distributing agricultural commodities for a 12-county trade area.

The city today has three main areas—residential, business-maritime-industrial, and recreational. Its growth has long been founded on its natural resources and attributes, including the water, which allows for transportation, commerce, and recreation; and the land, which is rich in petroleum and good for agriculture.

Its signature vista is the wide boulevard that borders the bayfront, beginning with the Bayfront Arts and Science Park at the north end and continuing southward until it reaches the Naval Air Station Corpus Christi. In the downtown section, this scenic boulevard is flanked by a 14-foot high, nearly two-mile long seawall of terraced facing that leads to the water and serves as a protective barrier for the downtown area.

This seawall, completed in 1941, was designed by sculptor Gutzon Borghum, whose most famous project is Mount Rushmore. With its 20-foot wide adjoining sidewalk, the seawall is a favorite for joggers, walkers, cyclists, skaters and those who just want to sit on a bench and enjoy the beautiful waterfront view.

The average summertime temperature is 83 degrees Fahrenheit, and 59.7 degrees in the winter, with an annual average of a balmy 71.2 degrees. Wintertime temperatures in the 70s and 80s are common. Such a temperate climate allows for year-round outdoor recreational activities, including fishing in the bay and offshore, outdoor tennis, sailing, golf, and windsurfing.

Nature lovers have increasingly been attracted to the region, and many birders flock to the area to view the variety of birds here. Of the nearly 800 North American bird species, an estimated 500 can be found in the Corpus Christi and coastal area. In addition to resident songbirds, shore birds, game birds and raptors, the area is a migratory flyway for birds heading south in the fall and north in the spring.

The city's proximity to Padre Island National Seashore, the world's longest barrier island, also attracts many beach-goers and nature enthusiasts. Padre Island, with over 130 miles of top-ranked beaches, contains Big Shell and Little Shell Beaches, famed for their seashells, and Seagull Park, a perfect site for a family picnic.

Corpus Christi, bordered on the east and south by the Corpus Christi Bay and Oso Bay, is located at an elevation of 27 feet above sea level. It encompasses a land area of 349.581 square kilometers. The population of the Corpus Christi Metropolitan Statistical Area, which includes Nueces and San Patricio Counties, has grown by over 100,000 since 1975, reaching 379,036. The median age of the population is 31 years old.

✧

Seagulls sit along the rock jetties in front of the downtown skyline of office buildings and hotels.

COURTESY OF THE CORPUS CHRISTI
CHAMBER OF COMMERCE

Above: Sailboats, pleasure boats and shrimp boats can be found along the T-heads that extend from Corpus Christi's seawall into the Corpus Christi Bay.

COURTESY OF THE CORPUS CHRISTI
CHAMBER OF COMMERCE

Right: A young girl dressed in a colorful folk costume dances during a multicultural performance.

COURTESY OF THE CORPUS CHRISTI
CHAMBER OF COMMERCE

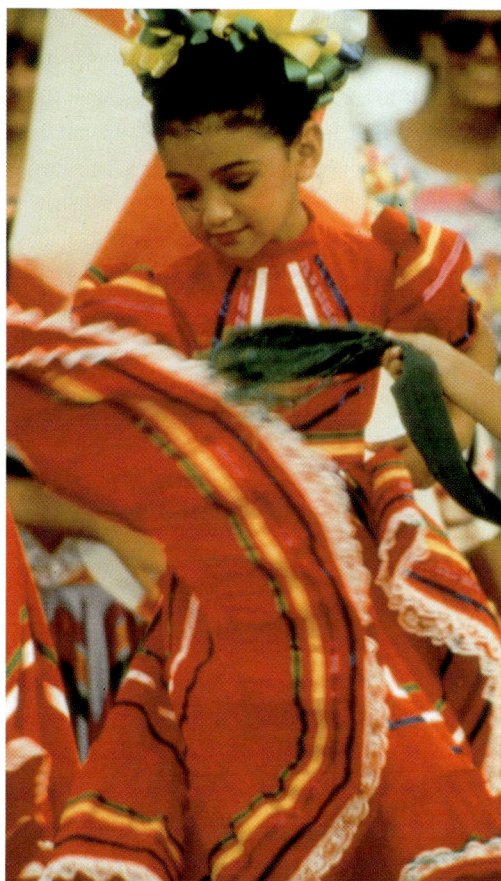

There are approximately 100,205 families in Corpus Christi, which is located 1,436 miles (as the crow flies) from Washington, D.C. and 181 miles from Austin, the state capitol. Residents enjoy cultural amenities including nine museums, a symphony orchestra, a jazz society, art center, two theater groups, two ballet troupes, and a national windsurfing regatta.

The city has a home-rule government with a mayor, eight council members, and a city manager. The city manager serves as a chief executive officer, carrying out policy and handling operations as directed by the City Council.

The 21st century has seen the city continue its path of growth and development. Early on, a key issue for the residents of this bayfront city was storm protection and bayfront development. It's an issue that still resonates today, as modern citizens grapple with concerns about whether and how to best develop the city's waterfront property, the community's trademark bayfront.

While keeping its eye on the future, the community is also working to preserve some of its

Left: A surfer catches a wave at Mustang Island State Park, a favorite haven for many beachgoers.

COURTESY OF THE CORPUS CHRISTI CHAMBER OF COMMERCE

Below: Birders find plenty to look at in Corpus Christi and the surrounding area, which is home to more than 500 species of birds.

COURTESY OF THE CORPUS CHRISTI CHAMBER OF COMMERCE

CHAPTER IX

75

Right: A burst of fireworks illuminates the downtown night sky during the city's Fourth of July festivities.

Below: Eight "miradores del mar," constructed along the city's seawall in 1991, are shaded outlooks that contain benches for passersby. The miradores contain plaques that recount the city's history.

COURTESY OF THE CORPUS CHRISTI
CHAMBER OF COMMERCE

Golfers find that they can play nearly year-round in Corpus Christi because of the moderate climate.

heritage. Fundraising efforts to restore the 1914 Nueces County Courthouse are working to raise the $950,000 necessary to receive a $1.9 million grant from the Texas Historical Commission. Organizers of the effort, including Friends of the Courthouse Inc. and the Nueces County Historical Society, hope to renovate the aging structure that has long been neglected. The building was designed by Harvey Page in a Neo-Classical Greek Revival style.

✧

Above: Sailing has always been a popular activity for many residents and visitors.

COURTESY OF THE CORPUS CHRISTI
CHAMBER OF COMMERCE

Right: The setting sun provides a dramatic backdrop for these joggers along the bayfront.

COURTESY OF THE CORPUS CHRISTI
CHAMBER OF COMMERCE

City leaders have also worked on revitalizing downtown, once the center of the community's existence. A variety of clubs, businesses and restaurants have opened in recent years, helping to draw both visitors and residents to the downtown area and strengthen the city's economic base.

One of the most significant areas in which Corpus Christi has advanced in recent decades is in the arena of higher education. There have long been two institutions of higher education in the city.

Del Mar College, founded in 1935, serves approximately 24,000 credit and non-credit students each year. It is ranked among the nation's top 50 community colleges granting associate degrees to Hispanic students. Degrees available are the Associate in Arts and Associate in Science degrees in over 50 university transfer majors; Associate in Applied Science degrees, Enhanced Skills Certificates, and Certificates of Achievement in more than 80 occupational fields.

The college prides itself on being affordable and accessible, providing more than $8 million per year to assist students with financial aid. Its east and west campuses cover 159 acres with facilities that house classes, laboratories, and the latest technology to prepare students for further study or employment in the Coastal Bend area.

Located on Ward Island, Texas A&M University-Corpus Christi originated as a Baptist college in 1947. In 1971, its affiliation with the Baptists ended and the state took over, running the then-University of Corpus Christi as an upper-level, two-year institution.

In 1973, its name was changed to Texas A&I University at Corpus Christi; four years later, it was again renamed, this time as Corpus Christi State University. In 1989, the university was merged into the Texas A&M University system and it received its current name, Texas A&M University-Corpus Christi, in 1993. The first freshmen and sophomore students arrived in 1994. Today, enrollment is

✧

Fulton Mansion State Historical Park near Rockport offers visitors a glimpse inside a stately Victorian mansion built in 1874.

COURTESY OF THE CORPUS CHRISTI
CHAMBER OF COMMERCE

more than 7,300 students, and there are 55 undergraduate and graduate degree programs.

Considered one of the state's fastest growing four-year universities, Texas A&M-Corpus Christi is also the only university in America located on its own island. Its palm tree-lined campus is surrounded by natural wetlands, and a newly restored beach provides an on-site laboratory for maritime studies.

Nearby is Texas A&M University-Kingsville, a comprehensive university of 6,500 students in Kingsville, about 40 miles south of Corpus Christi. A multi-cultural campus, its population mirrors that of the region; it also enrolls students from 31 other states and 50 countries.

Known as one of the most economical universities in Texas, it boasts nationally recognized programs in engineering, agriculture, and the sciences. Bachelor's degrees are offered in more than 65 fields. The university also has a College of Graduate Studies offering master's degrees in 38 major fields.

In addition, Texas A&M-Kingsville has developed joint doctoral programs in both educational leadership and adult education with the main Texas A&M University campus in College Station. A joint doctorate in wildlife science with Texas A&M is also being developed.

There are several organizations that are focused on the improving the business climate in the city and surrounding area, such as the Corpus Christi Chamber of Commerce, the Convention and Visitors Bureau, and the Corpus Christi Regional Economic Development Corporation.

As the largest city in the 12-county area known as the Coastal Bend, Corpus Christi serves as a healthcare, shopping and transportation hub for the surrounding area. There are a number of vibrant, smaller cities and towns nearby that grew along with Corpus Christi during the past 150 years of development.

One of the first to be established was Port Aransas, which went through several name changes. It was first called Mustang Island for

✧
A family of tourists enjoys the sun, sand and water along Corpus Christi Beach. The city's skyline is in the background.

❖

A picturesque view from the marina in downtown Corpus Christi in 2002.

COURTESY OF THE CORPUS CHRISTI CHAMBER OF COMMERCE

the wild horses that roamed the shores. Its first post office arrived in 1880. Later, the town was called Star, then Ropesville after promoter Elihu Ropes and then Tarpon for more than two decades—the fish beloved by anglers that populated its waters. The current name, Port Aransas, was chosen when the city was incorporated in 1911. Today, Port Aransas is a laid-back resort town with great fishing and a population that swells to 100,000 during summer months.

Rockport, once known as Rocky Point, is named for its famous rocky ledge. In the 1880s, it was known as Aransas Pass but it changed back to Rockport a few years later. In the meantime, the town of Aransas Harbor appropriated the name of Aransas Pass. Rockport is today a seaside village that attracts artists, nature lovers, and anglers. Nearby Fulton, too, draws visitors with its windswept, waterfront live oak trees and the Fulton Mansion, a three-story Victorian structure that dates back to 1874 and is now a state historical park.

Kingsville has a vivid history, populated with larger-than-life leaders, hard-riding *vaqueros*, racehorses, and cattle drives. In 1853, Captain Richard King purchased land on the Santa Gertrudis Creek and began building an empire that his widow, Henrietta,

continued. The ranch now encompasses 825,000 acres and is considered the birthplace of the modern cattle industry. One of King's children, Alice, married lawyer Robert J. Kleberg, and the two envisioned a city near the ranch with a railroad. The city dates its official birthday on July 4, 1904, when the first regular passenger train of the St. Louis, Brownsville and Mexico Railroad arrived.

A list of the other area towns offers a glimpse into the people and events that shaped this region's history: Agua Dulce, Alice, Aransas Pass, Banquete, Bayside, Beeville, Benavides, Bishop, Driscoll, Falfurrias, Freer, George West, Gregory, Ingleside, Ingleside-on-the-Bay, Mathis, Odem, Orange Grove, Petronilla, Premont, Portland, Refugio, Robstown, San Diego, San Patricio, Sinton, Taft, Three Rivers, Violet, and Woodsboro.

Visitors and new arrivals to Corpus Christi find a thriving and welcoming city that has managed to both retain a sense of its history and keep a steady focus on its future. At the 150th anniversary of its founding, it is a city that has surely exceeded the hopes of the forward-thinking pioneers who arrived on these shores more than a century ago. Today we pay homage to their vision, persistence, and courage, and hope that they may continue to inspire us.

SHARING THE HERITAGE

historic profiles of businesses, organizations, and families that have contributed to the development and economic base of Corpus Christi

In 1924 the Corpus Christi Chamber of Commerce as it is known today was born. On February 15, 1924, Henry B. Baldwin was elected the first president of the Chamber of Commerce. The organization was able to attract the influential leaders and businesspersons who knew how to get things accomplished. They were instrumental in developing many of the city's current assets.

Following official reorganization, the new Chamber of Commerce office was moved from a building on Starr Street, near the site of the old Federal Building, to the City Council Chamber of the City Hall, where it remained until 1940. It later moved to the fifth floor of the Nixon Building (now called the Wilson Building) and in 1951, it moved to its new headquarters at 1201 North Shoreline Drive, where it is currently located.

The Port was one of the first major Chamber achievements. The Chamber's directors aggressively lobbied for federal support, and financed the grandiose celebration ($50,000) of the opening of the Port on September 14-15, 1926. Chamber supporters named Robert Driscoll the Chairman of the Nueces County Navigation Commission and Roy Miller as vice-chairman. Today Corpus Christi is home to the fifth largest port in the nation, generating over forty thousand jobs.

The Chamber spearheaded efforts (which included obtaining Federal funds) that would build infrastructure securing the city's downtown from flooding and storm damage. The federal government informed the city leadership that this issue needed to be resolved before federal dollars would be made available for the dredging of the Port. The surrounding counties agreed to reroute tax dollars being sent to the state to Corpus Christi to be used solely and exclusively for the seawall project. The filling in of the area between Water Street and what is now Shoreline Drive and the building of the seawall followed.

With the advent of world unrest in the late 1930's and early 1940s, Chamber members began working to convince military and governmental officials in Washington to locate a naval station in the city. In 1941 the Corpus Christi Naval Air Station opened. The Chamber's support for the military includes working to maintain the Corpus Christi Army Depot in the city over the past several decades, as well as working to keep the Naval Air Station and to bring a homeport to the area. The Chamber played the key role in getting Washington officials to name Ingleside the site for the new Homeport. Through its Military Affairs Committee and the South Texas Military Facilities Task Force, the Chamber continues to monitor and respond to base closure discussions, considers opportunities for base expansions, and provide ongoing support to local military installations and their personnel.

In 1979 the Chamber and the Visitors Bureau agreed to work together and expand the Chamber's facility to accommodate both organizations. The Chamber and the Bureau shared the project cost. In early 1981 the Convention and Visitors Bureau relocated to the newly expanded 8,278 square foot Chamber building on Shoreline Drive. The Economic Development Corporation established offices at the Chamber when it was organized in 1986.

The list of Chamber-sponsored activities and developments is endless and includes such diverse projects as the Wesley Seale Dam, Harbor Bridge, the Texas State Aquarium, Deep Port, Choke Canyon Dam, Interstate 37, and the merger of Texas A&M with Corpus Christi State University.

The mission of the Chamber of Commerce is to be a "member-driven organization whose principle mission is to foster business growth by advocating business issues, enhancing the business climate, and providing services to our members." In the last decade, the Chamber has taken on several additional major projects for improvement and maintenance of the city. The Chamber was key in passing the vote in 2001 to fund the current repair project of the seawall, and the expansion of the Convention Center and new multi-purpose arena.

The Chamber also is currently supporting the proposition of a eighth-cent sales tax increase for economic development including the proposed baseball stadium as well as affordable housing. The Corpus Christi Chamber of Commerce remains a vital, active organization promoting the Corpus Christi area, serving the needs of the business community, and making Corpus Christi a better place in which to live and work.

CORPUS CHRISTI CHAMBER OF COMMERCE

SAM KANE BEEF PROCESSORS, INC.
BY JAIME POWELL

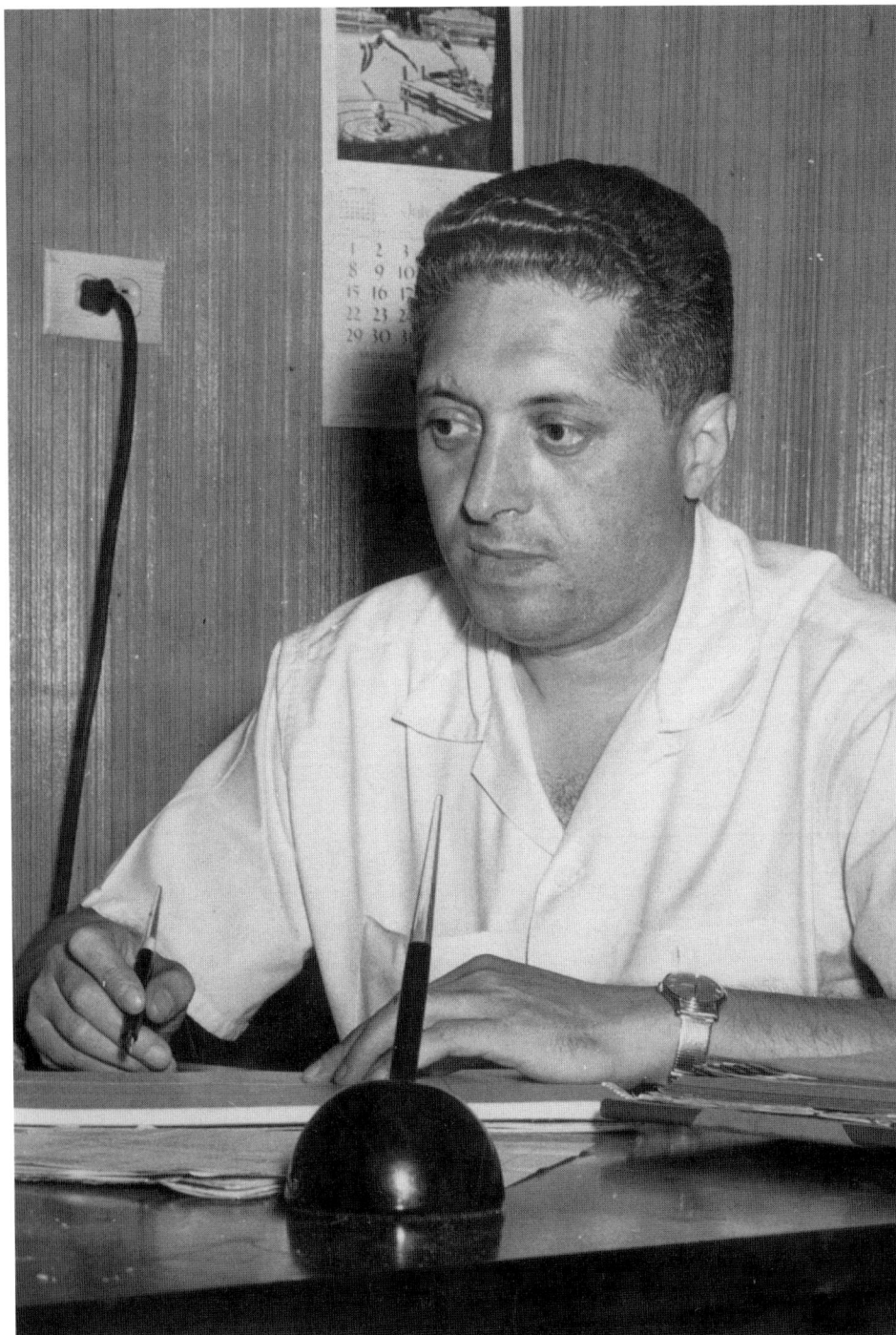

✧

Sam Kane.

Sam Kane and his family are living proof that the American dream is not a myth. Over the past fifty-four years, the Kane family has illustrated with the family beef processing behemoth that hard work; family values, faith and perseverance can pay off.

Sam Kane Beef Processors Inc. started in a tiny storefront grocery on Morgan Avenue in 1949. Since then Kane and his family have shepherded it into one of the largest independently owned beef processors in the United States.

Across the country, the number of independent beef processors has declined dramatically, while the Kane family business continues to thrive.

The company employs more than 750 people. Employees process 1,200 to 1,400 cattle a day, six days a week and produce more than fifteen percent of the beef graded "select" or "choice" in the country.

The company's success can be traced to the work ethic and old-fashioned business values Kane has passed down to his sons Harold and Jerry, who now run the company.

When Kane immigrated to America from post-war Europe, he had seen many of the atrocities life could offer. He and his brother, Bernard were the only survivors from a family of fourteen when Hitler's armies ravaged their homeland, Czechoslovakia during World War II. Kane was a resistance fighter and managed to evade the Nazis and almost certain death.

The woman who would become his wife, Aranka Feldbrandt and her sister were not so lucky. They were forced into the Auschwitz concentration camp destined for the gas chambers. The fact that they were talented seamstresses saved their lives. Instead of the death sentence inherent in the camps, they were reassigned to make clothes in a work camp.

When the war ended they were reunited and fled hours before the Russians brought down the iron curtain that would separate Eastern and Western Europe for decades.

Sam, Aranka, their one-year old son Jerry, and Bernard came to America and settled near Kane's aunt in Corpus Christi. Sam worked as a plumber's assistant and did other odd jobs before deciding he might have better luck in a bigger city.

While he was waiting for the bus that would take him to Chicago, Sam met a man who claimed that the real opportunities were in smaller communities like Corpus Christi because there was room to grow. Sam heeded the advice and the very next day found a job running a meat counter at a local grocery store.

A short time later, Sam started his own meat market, Sam Kane's Wholesale Meat where he cut meat and worked on his command of the English language.

After the long hours at the market, Sam came home talking about expansion. With his young family behind him, he invested the profits from his meat market into property in Annaville where he could build a business that would have room to grow. The dream started as a Quonset hut on Leopard Street where he slaughtered twenty-five head of cattle a day and has culminated in the high-tech operation that serves thousands of customers throughout the United States and many foreign countries.

The business has faced major setbacks like a 1991 fire that gutted the company's production facility and damaged the rest of the plant. It bounced back by selling stored projects and accepting assistance from the community, which immediately came to the family's aid.

The company turned the rebuilding process into an opportunity to modernize and now uses the latest technology to serve its customer base. The reconstruction process also allowed expansion into new areas of commerce not previously available due to construction constraints and streamlined operations to keep costs under control.

Innovative technology at the plant includes the newest vacuum packaging equipment,

✧

Left: Sam Kane Wholesale Meat, Inc., in 1953.

Below: Bernard (left) and Sam Kane (right), c. 1962.

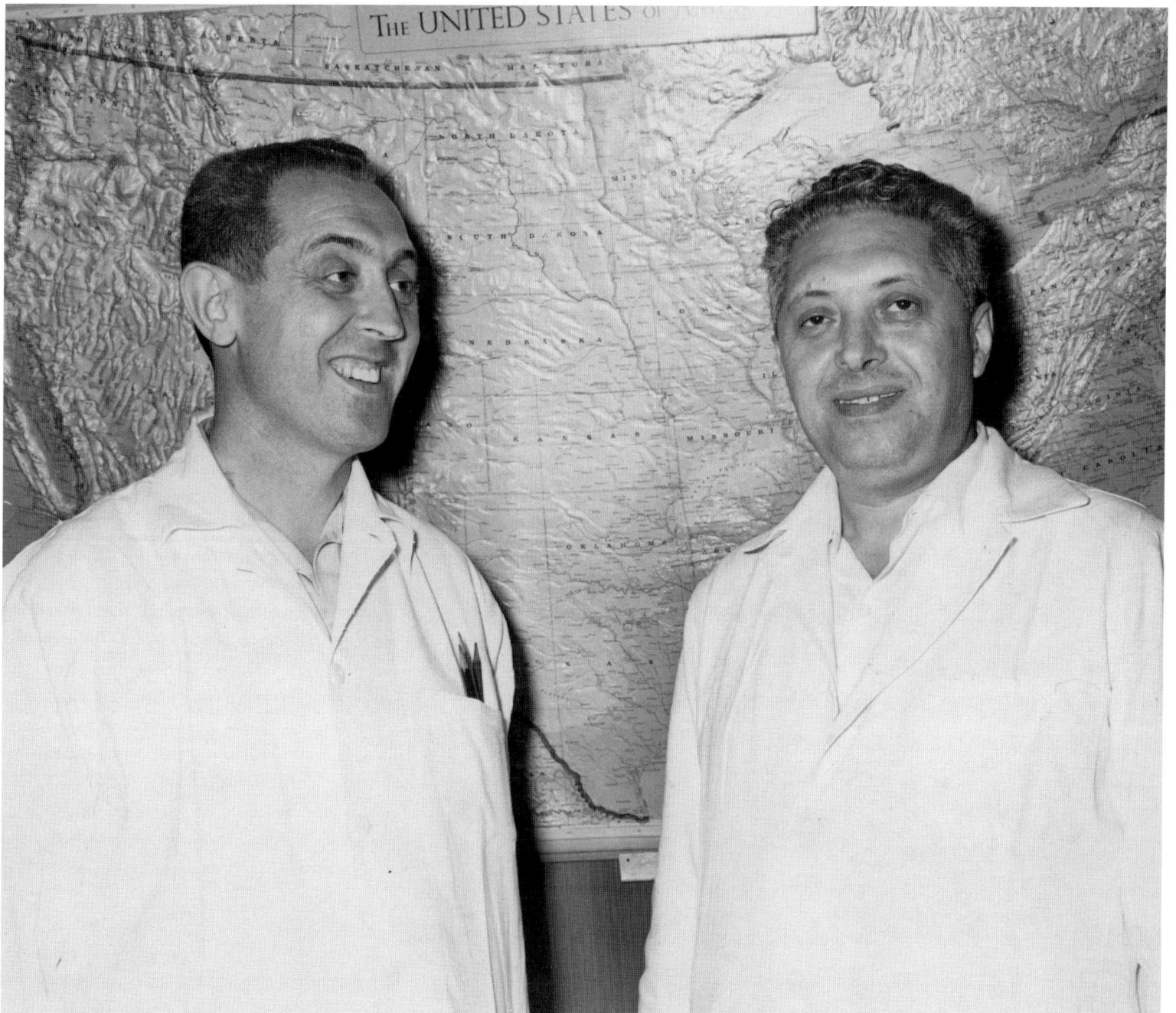

HRI steak and ground beef systems, industrialized robotics, highly efficient fabricating lines, automated carcass storage and retrieval and storage for seven million pounds of fresh boxed beef in a computer-operated warehouse.

The company also revolutionized the meat processing industry by using electro-stimulation to age all of its beef. The company, in conjunction with Texas A&M University and LaFiell Company developed the procedure. Sam Kane's was the first to utilize it on a high-volume assembly line and is the only company that continues to use the scientific process, which has been proven to enhance the quality, flavor, tenderness, value and palatability of beef.

Sam Kane Beef Processor, Inc., feeds and selects cattle that meet its customer's requirements for marbling and cutability, and places special emphasis on carcass selection, specialized fabrication, rigid quality control standards and order-matched product selection.

Its Corpus Christi facility produces a wide range of products for the largest supermarket chains and industry giants in the country and the world. Sam Kane's specializes in grain-fed, graded beef and produces high-quality beef products for grocery stores and restaurants.

The company prides itself on investing the resources necessary to achieve the safe, high quality meat products that to which Sam Kanes' consumers have become accustomed.

The company continues to meet consumer needs through the hard work and dedication to quality Sam espoused. The Kane family admits they will always be grateful for that bit of advice the unknown gentleman gave to Sam over fifty years ago. When he urged Sam to stay and find a future in Corpus Christi, he laid a cornerstone for a business that continues to operate independently and employs the old-fashioned business ethics and hard work that made it a success in the first place.

Today, Sam Kane Beef Processors, Inc., is owned and operated by Sam Kane, chief executive officer; Jerry Kane, president and chief operating officer; Harold Kane, chief financial officer and vice president; Bernard Kane, vice chairman and vice president; Esther Kan, vice president of marketing; Alfred Bausch, vice president and director of plant operations; David Kane; Jeffrey Kane; Leslie Kane; and Jordan Davis.

✧

Opposite: Bernard (left) and Sam Kane (right) in a holding room.

Left: Sam Kane Beef Processors, 1954.

Below: The present Sam Beef Processors, Inc., plant.

HOUSING AUTHORITY OF CORPUS CHRISTI

❖

Below: Examples of the unsanitary, unsuitable homes in which persons lived before the establishment of the Housing Authority, 1938.

Bottom: Dwelling units being demolished in order to construct Navarro Place public housing development, 1939.

Since the days of The Great Depression, the Housing Authority of Corpus Christi has worked to provide economical housing to low-income residents regardless of race. Its roots can be traced to the United States Housing Authority Federal Works Program spearheaded by President Franklin D. Roosevelt as part of his "New Deal" for the American people.

Following the enactment of the United States Housing Act of 1937, the Texas Legislature in 1938 passed the Housing Cooperation Law, providing for the creation of housing authorities in individual cities.

That same year, Corpus Christi set up a planning commission to determine the feasibility of launching a low-rent housing project. The plan provided for slum clearance and one new housing unit for every unsanitary, unsuitable building demolished.

Congress authorized the United States Housing Authority to lend $500 million over a three-year period for slum clearance and low-rent housing construction. Corpus Christi requested $1 million to build 1,100 units.

The USHA approved $938,710 for Corpus Christi to build 242 units. Slum demolition began immediately and by July of 1939, 54 units on what would become Corpus Christi's first low-income public housing project had been destroyed.

Eventually, 466 families would be removed from substandard and unsanitary shacks–many with no lights or water–and placed in new housing. The projects were designed to give people with low-income jobs decent homes at a monthly rental commensurate with their incomes.

In those days, Texas law mandated segregation in public housing projects, with residents divided into dwellings for "white persons, Negroes, and persons of Mexican descent."

The housing authority completed its first Corpus Christi project, named Kinney Place after the city's founder, in August of 1940. This 158-unit project, built for $350,000, was designed for Anglos and charged $13.50 to $14.50 a month.

Units were grouped around a new city park and recreation center, with playgrounds, softball diamonds, basketball courts, croquet, horseshoes, picnic areas and volleyball courts. Social programs provided on-site included homemaking classes, Girl Scouts, Camp Fire Girls, YMCA Boys Club, Garden Club and an annual picnic.

Completed at the same time as Kinney Place, the D.N. Leathers Center (122 units) and Navarro Place (210 units) served the housing needs of Corpus Christi's black and Hispanic populations. Due to popular demand, D. N. Leathers Center, named for Daniel Newton Leathers, founder of the city's Negro Business League, grew from 98 to 122 units.

Navarro Place, referred to at the time as the Latin-American Project, was built over one of the worst slums in the city. In La Pascua Addition, three or more shacks made from

scrap lumber, tin, tarpaper and other salvage material occupied 25-foot-by-50-foot lots.

Mr. and Mrs. Juan Garcia were the first residents of Navarro Place. Mrs. Garcia was the great-granddaughter of Jose Antonio Navarro, the Texas patriot for whom the project was named.

In June of 1940, the U.S. Navy announced plans to build Naval Air Station-Corpus Christi, at the time the world's largest naval air training station. A year later, the housing authority completed three projects designed for Navy enlisted men and civilian military employees.

La Armada I (250 units), the first defense housing project in the country, provided bus service to the air station. And when the air station doubled in size, the housing authority responded with La Armada II (400 units), and La Armada III (100 units).

"These homes were built by the people of the United States for the defenders of this nation," said President Roosevelt, describing projects like La Armada.

By the end of the first quarter of 1941, 323 of 385 unsafe Corpus Christi dwellings had been demolished, and an article in the local newspaper described the city as a model for slum clearance and construction of defense housing.

In response to an amendment to the 1956 Housing Act, the Housing Authority of Corpus Christi allowed single people older than 65 to live in public housing. And more than a decade later, the HACC board abolished the rule prohibiting unwed mothers from becoming tenants.

In 1963 the HACC purchased the Clairelaine Gardens I and II (186 units) from a private owner for $1.2 million to provide low-rent housing for the elderly. Through the years, the HACC has worked to provide tenants with a sense of community.

In 1968 the HACC set up a program to help tenants with needs such as housekeeping and children's health services, which were provided by eight aides employed by the HACC.

Tenants were given a voice in project operations in 1970 when Angie Garcia, president of the Corpus Christi Tenants Association asked that tenants be involved in HACC planning, development, program management, and grievance procedures.

On August 3, 1970, Hurricane Celia hit Corpus Christi, destroying numerous

✧

Above: Construction of D. N. Leathers Center, located on the north side of Corpus Christi, 1940.

Below: Construction of La Armada, the initial defense housing project in the country, 1940.

✧

Above: Completion of Kinney Place (now George Wiggins Homes), 1941.

Below: Youths playing at George Wiggins Homes, 1943.

dwellings. Within six months, the federal government announced plans to build 500 public housing units, with almost half to be built in Corpus Christi and the rest in surrounding cities.

For the first time in HACC history, builders were allowed to use their own discretion in deciding how many units to build on each site. The three sites, which broke away from stereotypical public housing designs, were designed as housing communities with greenways, playgrounds and a large park.

In 1974 Congress passed an act that included the Section 8 Program, which allowed qualifying tenants to pay no more than twenty-five percent of their income on rent, with the rest subsidized through the government.

On April 26, 1978, HACC celebrated its 40th birthday. It managed 11 housing projects at the time that, through the years, provided homes for more than 22,000 families. The HACC, which had a $1.5 million annual operating budget, boasted tenant associations in 11 projects.

Tenant associations continued to be the norm by 1980, along with on-site property managers and programs provided by the Corpus Christi Police Department and the Mental Health & Mental Retardation Center of Nueces County.

In 1991 Henry Flores, executive director of HACC, initiated a program called Target Independence designed to create transitional housing, where residents who met certain criteria could live in a better environment at no extra cost.

Residents with a steady income, good rental history, good school attendance, no recent criminal record and good housekeeping received money management classes, homeowner training and other information. HACC purchased the Hampton Port Apartments from a private business to house Target Independence.

In 1992 the Public Housing Drug Elimination Program, funded by the U.S. Department of Housing and Urban Development, began offering services designed to improve the quality of life for public housing residents. The program funded youth recreational services, police patrols, boys and girls club, basketball leagues and other social service programs.

In 1994 the Andy Alaniz Gardens (30 units) were completed and named after SPC Andy Alaniz (1970-1991), the only soldier from Corpus Christi to be killed in the Persian Gulf War. Three years later, Andy Alaniz Gardens II (12 units) was completed.

Today, HACC provides low-cost housing for more than 4,000 people and has more than 1,800 units available. The average rent is slightly more than $115 a month, while the average age of an HACC resident is 23.8 years, with more than half of HACC residents under age seventeen.

The HACC provides a variety of services to residents at its Family Educational Enrichment Center, family resource centers, and through other avenues. The Family Educational Enrichment Center offers on-site GED classes, computer training and help with job searches, resume preparation, financial aid and college applications.

The housing authority operates seven family resource centers around the city that are open to youth ages 7 to 17 after school and during the summer. The centers provide group mentoring, tutoring/scholastic skills, recreation, sports leagues, field trips, camping and fishing trips, fine arts, and drug and alcohol prevention.

The HACC maintains resident associations at each site, a resident advisory board, and a resident commissioner to provide input on programs, annual plans, and other activities.

HACC services include assistance to the elderly with daily living, medical needs, and transportation, while its family assistance programs provide help with childcare, transportation, counseling, dispute resolution, and housekeeping.

Other services include crime prevention training, fire prevention training, voter registration, homeownership opportunities, computer training and a monthly newsletter.

This wide array of social services supplements the Housing Authority of Corpus Christi's primary purpose, to provide economical housing to low-income residents, a mission it will continue to perform as long as the need exits.

✧

Above: Trailers were set up for the overflow of persons waiting to live in D. N. Leathers Center, 1944.

Below: Groundbreaking for D. N. Leathers Center II. Lillian Leathers, wife of the late D.N. Leathers, is pictured at right, 1951.

AMERICAN ELECTRIC POWER

A lot has changed since 1914 when two St. Louis, Missouri, entrepreneurs named Ralph W. Morrison and Warner S. McCall bought the electric, gas, water, and streetcar franchise in Laredo, Texas.

Little did they know that almost a century later their small company, which they eventually named Central Power and Light, would become part of a multinational energy company that today is America's largest generator of electricity—American Electric Power.

It all began in 1905 when Morrison was a salesman and McCall was sales manager for the St. Louis Car Company, one of the major streetcar manufacturers of the day. They struck out on their own in 1910 with a dream of pursuing careers in the utility business.

McCall became involved in the Texas utility industry at the turn of the century, purchasing the San Antonio Waterworks and a streetcar company in Beaumont. Leaving the streetcar business proved to be a wise move.

Two years after purchasing the Laredo franchise, the two men bought the electric franchise in Uvalde and quickly purchased additional electric plants in Alice, San Diego and Marfa. On November 2, 1916, they incorporated as Central Power and Light, choosing the name because their St. Louis headquarters was central to the rest of the country.

The company built its first transmission line (in those days referred to as the highline) in 1917 from Alice, Texas, to San Diego, Texas. That and other transmission lines helped the utility add communities to its system and convinced the company to move its headquarters to San Antonio.

Transmission lines also would allow the company to build central station generating units, which would further increase its efficiency. Morrison and McCall, however, lacked the capital needed to fund such a major upgrading, estimated to cost as much as $40 million.

They sold the company in 1925 to Middle West Utilities which, due largely to the stock market crash of 1929, declared bankruptcy seven years later. The company continued to service customers without interruption, however, in what was derisively referred to as the "cactus patch."

In order to be even closer to its customers, CPL moved its headquarters to Corpus Christi, where it has been located ever since.

By 1940, the end of the Great Depression was in sight, the oil industry began what would become a three-decade-long rebound, and the agriculture industry and South Texas population continued to grow.

During World War II, CPL meter readers rode bicycles to conserve gasoline and women assumed a larger role in the company's workforce. After the war ended, the company's business skyrocketed in response to increased electrical demand, which tripled between 1946 and 1955.

The 1960s brought all-electric living into vogue just as America's post-war baby boom was finally tapering off. Central Power and Light aggressively marketed its residential electric service in the late 1960s, working with builders in Corpus Christi and throughout South Texas on the Gold Medallion Home program, a utility industry program designed to promote the advantages of all-electric homes.

The energy crisis of the 1970s sent CPL's fuel prices skyward, forcing the company to diversify its fuel sources. A shortage of natural gas sent prices from 35 cents per million Btu in 1973 to 85 cents per million Btu in 1974. Price increases, combined with federal legislation, gave CPL the motivation and the means for diversifying its fuel sources, ensuring both production and affordability of its service.

CPL turned to coal and nuclear energy as alternative fuel sources. The coal-fired Coleto Creek Power Station came on line in 1980 and in 1988 the South Texas Project Electric Generating Station became the state's first operational nuclear plant.

As it entered the new millennium, CPL faced some of the most dramatic changes in its history—restructuring of the electric utility industry in Texas and a merger with its parent company, Central and South West (CSW) and American Electric Power (AEP).

Upon completion of the CSW/AEP merger, Central Power and Light Company became known as AEP-Central Power and Light. In January 2002 the retail electric market in Texas was opened to competition between electric companies. For the first time in Texas history, electric customers could choose their retail electric provider.

In the new market, integrated utilities like AEP-CPL were separated into three companies: an electric generation company, an energy delivery company and a retail company.

In April 2002, AEP announced the sale of its retail company CPL Retail to Centrica, a leading retail energy provider in the United Kingdom, Canada and the United States. Completion of the transaction is contingent upon regulatory approval. AEP and Centrica expect to complete the regulatory approval process and conclude the transaction by the end of 2002.

This transaction does not affect AEP's ownership of its power plants in Texas and its

✧

Above: A mule-drawn Central Power and Light ice cart.

Below: Central Power and Light meter readers.

transmission and distribution network that delivers electricity to consumers.

AEP stands today as an exciting, energetic company, with diverse resources and enormous opportunities for their application. Restructuring of the electric utility industry drastically changes this vital energy market and new technologies will meet the vastly divergent energy needs of the future. And as they do, AEP will continue to provide safe and reliable electricity to South Texas.

Although its size and scope have changed, AEP's strong commitment to the community remains the same as it strives to create a better place for all to live and work.

✧

Above: A Central Power and Light lineman with his equipment.

Right: A woman enjoys her modern electric refrigerator.

Wilson Plaza has provided the best service in the Corpus Christi office building market since 1927. This started with the construction of the first "skyscraper" in Corpus Christi; a 12-story structure located 50 feet from the water known as the Nixon Building.

In 1935 an eight-story structure called the Cotton Exchange was added to the Nixon Building. In 1947, Legendary oilman Sam E. Wilson purchased the two buildings.

Four years later, Wilson built a 17-story tower with a four-story penthouse and 400-car, six-story parking garage. The garage was built to allow for the future construction of a 6-to-10-story office building on top.

The penthouse was Wilson's pride and joy. The twentieth floor featured a card room and private bar and the view was described as rivaling that of the Top of the Mark Restaurant in San Francisco.

Today, Wilson Plaza is still a prime location for enjoying panoramic views of the blue coastal waters of Corpus Christi Bay. But the complex's interior and building systems have been totally updated to provide tenants with the most modern amenities.

Wilson Plaza provides tenants with reinforced concrete and steel construction that has withstood every hurricane through the years. Energy efficiency is a priority for the Wilson Plaza. It earned the Environmental Protection Agency's coveted EnergyStar recognition. No other office building in Corpus Christi has qualified for EnergyStar recognition.

Wilson Plaza provides tenants with communications flexibility via thirty telecommunication, Internet and broadband pro-viders. Its security system includes perimeter video monitoring and computerized card access doors and vehicle gates. Its fire/life safety includes a fire sprinkler system throughout the ground floor and the twenty-one-story West Building Tower.

Building operations are optimized through the latest computerized technology, AutoCAD

computerized design is offered for tenants and prospects for space planning.

The full-time staff includes electricians, plumbers, engineers, carpenters, painters, dry wall finishers and laborers that can complete tenant space quickly and professionally.

In 2000, Wilson Plaza commissioned a 112-foot-long mural portraying significant historical events and people of the city and region beginning with the arrival of the Karancahua Indians in the 1400s. The mural is visited by teachers and their students, families, and visitors.

Wilson Plaza has a longstanding reputation for providing the best service in the Corpus Christi office building market, a reputation that it is prepared to keep for many years to come.

For more information, call Wilson Plaza at 361-884-8855, contact the staff by fax at 361-887-2945 or visit the website at www.wilsonplaza.com.

H-E-B

The history of H-E-B encompasses a span of almost 100 years, from its humble beginnings as a small family shop in Kerrville, Texas, to its position today as a major supermarket presence in Texas and Mexico with more than 300 stores and 55,000 Partners (employees).

Described by industry experts as a daring innovator and smart competitor, H-E-B's commitment to excellence has made it one of the nation's largest independently owned food retailers. But one thing that has not changed at H-E-B throughout the years is the company's ongoing commitment to being the customer's champion when it comes to providing exceptional customer service, everyday low prices, superior quality and variety in product offerings and friendly shopping.

H-E-B's successful history began in 1905 when Florence Butt decided to open a grocery store in Kerrville, Texas, to support her family. With an initial investment of $60, Florence opened the C. C. Butt Grocery Store on November 26, 1905. By 1926, Howard E. Butt, Florence's youngest son, was at the helm of the company, now known as the Butt Grocery Company. He decided to expand the business and began by opening a new store in Junction, about 60 miles from Kerrville. Later, the company expanded into the Rio Grande Valley. By 1928 Howard moved his family and the company headquarters, now under the new corporate name of H. E. Butt Grocery Company, to Harlingen, Texas.

It was in the Valley that Howard's wife, Mary Holdsworth Butt, came into the forefront with her work on an array of community projects that addressed the serious health and educational needs of South Texas families. Howard enthusiastically embraced his wife's undertakings, as his mother had schooled him early on in the importance of public service.

As the company expanded into other areas in South Texas, including Corpus Christi in 1931, Howard and Mary Butt continued to invest directly in the communities they joined with an unwavering determination to provide a better way of life for their new neighbors. In Corpus Christi, this dedication translated into the Butts' donating a unique circular library building to the University of Corpus Christi, now a branch of the Texas A&M University System.

Before the State of Texas assumed responsibility for the university in 1973, the Butt family made countless contributions to the university, not only in bricks and mortar but also in meeting operational shortfalls that included everything from payroll needs to basketball uniforms to remodeling living facilities. Mary Butt also started a daycare center on the campus that later included a Kindergarten to help college students that had families be able to stay in school.

True to the vision of Howard and Mary Butt, the spirit of giving is still very much a part of everyday business at H-E-B and a tradition the company proudly continues. H-E-B routinely expands its commitment to its customers beyond the four walls of its stores with public service involvement in the communities it operates in.

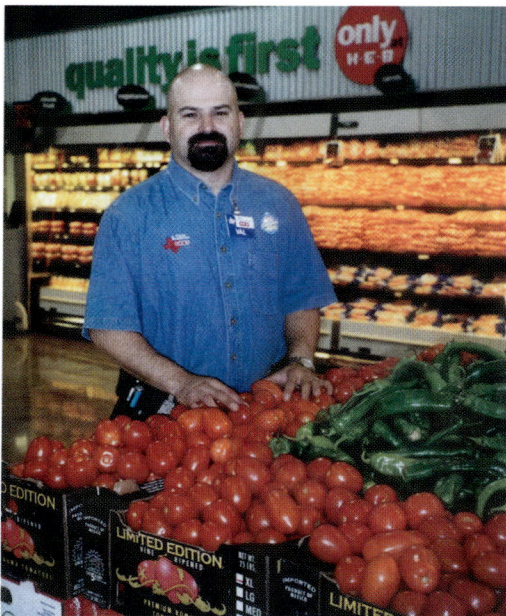

The company donates at least five percent of its pre-tax earnings each year to charitable organizations in the communities it serves and has instituted programs such as the H-E-B Excellence in Teaching Awards, the H-E-B Feast of Sharing Dinners and the H-E-B Food Bank Assistance Program.

In 2001, through the H-E-B Food Bank Assistance Program, they contributed products valued at more than $32 million to more than 15 food banks in Texas and Mexico. Also in 2001, H-E-B offered sustenance both physically and emotionally to more than 170,000 people in Texas and Mexico by offering a hot holiday meal set in a warm family setting at the H-E-B Feast of Sharing holiday dinners. The holiday dinners, which began in Corpus Christi and Laredo in 1989, were held in seventeen communities. Additionally, approximately 1,500 Texas schools were adopted statewide by H-E-B in the largest public/private education partnership in the state.

The history of H-E-B is one that is far from over. Instead it is one in which new chapters are begun every day, thanks to the innovative and continued leadership of the Butt family. In 1971, Charles, the youngest son of Howard E. Butt, became president of the H.E. Butt Grocery Company. Today, Charles is H-E-B's chairman and CEO, having grown the business from sales of $250 million in 1971 to $7.5 billion in 2000.

In many respects, H-E-B is an old-fashioned, American success story involving hard work, perseverance and dedication to the highest standards. It can be described as a company firmly rooted in the past with an eye toward the future.

W. W. Jones Family

The family of W. W. Jones is proud to have contributed greatly to the growth of Corpus Christi and the rest of South Texas. To this day the vast ranching and mineral holdings in five southern Texas counties continue to make W. W. Jones Properties one of the largest private and family-owned enterprises in the area.

The family's heritage can be traced as far back as Allen Carter Jones, a carpenter who was among the first American settlers to arrive in Texas. His son, Captain A. C. Jones, Jr., fought in the Civil War and served as Goliad County Sheriff before moving to Beeville in the early 1870s.

Proclaimed as the "Father of Beeville," Captain Jones organized the First National Bank of Beeville in 1886 and is credited with convincing two railroads to lay tracks through the city, assuring its future growth and dominant role as an area trade center.

His son, Colonel W. W. Jones, and his grandson, A. C. "Dick" Jones, followed in his footsteps as leading financial entrepreneurs, cattle and ranching operators, and community leaders. Both A. C. Jones High School and Bee County College were built on land donated by the Jones family.

William Whitby Jones was born in Goliad in 1857, and began riding the range at age twelve. Although his father wanted him to become a merchant or a banker, W. W. "Bill" Jones preferred cattle, spending months on horseback driving cattle through Indian Territory to Kansas City.

By the turn of the century, Jones, operating his own ranch near Beeville, had purchased extensive ranchland, which was the center of the Jones Properties, covering energy and ranching interests in parts of Bee, Jim Hogg, Duval, Brooks, Starr and Hidalgo Counties. In establishing his vast landholdings, the 6-foot, 4-inch giant of a man, who always wore a wide-brimmed hat, experienced numerous brushes with outlaws and cattle rustlers.

Colonel Jones, recognizing the opportunities in Corpus Christi, moved his home there in

1905 and began buying and developing property. He devoted his great energy and ability to widespread businesses, banking and community projects.

The Jones family owned and operated several important South Texas landmarks, including the three-hundred-room Nueces Hotel from 1913 to 1960. The city's premier hotel—and the center of civic and social activity—also acted as a refuge from the hurricane that struck the city in 1919. In 1935, the family founded Mestena Oil and Gas, still a very viable energy company, with offices in Corpus Christi.

From 1930 to 1979, the family also owned the 10-story Jones Building–Corpus Christi's first major office building–across the street from the hotel, and from 1935 to 1955 the W.W. Jones family home in the 500 block of South Broadway served as La Retama Public Library.

In addition to the hotel and office building, Jones served on the executive committee to secure the city's deep-water port along with other South Texas legends like Robert Kleberg, Roy Miller, John Kenedy, and John Scott.

In 1923 he joined Richard King, Robert Driscoll, John Kellam and Walter Timon as members of the port's first Navigation Commission. He also served as president of Alice State Bank and First National Bank of Hebbronville and as a director for several other banks.

Jones' oldest daughter, Lorine Jones Spoonts Lewis, served as the first female president of the Corpus Christi Chamber of Commerce in 1927-28, and planted or gave away thousands of palm trees in an effort to make Corpus Christi the "City of Palms."

W.W. Jones' son, A.C. "Dick" Jones, followed his father to become one of the largest individual landholders and financiers of South Texas, developing family property in several counties. He helped organize and served as president of the South Texas Hereford Association and served as a director of the Texas and Southwestern Cattle Raisers' Association. He also served as the first county judge of Jim Hogg County and president of First National Bank of Beeville.

The family's grandchildren and great-grandchildren proudly continue to live and

work in the South Texas area. Future generations will no doubt continue the family tradition of service to the South Texas community, a community that owes much of its character and success to W. W. Jones and his heirs.

FIRST UNITED METHODIST CHURCH

First United Methodist Church of Corpus Christi is the oldest and largest Protestant church in the city.

The Methodist presence in Corpus Christi dates back to as far as February 8, 1846, when the Reverend John Hayne preached the first Methodist sermon in the city to a congregation that included future presidents of the United States Ulysses S. Grant and Zachary Taylor, as well as the future president of the American Confederacy, Jefferson Davis.

In 1853 the Reverend Henderson Lafferty arrived to lead the Methodists in Corpus Christi, one year after Henry L. Kinney incorporated the city under the name Corpus Christi.

The Reverend Lafferty immediately recognized the need for a church building as well as a formal organization. So he built a small adobe building that could hold as many as 200 people on the corner of Mesquite and Mann Streets, and the church organized with 24 members.

By 1872 the growing congregation built a frame church with bright red carpet, earning it the nickname "the red carpet church," and by 1903 the congregation added a tall steeple with a belfry and bell.

In 1911 church officials decided to incorporate the church. They drew up a charter and filed it with the state under the name of

First Methodist Episcopal Church South of Corpus Christi. As the church continued to grow, church leaders realized they needed a larger facility and on March 27, 1911, a building committee appointed by trustees began the process of erecting a new church.

The new church, also built on the corner of Mesquite and Mann Streets, was known as the "round church." It had a basement, main floor, balcony and several stained-glass windows that opened for ventilation.

The church was the first in Corpus Christi to be fitted with a pipe organ, which had to be pumped by someone in the basement when it was played.

From 1937-1938, Del Mar College held classes in the education building of the "round church," continuing a tradition from the earliest days when public schools conducted classes at the church.

In the early 1960s, the church organized half-day programs for weekly kindergarten and preschool classes, and in 1973 expanded the program to an all-day schedule to meet the needs of working parents.

In 1996, the Vinson Morris Children's Center, which celebrates its fortieth anniversary in 2003, became the first church-sponsored daycare

✧

Right: A rendering of the 1872 "red carpet" church.

Below: A rendering of the 1853 adobe church.

center in Corpus Christi to be fully accredited by the National Association for the Education of Young Children.

In 1947 church leaders began buying property on Shoreline Boulevard, securing property in one of the most beautiful locations in the city. In 1954, work began on a completely new facility, with Fellowship Hall (which acted as a temporary sanctuary), offices, a dining room, kitchen and classrooms completed in 1955. The new sanctuary, chapel and music facilities were added in 1962.

In May 1989 the church added the Stewart Activities Center featuring a gymnasium, locker rooms, youth activities center and additional classrooms.

Since the 1930s, parishioners had dreamed of bringing a statue of Christ to Corpus Christi, which is Latin for "Body of Christ." Following a lengthy fundraising effort, the church commissioned world-renowned sculptor Kent Ullberg to create a new artistic gift to the community entitled "It is I," a larger-than-life sculpture of Christ standing in a boat calming the seas.

The statue of Christ, installed in the fall of 1995, stands in front of the church on Shoreline Boulevard, arms outstretched toward Corpus Christi Bay. The church continues to maintain and improve its facilities. In 2002 First United Methodist

Church began a multi-million-dollar campaign to refurbish existing buildings and began construction on a Columbarium on the north side of the church.

The historic church hosts a wide range of activities, meetings, study groups and other ministries important to members and the community.

And although it's the largest Protestant church in the city, its members are noted for their warm, welcoming and friendly spirit, thereby contributing to the reputation of Methodists as people with open hearts, open minds and open doors.

❖

Above: The 1912 "round dome" church.

Below: The present worship complex on South Shoreline Drive.

VALERO CORPUS CHRISTI REFINERY

Valero's Corpus Christi Refinery is highly regarded in the refining industry and the South Texas community it calls home. The refinery is owned by Valero Energy Corporation, a Fortune 500 company based in San Antonio with more than 22,000 employees and $30 billion in revenues.

In Corpus Christi, the company operates one of the world's most modern and efficient facilities, and with the support of its employees—the company's most valuable resource—contributes both time and money to making the region a great place to live and work.

Commissioned in June of 1983 on the site formerly occupied by Corn Products, Bluebonnet International and Saber Refining Company, Valero's Corpus Christi Refinery, the last grass-roots refinery built in the United States, was dubbed the "refinery of the future."

The initial project enabled Valero to produce high-quality, premium products from primarily low-quality residual oil, while utilizing "Best Available Control Technology" to protect the environment.

Protecting the environment has always been a top priority for Valero, along with producing high-quality products in a workplace that assigns paramount importance to worker and community safety.

Valero specializes in the production of environmentally clean transportation fuels and products, primarily reformulated gasoline (RFG)

and low-sulfur diesel. Other products include California Air Resources Board (CARB) gasoline and oxygenates. Valero has invested more than $1 billion to produce these fuels and products and more than $40 million in voluntary environmental initiatives.

Valero's environmental leadership has earned the company numerous accolades. Valero was the first petroleum refiner ever to earn the prestigious Texas Governor's Award for Environmental Excellence. The company was also one of the only refiners to receive a national Environmental Achievement Award at America's Clean Air Celebration in 2000.

In 2001, Valero purchased another Corpus Christi refinery from the El Paso Corporation that was previously owned by Coastal Corporation. The facility is located less than a mile from Valero's original refinery, and the company is making improvements to fully integrate the two refineries in the coming years.

The combined operations will increase Valero's Corpus Christi feedstock refining capacity from 340,000 barrels per day to 400,000 barrels per day, transforming it into the fifth-largest refinery in the United States.

Also in 2001, Valero Energy Corporation acquired Ultramar Diamond Shamrock (UDS) in a $6 billion transaction that made it one of the largest refining and marketing companies in the United States, with 12 refineries and nearly 5,000 retail outlets.

In Corpus Christi, Valero employs more than 800 people on a full-time basis and more than 200 contractors, and has an annual payroll of $59 million.

Community involvement is an integral part of Valero's corporate culture–from its organized Valero Volunteer Council to financial support of countless community organizations. Valero and its employees work hard to make a difference in the community where they live and work.

One of the company's highest priorities in terms of community service involves strong support of the United Way. In 2001, 99.9 percent of Valero's Corpus Christi employees gave to the United Way, including 94 percent who gave to the "Care Share" level (1 percent of salary) or higher.

And, with employee and corporate contributions, Valero became the first company in the Coastal Bend to surpass $500,000 in giving to the United Way as its 2002 United Way Pacesetter campaign raised more than $576,000.

Valero employees also spend thousands of hours each year volunteering for hundreds of worthwhile causes. In fact, in 2001, Valero employees donated more than 10,000 volunteer hours to mentoring students, organizing fundraisers, participating in cleanup events, volunteering at youth centers and much more.

The caring and sharing spirit of Valero and its employees has been the foundation for the company's past and present success, and will continue to play a big part in its future success.

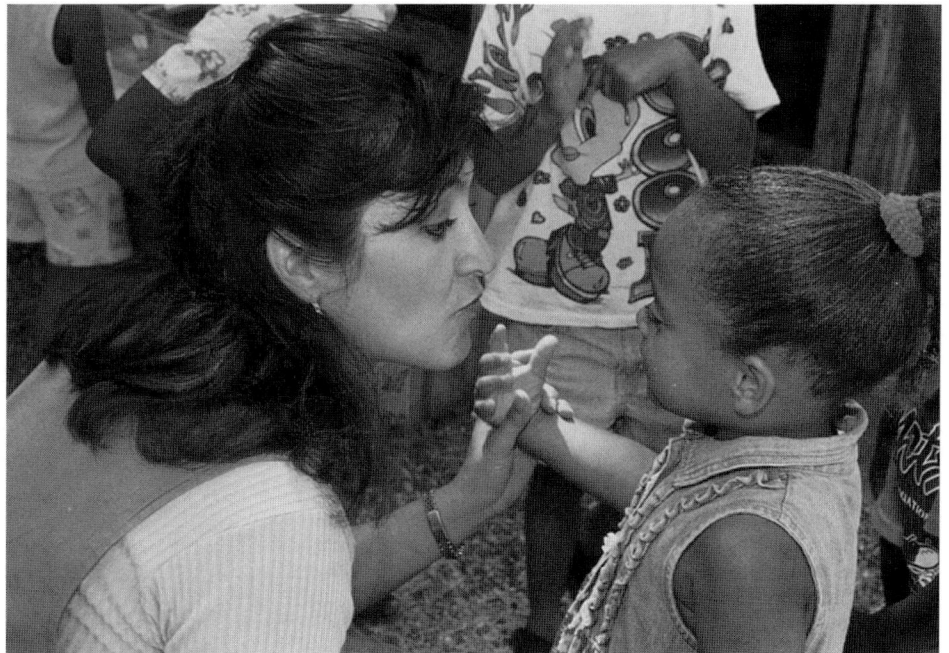

CORPUS CHRISTI RADIOLOGY CENTER

✧

Above: Corpus Christi Radiology's main office at 3554 South Alameda in Corpus Christi.

COURTESY OF GRAY PHOTOGRAPHY.

Below: Dr. Alvaro J. Ramos and his wife, Carmen.

COURTESY OF GRAY PHOTOGRAPHY.

Corpus Christi Radiology Center has been a leader in diagnostic imaging since Dr. Alvaro J. Ramos and his wife, Carmen Ramos, opened their main office at 3554 South Alameda, across from Driscoll Children's Hospital in 1984.

Through the years, Corpus Christi Radiology Center has grown from a private office providing general x-rays to a complete and modern freestanding, outpatient-imaging center offering state-of-the-art equipment and services to referring physicians and patients.

Dr. Ramos, a 1969 graduate of the University of Cartagena in Colombia, South America, interned at St. Raphael Hospital at Yale University and completed his residency in general diagnostic radiology at Harper Hospital Wayne State University in Michigan.

He later completed a fellowship in pediatric radiology at Detroit Children's Hospital, and was assistant professor of Radiology at Wayne State University. In 1977 he moved to Corpus Christi to join Dr. Joseph H. Jackson in pediatric radiology at Driscoll Children's Hospital. He was also a radiologist at the Corpus Christi Naval Hospital from 1980-1982 and at the Corpus Christi Veterans' Administration Outpatient Clinic from 1989-2002. Dr. Ramos is also a certified "B Reader" by NIOHS.

Dr. Ramos is a diagnostic board certified radiologist, and his staff at Corpus Christi Radiology Center is well qualified in assisting patients. Corpus Christi Radiology Center provides quality images to physicians using state-of-the-art equipment, while the Mammography Department exposes the lowest dose of radiation possible.

Corpus Christi Radiology Center began as a small, private outpatient radiology office that, at first, provided general x-rays in one room and ultrasound from another.

Six months later, Corpus Christi Radiology Center expanded to a second x-ray room, and in 1985 became the first radiology office in Corpus Christi to employ film-screen mammography for its patients.

Three years later, Corpus Christi Radiology Center became the first private radiology office to include a CT scanner with exams performed in a mobile unit that served small, rural hospitals in the area.

As demand for CT scans grew, it became obvious that the unit needed to remain in Corpus Christi to better serve the public and our community, and Corpus Christi Radiology Center continued on its quest to become a complete diagnostic imaging center.

In 1990 the privately owned radiology center became the first private office to offer computerized nuclear medicine, and 1994, due to increasing demand, opened its second office

at 1621 South Brownlee, located between two major Corpus Christi hospitals.

The Brownlee facility became the first non-hospital diagnostic imaging facility in Corpus Christi to provide outpatient MRI services to the community. The Brownlee facility also provides high resolution CT scans and an "Open" MRI with state-of-the-art, high field scanning. This facility also offers screening mammography, general x-rays and bone densitometry studies for detecting osteoporosis.

Corpus Christi Radiology Center opened its third facility in 2000 at 3945 U.S. Highway 77 in the Five Points area of Corpus Christi. Its newest facility serves the Northwest section of Corpus Christi and outlying areas by providing general x-rays and ultrasound.

Corpus Christi Radiology Center understands that, for a patient who comes to them for diagnostic testing, there is no such thing as a "routine" test. Their services have been designed around their patients and they put their patients' individual medical needs first. The administrative and procedural services have all been planned around the patients' comfort, convenience and peace of mind by offering "personalized" service with Dr. Ramos himself talking to the patient about his/her exam results.

Corpus Christi Radiology Center files all insurance forms for its patients, participates in every health insurance plan available in the Coastal Bend and accepts Medicare and Medicaid assignments.

Other services provided by Corpus Christi Radiology Center are courier services as well as a courtesy van five days a week for patients who need transportation or special assistance. Corpus Christi Radiology Center is committed to keeping fees for its services to levels comparable with other providers of diagnostic imaging services.

What began as a single office staffed by four people has grown to three offices and 22 people including registered technologists in all disciplines. The key to their success is hard work and dedication to providing the latest in equipment and services, and a commitment to living up to the company's motto: "Where Patients Are First."

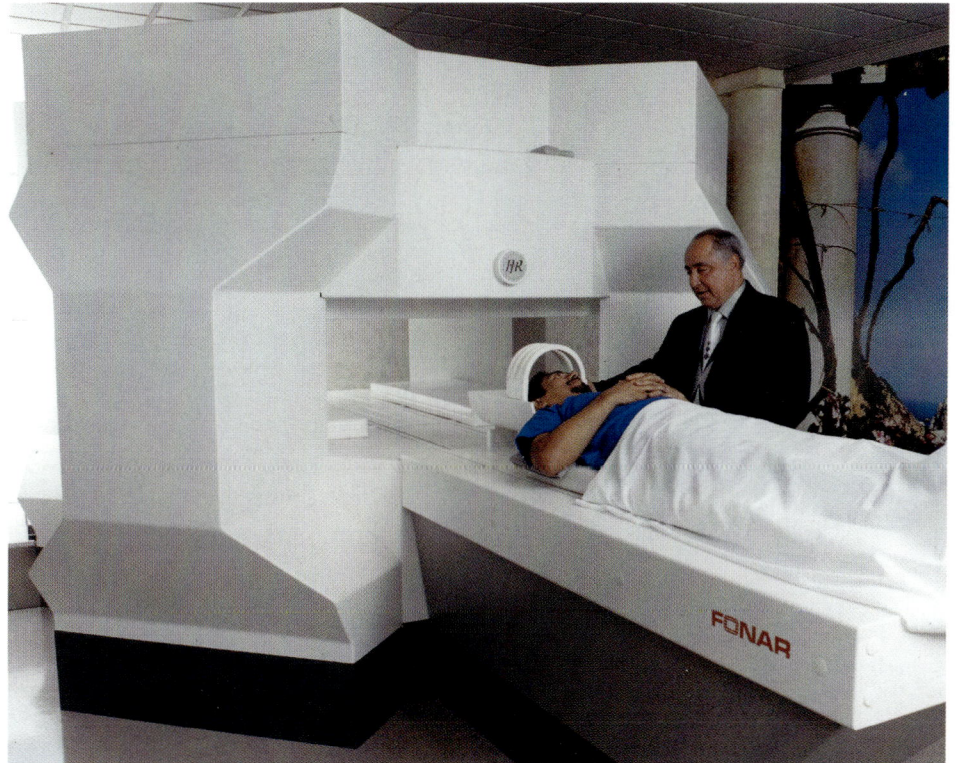

✧

Above: Open-field MRI (Magnetic Resonance Imaging).
COURTESY OF GRAY PHOTOGRAPHY.

Below: The staff of Corpus Christi Radiology. Front row (kneeling, from left to right): Rosie De La Cruz, Ana Hernandez, Cassie Walts, Oscar Ramos, M.D., Juan Garibaldo, Michael McColgan, Sandra Garza, and Diane Martinez. Second row (standing, from left to right): Lydia Soliz, Marisela Miranda, Vilma Boyles, Yolanda Olivarez, Brandie Nolen, Tammy Zipprian, Eleanor Garza, Dr. A. J. Ramos, Carmen Ramos, Daniel Porras, Mary Roche, Esmeralda Porras, and Michelle Perez. Third Row (standing, center): Cliff McDonald.
COURTESY OF GRAY PHOTOGRAPHY.

BRASELTON CONSTRUCTION COMPANY

The scripture that guided Guy Braselton's business philosophy when he founded Braselton Construction Company in 1945 continues to inspire this third-generation company in the new millennium. To this day, company literature bears a reference to Psalms 37: 3, 4, and 5, which advises Christians to trust in the Lord and do good things.

That philosophy may seem outdated in today's modern world, but at Braselton Construction, the oldest general contractor in Corpus Christi, it is still very much a part of the way they do business. People turn to Braselton Construction time and again, in part, because they know they will be treated with fairness, honesty and integrity.

Guy Braselton, whose grandson now owns and operates the company, worked as a carpenter and construction superintendent in West Texas before moving to Corpus Christi to start his own business.

From the very beginning, Braselton Construction concentrated on the commercial sector, shifting its focus in response to changes in the marketplace. Through the years, the company has expanded with branch offices in San Antonio and Houston, and seeks out projects in the $1 million to $20 million range in an area bounded by New Braunfels, Del Rio, the Rio Grande Valley and the Houston market.

In the 1950s, the bulk of the firm's projects came from schools and public buildings like the original Corpus Christi City Hall and the Corpus Christi International Airport. Guy Braselton's two eldest sons, Bobby and Billy, who joined the company in 1950, worked alongside their father during this period until 1955, when Guy Braselton retired from the business.

The brothers ran the company for the next thirteen years until in 1968 Billy Braselton bought out his brother's interest. It was during the 1960s that the company expanded to the Rio Grande Valley and throughout the next two decades worked there continuously.

In the 1970s, in response to the South Texas area's growing tourism industry, the company worked largely on private hotels, motels and condominiums. During that time, Bill Braselton, the company's current owner and president, joined the business full time. He worked alongside his father, Billy, to help the company through the 1980s oil bust that sent the Texas economy into a tailspin. In 1989, Bill became president and, in 1992, Billy retired. Since that time, the company has enjoyed a healthy workload and once again finds a large percentage of its work in the private and public sectors.

As one of the older family-owned businesses in Corpus Christi, Braselton Construction enjoys stability and commitment to quality that generates repeat customers, which, along with changes in state law, has led to a boom in business.

Texas law now allows public entities to choose the best candidate for a job rather than the rock-bottom bidder, and Braselton's stellar reputation has convinced several public entities to select their services based on the best value for the owner.

Above: The entrance to the Flour Bluff High School cafeteria in Corpus Christi is among the many attractive features incorporated into the 90,000 square feet of additions made to the campus in 1999. The $8 million project also included a science wing, cafeteria, administrative area and classrooms.

Below: Construction of the Parkdale Branch Public Library required the expertise of an experienced and skilled company like Braselton Construction Company, which met the special challenges associated with constructing a round building situated next to an active drainage ditch.

PHOTOS COURTESY OF SAMMY GOLD PHOTOGRAPHY

Customers have come to rely on the skills and knowledge that Braselton Construction Co. employees bring to their projects. The average employee has been with the company for 15 years, including some who have been there for decades and others who are second- or third-generation employees.

Braselton continues to invest in its people through training programs designed to keep them up to date on the latest construction techniques and advanced management practices. This attention to training has helped the company win several national safety awards for zero accidents.

The company has earned a reputation for using innovative techniques and taking on complex projects that less qualified contractors avoid. In recent years, more than half its projects have been renovations and additions, which require a high level of skill to deal with the array of materials and construction techniques employed by the original builders.

The people at Braselton Construction are committed to helping owners obtain the best value for their money by offering an assortment of project delivery methods, and continue to take pride in their work. This is because they understand what Guy Braselton understood more than a half century ago, that nothing is more satisfying than exceeding the owner's expectations and creating a building that will stand for decades to come.

✧

Above: Allen Samuels Chevrolet in Corpus Christi is among the many repeat customers who turn to Braselton Construction Company for their construction needs. In 1996 the car dealership hired Braselton Construction to build a sixty-five-thousand-square-foot new car facility and two years later hired the company to build a ten-thousand-square-foot used-car facility.
PHOTO COURTESY OF LANMON AERIAL PHOTOGRAPHY, INC.

Below: Owners of the Port Royal Condominiums on Mustang Island turned to Braselton Construction Company in 1984 to build this 210-unit, 500,000-square-foot project. Braselton Construction is the only general contractor in the Coastal Bend with the expertise needed to build such a complex concrete structure. The Port Royal Condominiums remain the largest concrete building south of San Antonio.

CATHOLIC DIOCESE OF CORPUS CHRISTI

The Catholic Diocese of Corpus Christi traces its roots to as far back as 1853, when Father Bernard O'Reilly built the first St. Patrick's Church in Corpus Christi. Workers completed this tiny adobe-and-shell building in the same year that Henry L. Kinney started what would eventually become Corpus Christi.

In 1874 the Diocese of Galveston, which at the time comprised the entire State of Texas, was divided into the Diocese of San Antonio and the Vicariate Apostolic of Brownsville. A year later, Bishop Dominic Manucy, the first Vicar Apostolic of Brownsville, moved his residence to Corpus Christi. Then, in 1912, the church elevated the vicariate to the rank of diocese, with Corpus Christi designated as the Diocesan See.

Today, the Diocese of Corpus Christi has grown along with Corpus Christi and the South Texas area to serve the spiritual, educational, and charitable needs of a rapidly growing Coastal Bend population.

The Most Reverend Edmond Carmody, D.D., installed as the seventh bishop of the Diocese of Corpus Christi on March 17, 2000, leads the diocese. Bishop Carmody serves as pastor of the Corpus Christi Cathedral, the spiritual cornerstone for the diocese and a significant historical and architectural landmark.

Workers laid the cornerstone of the Cathedral on March 1, 1940, and, on July 17,

church officials renamed and dedicated it as the Corpus Christi Cathedral at the direction of Pope Pius XII who told Bishop Ledvina, "Corpus Christi is the Diocese with the most beautiful name in the world." Its Spanish- and Mission-style architecture includes tower domes made of glazed terra cotta, a red Spanish clay tile roof and a marble pulpit.

The Chancery Office is located adjacent to the Cathedral in downtown Corpus Christi

❖

Above: Corpus Christi Cathedral.

Below: Catholic Charities employees and volunteers participate in a workshop given by the American Red Cross on how to best assist victims of flooding in South Texas. Emergency aid is one of the many services provided by Catholic Charities.

COURTESY OF *SOUTH TEXAS CATHOLIC.*
PHOTO BY PAULA ESPITIA.

where Bishop Carmody, Vicar General Monsignor Richard Shirley, Chancellor Father Emilo Jiménez, and numerous other vicars and directors oversee the diocese's administrative and pastoral functions.

They supervise a wide range of activities designed to meet the needs of Catholics and non-Catholics alike. The principal ministries of the diocese include Catholic Charities, a social services agency that serves the poor with counseling, emergency aid, and immigration and naturalization programs.

The diocese operates its own fully accredited school system, providing top-notch education to students at seventeen Coastal Bend campuses, including a charter school for students at risk for dropping out of high school.

The diocese also works to form youth leaders through its pastoral care program, and on the parish level gives children a foundation in the Catholic faith through its religious education program and its ongoing training of catechists and directors of religious education. In addition, the Youth Ministry of the diocese operates an active youth retreat movement for junior and senior high school students. Other spiritual and retreat movements that serve the adult population are the Cursillo, Charismatic Prayer Groups, and the recently formed Journey to Damascas, which serves both Catholics and Protestants alike.

The Diocesan Pastoral Institute trains adults in a wide array of lay ministries, giving them the skills they need to provide valued assistance to the staffs of local parishes. Pastoral services include visiting inmates in jails and prisons within the diocese, as well as providing support to women and girls who become pregnant out of wedlock.

The diocese shares its activities and those of the Catholic Church worldwide through broadcasts on the diocesan-owned radio station, KLUX, and through the *South Texas Catholic*, a bi-monthly newspaper.

The Villa Maria apartment complex for the elderly, owned by the diocese and operated by a Catholic lay group, is home to 100-150 residents, and plans call for future expansion.

The diocese oversees a number of spiritual movements designed to support Coastal Bend families. These programs provide services such as parenting skills and marriage preparation classes.

The Permanent Diaconate Program, which recently celebrated its twenty-fifth year, trains married men to assist in weddings, funerals and other diocesan ministries. Through the Rite of Christian Initiation of Adults Ministry, individuals of catechetical age are gradually initiated into the Body of Christ, becoming full, active, conscious participants in the prayer and life of the parish communities of the diocese.

A presence that began with the tiny St. Patrick's Church has grown to a widespread network of churches, schools, and ministries that serve and will continue to serve the varied needs of a diverse and growing Coastal Bend community.

✦

Above: Area youth rallies are among the activities sponsored by the Diocese of Corpus Christi's Office for Youth and Young Adult Ministry.
COURTESY OF *SOUTH TEXAS CATHOLIC.*

Below: Jim and Glenda Tansey and Father Michael Lenihan interact with soon-to-be married couples at an Engaged Encounter Weekend, sponsored by the Office of Family Life of the Diocese of Corpus Christi. During the weekend, couples learn how to communicate and go into marriage with their eyes wide open.
COURTESY OF *SOUTH TEXAS CATHOLIC.*
PHOTO BY PAULA ESPITIA.

SARATOGA MEDICAL CENTER

Saratoga Medical Center is a leading outpatient center offering diagnostic imaging, primary and specialized medical care in Corpus Christi. The mission of the center is to provide the best possible medical care and diagnostic imaging in a pleasant environment, accessible and convenient, without hassles found in a hospital setting and at prices substantially lower.

SMC was founded by Jairo A. Puentes, M.D., a leading medical doctor and specialist, who after practicing and teaching in Houston at Baylor College of Medicine for more than ten years, moved to Corpus Christi to develop a Rehabilitation Hospital.

Under his leadership as the first Physical Medicine and Rehabilitation specialist in Corpus Christi, he also founded and became director of the inpatient Rehabilitation Center at Spohn Hospital Shoreline. Dr. Puentes' experience in pain medicine and treatment of musculoskeletal injuries provided the base to create a new center where patients could find under one roof all the necessary diagnosis and treatment for injuries to the spine, bones, joints, muscles and nerves. SMC opened its doors in December 1995 at 3434 Saratoga Boulevard. The Center is organized in several centers of excellence.

- The Center for Backpain and Muscle Injuries specializes in non-surgical treatment and rehabilitation of injuries of the spine, joints, bones, ligaments and nerves. The Center offers state-of-the-art diagnostic and therapy services. Treatments may include medication, therapeutic nerve blocks, physical therapy, joint injections, and exercise and water therapy. The center offers a pain management program to patients with chronic pain to help them to manage their pain and reduce the use of narcotic analgesics.

- The Physical Rehabilitation Center offers a full range of physical therapy modalities under the direction of a licensed physical therapist. A state-of-the-art gym offers the latest exercise equipment to strengthen almost any muscle. The Center offers a modern, heated swimming pool, sauna and whirlpool including an underwater treadmill for patients with hip, knee or ankle problems.

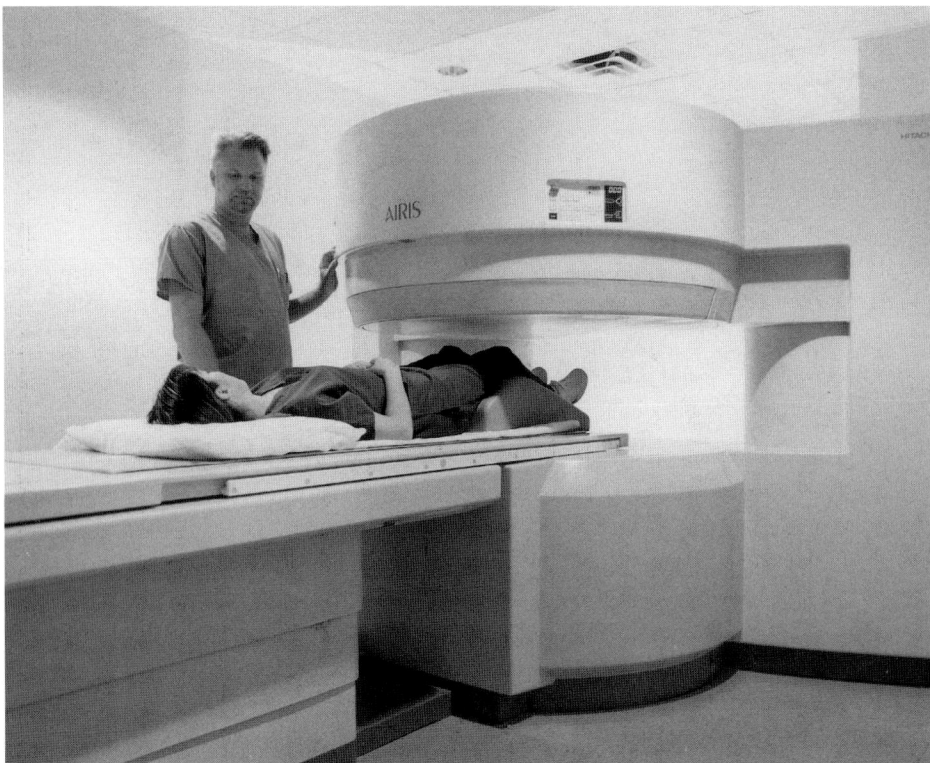

- The Diagnostic Imaging Center offers open MRI technology, spiral CT scanning, general radiology and ultrasound. The open MRI was the first MRI scanner available to the community of South Texas in 1996. This technology offered a relief to claustrophobic and large-framed patients who could not be scanned with the old "tunnel effect" technology.

- The Neurodiagnostic Center offers computerized testing and analysis of the peripheral nerves and muscles also known as EMG (electromyogram). The tests are performed by Dr. Puentes, a certified specialist in the field. Problems such as carpal tunnel syndrome, compression of nerves in the spine (pinched nerves), muscle and nerve diseases can be diagnosed with this equipment.

- The Urgent Care Clinic offers immediate medical care without the need of an appointment at prices substantially lower than hospital emergency rooms. These services have grown due to the convenience and affordability. The vision of the future for the center is to expand medical services and add more specialists. The need for affordable quality and compassionate care is absolutely necessary for successful expansion. As Corpus Christi expands to the Southside, the Center is in a prime location to become one of the most technologically advanced clinics with outstanding physicians and staff.

Please visit www.back-jointpain.com for more information.

✧

Above: Saratoga Medical Center founder/CEO Jairo A. Puentes, M.D.

Below: Diagnostic Imaging X-Ray Reading Room.

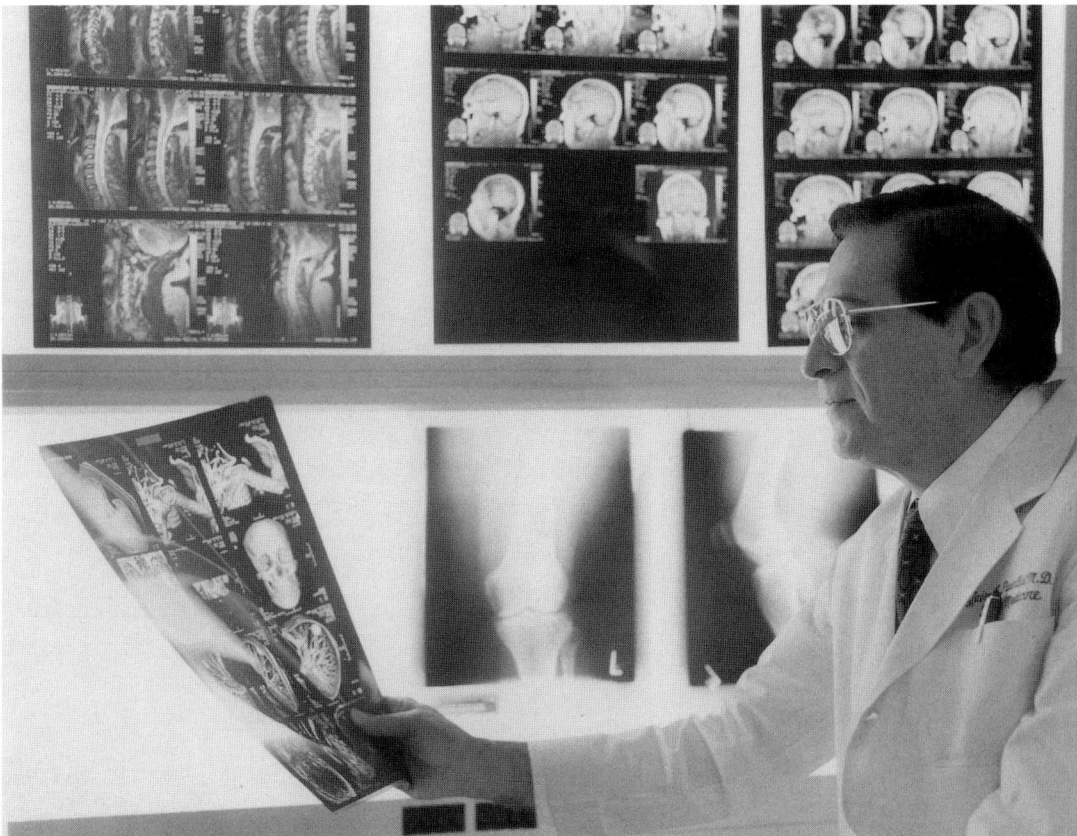

CORPUS CHRISTI COUNTRY CLUB

Corpus Christi Country Club, the only private member-owned country club in the area, has been an integral part of the city's history since its inception on January 24, 1922.

The club's founders purchased the Old Kaler farm (82.71 acres) in north Corpus Christi as the site for the new club. Golf professional John Bredimus was hired to design and oversee installation of the original nine-hole course.

Members used the original Kaler farmhouse as their clubhouse and, later that year, added two tennis courts. The opening event, a golf tournament held on Labor Day 1922 attracted twenty-four players in a competition won by businessman Pat Grogan.

In 1924 the club erected its first building, later adding locker rooms, and a kitchen and dance floor. The club eventually added a grill, bar, golf shop, dining room, swimming pool and tennis courts.

The Depression brought financial troubles to the region. In 1932 the club authorized Gulf Coast Oil Company to erect an oil well on the third hole, clearing the way for five producing wells. By 1937 the club had expanded the golf course to 18 holes and built a new clubhouse and swimming pool.

In its day, the course, with its view of the Nueces River, was one of the most beautiful courses in the country. It attracted celebrities such as President Howard Taft, Bing Crosby, Ben Hogan, Babe Didrikson Zaharias and Byron Nelson.

But the location eventually proved too small and in 1963 the club purchased a 156-acre parcel at what is now 6300 Everhart Road. The present course, designed by Robert Trent Jones, uses an extended irrigation system to water fairways, greens, and more than two thousand trees, making it the most beautiful course in South Texas.

Amenities at Corpus Christi Country Club include a driving range, chipping and putting greens, 11 lighted tennis courts, golf and tennis pro shops, adult and children's swimming pools, fitness center, formal ballroom, banquet facilities, meeting rooms, mixed grill and pub, snack bar and men's and women's nineteenth holes.

With an active membership and professional, dedicated staff, Corpus Christi Country Club is poised to continue playing an important role in the city's history.

❖

Above: Corpus Christi Country Club on July 22, 1938.

COURTESY OF THE DR. FRED K. MCGREGOR PHOTO COLLECTION OF THE CORPUS CHRISTI MUSEUM.

Right: Corpus Christi Country Club as it appears today.

COURTESY OF GRAY PHOTOGRAPHY.

Nueces County Judge Richard Borchard began his life as a migrant worker in the cotton fields of West Texas and through hard work and perseverance rose to the highest office in the county.

Borchard, a native of nearby Robstown, became the first Hispanic to serve as Nueces County judge following his election in 1994. The former Nueces County commissioner, who gave up his seat on the commissioners' court to run for the higher office, was the county's first new county judge in twenty-four years.

Borchard's tenure, which began in late 1994 following the unexpected resignation of his predecessor, ended on December 31, 2002, after Borchard decided not to seek reelection.

Working as the presiding member of the Nueces County Commissioners Court, Borchard helped keep the county in good financial standing by maintaining a bond rating as good as or better than 250 of the state's 254 counties.

During Borchard's tenure, the county negotiated a long-term lease with Spohn Health System to run Spohn Memorial Hospital, allowing the county to twice reduce its hospital tax rate and improve healthcare to indigent patients.

Another success during Borchard's tenure has been the inclusion of Corpus Christi in the I-69 corridor project linking Corpus

Christi to a major trade route between Mexico and Texas. Original plans would have bypassed the city.

A landmark lawsuit filed by the county forced the state to live up to its obligation to house state prisoners. The court decision forced the state to build new prisons rather than leaving them in county jails.

The county also filed legal documents to receive its rightful share of the state's $17-billion settlement from tobacco companies when it was discovered that the state had decided to bypass Nueces County in distributing the funds.

Borchard believes it is important to allow more children to participate in the annual livestock show. As such, he negotiated the County's purchase of 162 acres of land, making the County Fairgrounds a reality. He also negotiated a public-private partnership to bring professional baseball and a new stadium to the Fairgrounds. In addition, Borchard will leave office with a plan to restore the old Nueces County Courthouse.

His retirement plans include spending more time with his wife and high school sweetheart, Norma, and their daughter Nicole, a student at Southwest Texas State University.

JUDGE RICHARD BORCHARD

✧

Above: Judge Richard Borchard.

Below: Judge Richard Borchard with wife, Norma, and daughter, Nicole.

SISTERS OF THE INCARNATE WORD AND BLESSED SACRAMENT

INCARNATE WORD ACADEMY

Incarnate Word Academy of Corpus Christi is one of several religious educational institutions throughout the world that owes its existence to the Sisters of the Incarnate Word and Blessed Sacrament.

Founded by Jeanne Chézard de Matel on July 2, 1625, the Sisters are called by Christ to extend His incarnation in time, to respond to the needs of the world through ministry, and to be God's gospels of love to the world. Answering the call of Bishop John M. Odin of Texas, four Sisters set sail from France in March 1852 to assist in the vast mission diocese of Texas in the work of education. They established their first American foundation in Brownsville, Texas, and opened Incarnate Word Academy there on March 7, 1853. From the humble beginnings of the first community in Brownsville, other Incarnate Word groups and schools were established in various parts of Texas and Mexico.

The Sisters of the Incarnate Word arrived in Corpus Christi and opened Incarnate Word Academy in 1871. Through the years, thanks to the support of parents, alumni, past parents, and friends, enrollment expanded and the convent and school moved from downtown to its present facilities at 2900 South Alameda Street. Currently, a significant number of students are second-, third-, or fourth-generation Incarnate Word Academy students, many of whose parents participate in a vibrant alumni association.

Motivated by a Catholic philosophy of education, each level—Montessori, elementary, middle, and secondary—aims to integrate faith development with high academic standards. Incarnate Word Academy strives to make quality Catholic education affordable and offers financial assistance in a variety of ways.

Incarnate Word Sisters promote collaboration and involvement in the educational ministry within the school community. Administrators, teachers, coaches, counselors, staff members, and parents form a Christian community helping students grow and meet their potential in thinking logically, open-mindedly, accurately, and critically. Students are encouraged to use their God-given gifts responsibly, to live Gospel values, and to care for one another and the global community.

With a highly trained faculty who have chosen to teach at a school that values faith formation, scholarship, and individuality, Incarnate Word Academy fosters an environment that encourages lifetime learning, a commitment to following Christ and His Gospel, and faith expressed in worship, prayer, and service to others. Incarnate Word Academy embraces a standard of excellence and requires progressive mastery in religious studies,

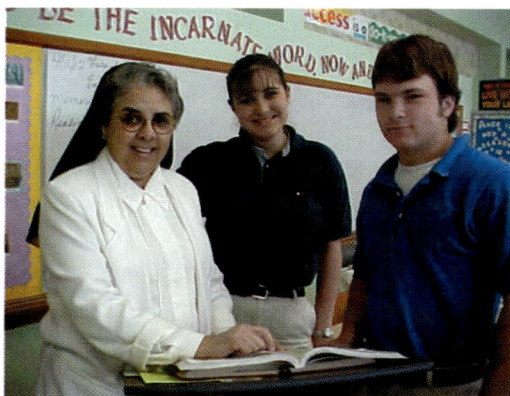

activities at all levels emphasize leadership, community service, the arts and sports.

Incarnate Word Academy's continued success is due in great measure to a strong school board that received national recognition from the National Catholic Education Association. The school board serves as an opportunity for parents, alumni and friends to share in ensuring that the Academy continues to flourish in the future, building on the mission and traditions of the Sisters of the Incarnate Word.

language, mathematics, social studies and science, thus preparing students to become committed adult Christians and to excel at the university level.

The elementary level offers two programs of instruction—Montessori and traditional. Both accelerated educational programs allow children to learn in a setting that fosters independent thinking and progress. The middle level, grades 6 through 8, offers a full curriculum including an inter-disciplinary approach that emphasizes the relationship among subject areas. The secondary level follows a four-year college preparatory curriculum including numerous Advanced Placement courses. Ninety-nine percent of Incarnate Word Academy graduates pursue higher-level education in colleges and universities. In addition, extracurricular

In addition to serving at Incarnate Word Academy in Corpus Christi and other schools, the Sisters of the Incarnate Word serve in hospital pastoral care, hospice work, parishes and diocesan offices. The Sisters also share their commitment to Christ and His Gospel message through a lay association. Incarnate Word Associates provide a way for laity and diocesan clergy to share the spiritual heritage of the Order of the Incarnate Word.

Today, Incarnate Word Sisters can be found in the United States, Mexico, Central and South America, France, Spain, Kenya, and Tanzania. The Sisters are dedicated to helping people come to know and love Jesus, the warm, gracious, loving Person who walked among the people and lived in communion with them.

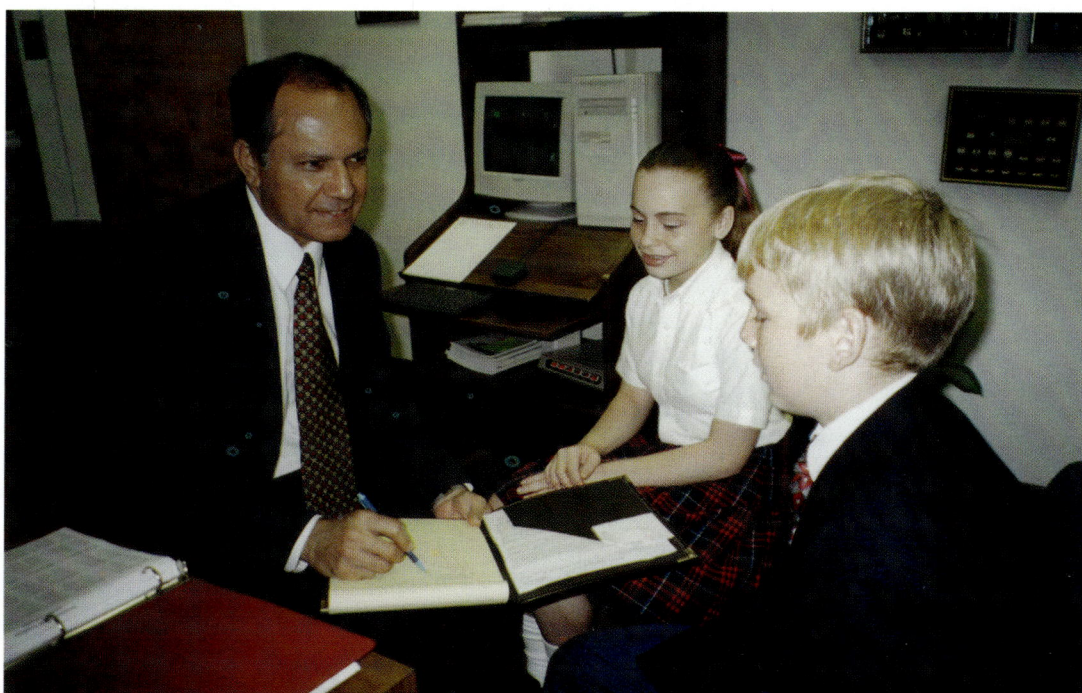

CITY OF CORPUS CHRISTI WATER DEPARTMENT

The City of Corpus Christi Water Department serves nearly five hundred thousand citizens of Corpus Christi and the Coastal Bend. Its mission is to effectively manage the City of Corpus Christi's water supply, production and distribution system in order to meet the water supply needs, and to provide safe drinking water that meets state and federal regulations; to review the design and construction of water facilities to ensure the adequacy of the water system to reach projected growth requirements; and to identify and acknowledge consumer needs and expectations.

The Water Department supplies water for municipal and industrial use in a seven-county service area covering 140 square miles. Major raw water customers include Alice, Beeville, Mathis, San Patricio Municipal Water District, Celenese, and Flint Hills Resources. Treated water customers include Nueces County Water Improvement District No. 4 (Port Aransas), San Patricio Municipal Water District, South Texas Water Authority, and the Violet Water Supply District. Water is drawn from the Lake Corpus Christi/Choke Canyon Reservoir System within the Nueces River Basin, and from Lake Texana via the Mary Rhodes Pipeline.

Lake Corpus Christi, which stores 242,241 acre-feet of water, was dedicated April 26, 1958 with the construction of Wesley Seale Dam. The Lower Nueces River Water Supply District built and owned the reservoir until the bonds were paid off in 1986 and the City of Corpus Christi assumed ownership.

Choke Canyon Reservoir stores 695,271 acre-feet of water. The Bureau of Reclamation financed, designed and built the reservoir. The reservoir was dedicated on June 8, 1982. The City operates and maintains the facility.

The 101-mile long Mary Rhodes Pipeline draws water through a 64-inch pipeline from Lake Texana near Edna to supplement the water supply drawn from the City's two reservoirs. The pipeline, named for the former mayor who fought to build it, came online in September 1998. In 1993 Corpus Christi entered into a contract with the Lavaca-Navidad River Authority to purchase 41,840 acre-feet of water per year. Approximately fifty percent of the water delivered to homes in Corpus Christi comes from Lake Texana.

Other department functions include operation of the O. N. Stevens Water Treatment Plant. The City diverts raw water from the Nueces River and Lake Texana into the plant to be treated and turned into drinking water. Approximately 28 billion gallons of water are treated each year. Its rated capacity of 167 million gallons per day is well above the peak summer demand of as much as 110 million gallons per day. The department operates five pumping stations, four elevated storage tanks and maintains 1,600 miles of pipeline.

The Water Department operates in full compliance with all state and federal requirements. Water professionals work hard to ensure measures are taken to provide customers with the best quality water possible. The city meets or exceeds requirements set forth by the U.S. Environmental Protection Agency.

The Water Department also maintains a water laboratory and a water maintenance activity that oversees the repair and replacement of sixteen hundred miles of transmission and service water lines.

The Water Department has a long-standing commitment to promoting water conservation in the community. Its public education and communications functions promote community awareness. The department provides free water-related educational materials to local school districts.

Through the reengineering process, the Water Department is promoting effective, efficient and economical ways to operate. To that end, the department is committed to a streamlined operation.

To meet the demand of a growing community, the City has taken steps to assure a future water supply. In 1999 the city purchased senior water rights to thirty-five thousand acre-feet of water per year in the Colorado River from the Garwood Irrigation Company. This water will be transported to Corpus Christi via a pipeline that will be constructed in the future from the Colorado River to the Mary Rhodes Pipeline at Lake Texana.

The City also is exploring the feasibility of desalination–the process of turning seawater into drinking water. A desalination plant is possible once the cost falls below the cost of acquiring additional fresh water resources.

But no matter what the future might bring, the Water Department is committed to providing professional and technical services.

❖

Barrilleros line up to pump water into wooden barrels.

COURTESY OF THE DOC MCGREGOR COLLECTION.

Port Aransas Chamber of Commerce & Tourism Bureau

Port Aransas, once a sleepy fishing village on the northern tip of Mustang Island, has transformed itself over the past three decades into a major Texas tourist attraction while preserving the village atmosphere that visitors enjoy.

The island's original inhabitants were the Karankawa Indians, who were there to greet early explorers such as Alonzo Alvarez de Pineda and Alvar Nunez Cabeza de Vaca. Jean Lafitte and his buccaneers later frequented the island, and legend has it that a Spanish dagger with a silver spike driven through the hilt marks the spot where LaFitte buried a chest of gold and jewels.

Originally called Wild Horse Island for the horses brought there by the Spaniards in the early 1800s, Mustang Island recorded its first permanent settler in 1853 with the arrival of an Englishman from Lancaster by the name of Robert Ainsworth Mercer.

He built a ranch house, imported cattle and sheep herds and sent for his wife and three youngest children. Four years later, construction ended on the nearby Harbor Island Lighthouse, which helped ships navigate through gulf passages and today stands as a historical link to a simpler time.

This island settlement grew until the Civil War when Yankee incursions forced settlers to abandon the island. They returned in 1866 with a few newcomers to repopulate the island, which grew slowly throughout the next a hundred years.

Congress approved the U.S. Coast Guard Station known as the Aransas Life Saving Station on June 16, 1878, beginning a long association between the Coast Guard and Port Aransas that continues to this day.

Another historic landmark is the Tarpon Inn, which opened for the first time in 1886. Destroyed or damaged by fire and hurricanes over the years, the Tarpon Inn preserves a piece of the city's history in the Inn's small lobby with a wall covered with autographed tarpon scales, including one caught by President Franklin D. Roosevelt.

Port Aransas remained a sleepy fishing village until 1965 when Wanda and J.C. Barr built the first condominium in Texas, Sea Isle

Village, in Port Aransas. Its construction kicked off a building boom that transformed the town into a year-round tourist destination.

Today, anglers, surfers, beach-lovers, bird-watchers and spring-breakers, who enjoy its laid-back lifestyle and visitor-friendly nature, favor Port Aransas. Visitors enjoy the trip along Texas Highway 361 and the ferry ride to the Port Aransas landing. The free ferry is operated by the state twenty-four hours a day year-round.

Port Aransas, known as the Fishing Capital of Texas, is home to the oldest and largest fishing tournament on the Gulf Coast–The Deep-Sea Roundup, originally known as the Tarpon Rodeo. The town pays tribute to its fishing heritage almost every summer weekend with a fishing tournament.

Anglers enjoy the bountiful catches common to Port Aransas. Spanish mackerel, redfish, speckled trout, flounder and black drum frequent Port Aransas bays and channels, while kingfish, sailfish, marlin, and tuna inhabit the deeper waters of the Gulf of Mexico.

Search for seashells along Mustang Island or take a day trip to uninhabited St. Joseph's Island. Board a boat for a nature tour of the channel and watch the bottle-nosed dolphins swim and frolic in the waves.

Nature is very much at home on Mustang Island. Located in the heart of the spring and fall migrations, the island has one of the highest bird counts on the Gulf Coast. Several bird-watching sites are listed on the Great Texas Birding Trail. And the Aransas National Wildlife Refuge, winter feeding grounds for the endangered whooping cranes, is a short drive away.

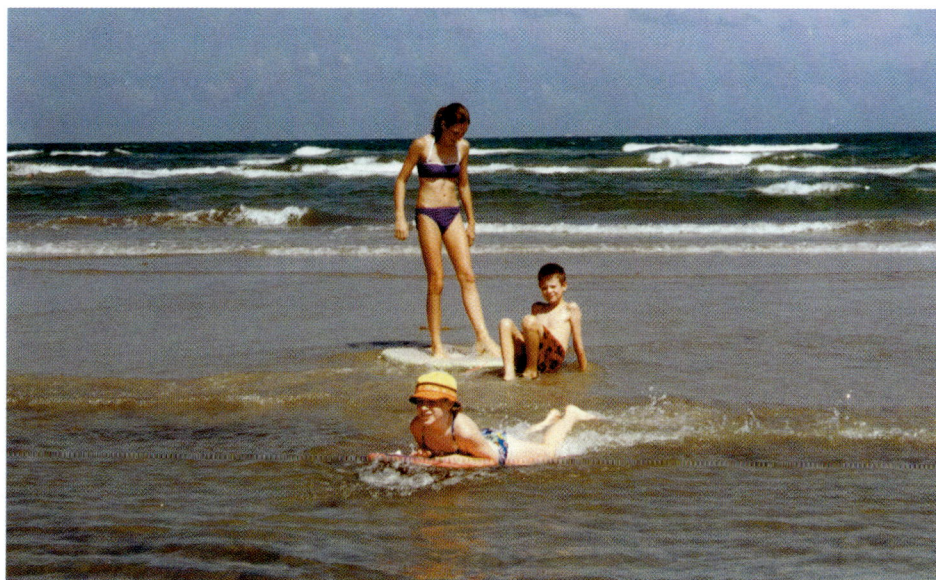

Sports enthusiasts can enjoy horseback riding on the beach, jet skiing, parasailing, surfing, biking, golfing, rig diving, sailing, windsurfing, kite flying and tennis.

The University of Texas Marine Science Institute serves as the center for the study of Texas bays, the Gulf of Mexico and the world's oceans. The institute's visitor center maintains various aquaria and features regularly scheduled movies.

Take a free trolley for a fun trip around the island, and visit one of the many souvenir shops for something to commemorate your trip. Shop at a boutique, dine in fine restaurants or visit an art gallery, where you can purchase an island seascape to take home with you.

Before you visit Port Aransas in person, please visit www.portaransas.org, or call us at 1-800-45COAST. Experience Port Aransas, Texas—Island Style!

✧

Above: Port Aransas is a popular family vacation spot.

Below: Fishing boats going out from Port Aransas for tarpon.

CORPUS CHRISTI BAYFRONT INN

The Corpus Christi Bayfront Inn is perfectly situated along the Corpus Christi bayfront to provide guests with a beautiful view of the water as well as easy access to the city's major tourist attractions.

This 120-room hotel at 601 North Shoreline Boulevard is across the street from the historical Corpus Christi Seawall, the Corpus Christi Marina and a memorial statue commissioned to honor the life of slain Tejano singer Selena Quintanilla-Perez.

Guests stay in beautifully decorated and comfortable king and double bed family rooms or executive suites. Many of the rooms have excellent views of Corpus Christi Bay and its many amenities.

The two-mile-long Corpus Christi Seawall, completed in 1941 to protect the city from devastating hurricanes, is a popular place to walk, jog, skate or ride a bicycle. Visitors can enjoy a snow cone or other cooling treats, while watching the sailboats or studying the memorial statue to Selena, a Tejano singer from Corpus Christi who was widely revered in the Hispanic community.

The hotel is within walking distance of the Peoples Street and Lawrence Street T-Heads as well as the Cooper's Alley L-Head. All three are man-made peninsulas that jut into Corpus Christi Bay and are home to boat slips, restaurants, shrimp boats and other tourist attractions.

Here you can buy freshly caught shrimp, take a deep-sea fishing trip, enjoy a tour of Corpus Christi Bay or dine in excellent seafood restaurants before retiring to your hotel a short walk away.

Hotel amenities include a large work desk in most rooms, cable TV including premium movie channels, a large outdoor pool, coin-operated laundry, free local calls and a free Continental breakfast.

Breakfast is served in the hotel's on-site restaurant adjacent to the swimming pool. Enjoy fresh coffee, fruit, sweet rolls and more. The restaurant also is open for lunch and dinner.

You'll enjoy the Corpus Christi Bayfront Inn for its combination of elegant surroundings and down-home comfort. Its well-trained staff will get you to your room quickly and will assist you in making your stay as pleasant and memorable as possible.

Meeting and banquet rooms are available for conferences, business or social functions or for those events destined to be among life's most memorable occasions.

Anniversary celebrations, wedding receptions and baby showers are popular events at the Corpus Christi Bayfront Inn. Its meeting/banquet facilities can accommodate 75 to 150 people depending on your needs.

The Corpus Christi Bayfront Inn is located minutes away from major attractions such as the U.S.S. *Lexington* aircraft carrier, Texas State Aquarium, South Texas Institute for the Arts, and the Corpus Christi Museum of Science and History.

The hotel is also close to several performing arts venues as well as downtown Corpus Christi and its many restaurants, shops and nightclubs.

The Corpus Christi Bayfront Inn has upgraded its facilities in recent times to better serve its customers and to play its part in downtown and bayfront development.

The hotel's rooms received new carpeting, marble vanities and upgrades in each of the bathrooms. Outside, the Corpus Christi Bayfront Inn has received a facelift that makes it among the most attractive structures along the scenic Shoreline Boulevard.

The hotel is easy to find whether you're arriving via Corpus Christi International Airport, Interstate 37 or U.S. Highway 181 from the north. Take the Shoreline Boulevard exit, turn right and drive four blocks. The hotel, with its stately fountain, eye pleasing landscaping and comforting outdoor lighting, is on the right.

The Corpus Christi Bayfront Inn is the place to be whether you're planning a trip in the next few days or considering a visit in the years to come.

As Corpus Christi's downtown and bayfront continue to grow, the Corpus Christi Bayfront Inn is poised to take advantage of proposed development along the city's marina as well as expansion to the city's convention center, construction of a multi-purpose arena and possible construction of a minor league baseball stadium.

The Corpus Christi Bayfront Inn is the perfect choice for business and vacation travelers alike.

✧

Above: Relax by our large outdoor pool.

Below: Friendly, courteous staff greet guests upon their arrival in the newly remodeled lobby.

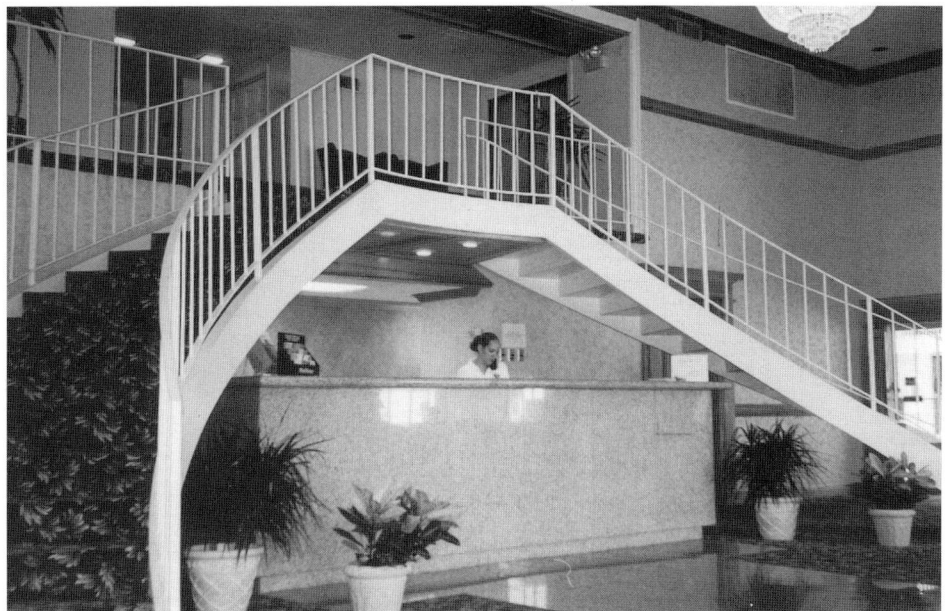

SWANTNER & GORDON INSURANCE AGENCY

Swantner & Gordon Insurance Agency, LLP, Corpus Christi's largest independent insurance firm, has been growing with the city and protecting its citizens and their property since 1936.

As an independent insurance agency, Swantner & Gordon represents many of the top insurance companies in the country. That means quality coverage at a competitive price. Swantner & Gordon Insurance Agency is ranked in the top 150 Independently Owned Agencies in the nation.

Because of Swantner & Gordon's substantial size and strength, the commercial staff handles the placement of large or difficult accounts

quickly and accurately. The agency's primary business territory covers the state of Texas. Swantner & Gordon Insurance Agency also has clients in twenty other states as well as foreign operations.

Jamin Gordon and Bob Swantner formed Swantner & Gordon Insurance Agency in May 1936. They started out in the old City National Bank Building at Chaparral and Peoples Streets with a staff of two. In October 1941 construction began on the Swantner Building at 401 North Shoreline Boulevard. It was the first private construction on Corpus Christi's newly created bayfront seawall improvement program.

Swantner & Gordon operated as a partnership until 1972 at which time the agency incorporated under the direction of John Richard Swantner. In January 1986 the agency dissolved the corporation and formed a partnership for the purpose of buying out John Richard Swantner and three minor shareholders.

In August 1995 the agency formed a limited liability partnership, bringing in three new partners, while buying out two existing partners. In October 2002 the agency named its fifth partner. Currently, Swantner & Gordon Insurance Agency employs more than 130 people with offices in Kingsville, Portland, and Houston.

Randal Mark Lee, managing partner of Swantner & Gordon Insurance Agency, has been employed by the agency since 1976. Lee is a graduate of Rice University, with a bachelor of science degree in commerce. American General Insurance Company employed him from 1972 to 1976 as marketing manager for the South Texas region. He subsequently came to work at Swantner & Gordon, where as managing partner he oversees all aspects of the agency operations.

Jerry Jerome Crider, CIC, partner, has been employed by Swantner & Gordon since 1993. Crider is a graduate of Texas A&M University at College Station with a bachelor of science degree in sociology. He was employed by Employers Insurance of Texas upon graduation in 1966 and resigned in 1991 as a senior marketing executive. He then opened an office in Corpus Christi. In 1993, after developing a

Opposite, top: Swanter & Gordon, 1951.

Opposite, bottom: Swanter & Gordon, 1958.

Left: Standing (from left to right): Steve
Addkison, CIC, CPCU, partner; Trey
Tollett III, CIC, partner; and Jerry Crider,
CIC, partner. Seated is Randy Lee,
managing partner of Swanter & Gordon
Insurance Agency.

Below: Swanter & Gordon, 2002.

new large commercial clientele, he merged with Swantner & Gordon. Two years later, he became a partner.

John Thomas (Trey) Tollett III, CIC, partner, has been employed by Swantner & Gordon Insurance Agency since 1988. Tollett has a bachelor of business administration degree from Corpus Christi State University. His insurance career began in the Life, Health and Financial Services area with MassMutual Life. After joining the agency, he expanded his career in insurance to include the Property and Casualty area.

James Steven Addkison, CIC, CPCU, partner, has been employed by Swantner & Gordon Insurance Agency since 1980. Addkison graduated from the University of Texas at Austin with a bachelor of science degree in education. Addkison received the CPCU designation in 1991. In 1995 he received the CIC designation. Addkison is past president of the Independent Insurance Agency of the Coastal Bend. Besides his insurance licenses, Addkison maintains a Risk Manager's license.

Dudley C. Ray, CIC, partner, has been the production manager for Swanter & Gordon's Houston branch since 1999. Ray has a bachelor of business administration degree in finance from Sam Houston State University. Ray is a

past president and director of the Independent Insurance Agents of Houston, and is a member of the CNA Pacer Panel.

Swantner & Gordon Insurance Agency, LLP, is professionally affiliated with Independent Insurance Agents of the Coastal Bend, Texas Association of Independent Agents, Independent Insurance Agents of America, The Council of Insurance Agents and Brokers, the Group 500 and Globex International Group.

PORT OF CORPUS CHRISTI

The Port of Corpus Christi was born on November 13, 1922, when county commissioners voted to create a navigation district to manage the deepwater port authorized by Congress two years earlier. Corpus Christi's selection as the site for the new port assured its place as the dominant Coastal Bend city, and decades later the Port continues to serve as the economic engine that drives South Texas.

The nation's fifth-largest port, positioned halfway along the Texas coast on the Gulf of Mexico, provides ready access to Mexico, Texas, Central and South America, and Asia. This Gateway to the World is centrally located between North and South America, links the Caribbean and Asia, and, for many countries, is the closest port to Los Angeles.

Customers benefit from the Port's 45-foot channel depth, 125 acres of open storage and fabrication sites, heavy lift capabilities, quick access to the Gulf of Mexico and dockside rail from multiple carriers. Port customers also enjoy excellent highway access, a productive labor force and 338,500 square feet of covered dockside storage.

The Port, which originally served as a distribution point for the agriculture industry, serves as the hub for the region's petrochemical industry, with numerous refineries and chemical plants situated along the Port channel. Refineries here produce roughly five percent of the gasoline used in the United States, while area chemical plants manufacture base commodities used worldwide.

Port industries produce 870,000 barrels of crude oil per day and account for 13 percent of Texas refinery capacity. Austin gets ninety percent of its gasoline from Corpus Christi refineries and Dallas/Fort Worth International

Airport gets sixty-seven percent of its jet fuel from refineries here.

Throughout its existence the Port has sought to increase and diversify its contributions to the South Texas economy. Additions and improvements to Port facilities include:

- Cold storage: A 100,000-square-foot refrigerated warehouse features three rooms, two of which can chill products to as low as twenty degrees below zero. The facility, served by three railroads, provides blast freezing, repacking and warehousing.
- Congressman Solomon P. Ortiz International Center: This state-of-the-art meeting and banquet facility features a 16,000-square-foot banquet hall, five meeting rooms ranging from 580 square feet to 3,140 square feet and a 42,000-square-foot outdoor plaza. The center is the cornerstone in plans to change the face of waterfront development, eventually creating a tourist destination with shops and restaurants.
- Joe Fulton International Trade Corridor: This 11.5-mile road and 7-mile rail project will improve access to more than 2,000 acres of land along the north side of the Corpus Christi Ship Channel. The $42-million project will make approximately 1,000 acres of land available for use as marine terminals and industrial sites.
- Channel improvements: The Corps of Engineers has recommended that the Corpus Christi Ship Channel be widened to 530 feet and deepened to 52 feet. It also

recommends that 7,200 feet at a depth of 40 feet lengthen the La Quinta Channel.
- The Port of Corpus Christi serves as a strategic deployment seaport for U.S. military forces. The Port is working to enhance its role and military readiness through a partnership with the Department of Defense to construct a Surge Sealift Homeport adjacent to Naval Station Ingleside.
- La Quinta Trade Gateway: The Port of Corpus Christi has plans to develop eleven hundred acres into a major container terminal that is expected to handle significant amounts of cargo.
- The vacation cruise industry: The Port is positioning itself to take advantage of future growth in this rapidly expanding industry. Corpus Christi could serve as the gateway to South Texas and San Antonio, the No. 1 tourist destination in the state.
- Harbor Island: The Port of Corpus Christi is determining the best use for this 350-acre tract on the Gulf of Mexico. A recent study found the area suitable for industrial, residential or resort development.

The Port of Corpus Christi will continue to focus on its core business, while looking for ways to stimulate the local economy and improve life for all South Texans.

Meanwhile, the Port is prepared to become a primary player in national and international trade, or, as they say at the Port of Corpus Christi: "The Twenty-first Century Will Move Through Us."

THE SISSAMIS FAMILY

The Sissamis Family has been instrumental in the growth of the Corpus Christi restaurant industry for more than half a century.

It all began in 1940 when Louis Sissamis, known for years as "Papa Louis" by Corpus Christi residents, emigrated to the United States from the Island of Karpathos off the coast of Greece in search of a better life, leaving behind a wife, Maria Sissamis, and three children, Paul, Bill and Stacy (Tessie), for whom he eventually planned to send.

Landing at Ellis Island, "Papa Louis" worked in several restaurants to learn the trade. He eventually worked his way to Corpus Christi, where he later joined his brother-in-law, Chris Hartofilax, and Chris' brother, George Hartofilax, in opening an American-style restaurant on Leopard Street known as the Hasty Tasty.

World War II made it impossible for "Papa Louis" to communicate with or send money home to his family. His oldest son, Paul Sissamis, quit school at age twelve and worked to support his mother, brother and sister, sometimes even chopping wood for the German army in exchange for a loaf of bread.

After the war ended, Paul was determined to come to the United States to join his father. He saved his money and borrowed a pair of shoes in order to be allowed to board a ship to America. In 1947, at the age of nineteen, Paul boarded a cargo ship that set sail for New York, where he planned to gain citizenship and make his way to Corpus Christi.

He made his way to the states and eventually worked his way to Corpus Christi. He washed dishes at the Hasty Tasty and used his first paycheck to buy a pair of shoes, clean the borrowed pair, and return them to their owner.

"Papa Louis" sent money to Greece to bring his other son, Bill, to the states and help with the family business, and after a brief period sent for his wife and daughter to join them. In 1952 Paul opened The Pirate Grill on Chaparral Street in downtown Corpus Christi before moving to Brooklyn, New York, where he met, and on May 11, 1958, married his loving wife of forty-three years, Frances Kapetanakes.

During this time, "Papa Louis" sold his interest in the Hasty Tasty to brothers Chris and George Hartofilax, and together with son Bill Sissamis opened The Astor Restaurant in 1957. Paul later returned to Corpus Christi with his new wife and became co-owner of the Astor Restaurant with his father and brother.

"Tessie" Sissamis later married Gus Papakostas of Greece and together they made a home in Corpus Christi. In 1970, Gus purchased the interest of Bill Sissamis, who returned to Greece to pursue a successful career in property development until his death in 1983. Later that year, Paul retired from the restaurant business to pursue a career in commercial fishing and cattle ranching, selling his interest to Mike Chrissos, Gus Papakostas' son-in-law. In 1984, "Papa Louis" passed away after a brief illness.

In the years to follow, one of Gus Papakostas' sons, Angelo Papakostas, formed a partnership with Bill Hartofilax, son of Chris Hartofilax, to open the Longhorn Restaurant on South Padre Island Drive in 1988. That partnership lasted until 1990, when Bill Hartofilax moved to Greece, selling his interest to Angelo. Angelo, eventually joined Louis Sissamis, son to the late Bill Sissamis, and together they operated the Longhorn Restaurant.

In 1993, Angelo and Louis brought in Bill Sissamis, son of Paul Sissamis, to assist in operations and open more restaurants. In April 1994 the trio opened the Longhorn Steak & Ale on Alameda Street and later that same year opened another Longhorn Steak & Ale in Calallen.

In March 1995 the three men dissolved their interests, with Bill Sissamis retaining ownership of the two recently opened restaurants and Angelo Papakostas retaining his interest in the Longhorn Restaurant. In that same month, Nick Sissamis, another son of Paul Sissamis, joined his brother Bill as a partner in both Longhorn Steak & Ale

restaurants. The Longhorn Steak & Ale in Calallen eventually became the Silverado Steakhouse, which sold in 1997. Their partnership continued until 1999, when Nick Sissamis bought out his brother's interest.

Bill Sissamis went on to earn a real estate license and form Sissamis Properties, which owns Weber Mini Storage, Morgan Street Mini Storage and Tradewinds Mini Storage. In 2001 Nick Sissamis purchased Bonus Q-Pons, a direct mail advertising company and later that same year opened the Sugar Shack nightclub.

The story of the Sissamis Family's involvement in the Corpus Christi restaurant business has yet to come to a close. Bill Sissamis is building a buffet-style cafeteria at Weber Road and Gollihar, and Nick Sissamis plans another steakhouse in 2003 at Staples Street and Saratoga Boulevard.

❖

Above: Longhorn Steak & Ale on Alameda Street opened in 1993.

Below: The Longhorn Steak & Ale offers comfortable surroundings.

CHRISTUS SPOHN HEALTH SYSTEM

❖

Above: Dr. Arthur E. Spohn.

Below: Spohn Sanitarium on North Beach.

Opposite, top: Spohn Cancer Center.

Opposite, middle: A heart catheterization lab.

Opposite, bottom: Spohn Hospital South.

The heritage of CHRISTUS Spohn Health System began in 1905 when the Sisters of Charity of the Incarnate Word agreed to operate the first hospital built in Corpus Christi: Spohn Sanitarium located on North Beach.

Today this comprehensive, value-driven, faith-based health care network consists of six hospitals located throughout South Texas, offering technologically advanced cardiac and cancer services, a network of family health centers and a variety of wellness programs designed to be responsive to community needs.

CHRISTUS Spohn hospitals in Alice, Beeville, Memorial, Kleberg, Shoreline and South along with CHRISTUS Spohn Cancer Center, CHRISTUS Spohn Diabetes Centers, CHRISTUS Spohn Rehabilitation Services and the CHRISTUS Spohn Heart Institute located within the Pavilion at CHRISTUS Spohn Hospital Shoreline, are the major components of CHRISTUS Spohn Health System.

CHRISTUS Spohn Hospital Shoreline is the modern incarnation of the Spohn Hospital built by the bay in 1923 following the 1919 hurricane destruction of the North Beach Sanitarium. This 432-bed hospital is the largest and foremost acute-care medical center in South Texas, offering a full range of diagnostic and surgical services. The Pavilion located at CHRISTUS Spohn Hospital Shoreline houses the CHRISTUS Spohn Heart Institute, which has been recognized among the top one hundred cardiovascular hospitals in the United States.

CHRISTUS Spohn Hospital South was built in 1994 to address the needs of Corpus Christi's growing south side, offering convenience to physicians and patients. In

2002, two additional floors were added to the hospital. This 142 bed, full-service hospital offers diagnostic, surgical, emergency, OB/GYN, orthopedic and geropsychiatric care. CHRISTUS Spohn is home to Driscoll Children's Hospital Neonatal Nursery, a 12-bed neonatal intensive care unit. This special care nursery allows premature babies and newborns with special needs to receive treatment while remaining close to their mothers.

CHRISTUS Spohn Hospital Memorial became a part of the Spohn System in 1996 and, with 397 beds, is the second largest hospital in Corpus Christi. The Level III Trauma Center at Memorial is the only one in the region and receives patients from thirteen South Texas counties. Memorial also has the only civilian Burn Center south of San Antonio. The Corpus Christi Family Practice Residency Program located at Memorial is affiliated with the University of Texas Health Science Center and provides a three-year program for young physicians to become family practitioners.

CHRISTUS Spohn is committed to building healthier communities and to extend its healing ministry to the poor and underserved—this is a vision of CHRISTUS Spohn Health System—to keep communities healthy by focusing attention on awareness and early detection and promoting a healthier lifestyle. Throughout South Texas, CHRISTUS Spohn is involved in outreach programs including free risk assessments, annual screenings and educational presentations. CHRISTUS Spohn gives back to the community a wealth of services plus care for the indigent. The cost of charity care provided by CHRISTUS Spohn Health System on a yearly basis through

charity care, unbilled community benefits and non-reimbursed Medicare is in the multimillions.

Three CHRISTUS Spohn hospitals located in Alice, Beeville and Kingsville serve rural South Texans. CHRISTUS Spohn Hospital Kleberg became a part of the System in 1985 and is a general acute care hospital licensed for 100 beds. Hospital services include complete medical and surgical and intensive care. It offers OB/GYN and skilled nursing, as well as comprehensive diagnostic services. The Emergency Department is designated as a Level IV Trauma Center. CHRISTUS Spohn Kleberg Health Plaza houses the hospital's birthing services—modern, home-like birthing suites that include labor, delivery, post-partum rooms, a nursery and the Cissy Horlock Taub Women's Center. Recently opened is the CHRISTUS Spohn/H-E-B Education Center built entirely from donated funds and available for use by community nonprofit agencies.

CHRISTUS Spohn Hospital Beeville is licensed for sixty-nine beds. This full service hospital is newly renovated and has been updated with the addition of three new surgical suites and several outpatient day surgery rooms. The women's care unit includes nine modern birthing suites and a full service nursery. The recently expanded, modern emergency department is designated as a Level IV Trauma Center. The intensive care unit provides quality critical care twenty-four hours a day. A new lobby and admitting area are slated for completion in 2003.

CHRISTUS Spohn Hospital Alice was built in 1999 to serve the needs of people in Jim Wells, Brooks, Live Oak, Duval and Jim Hogg Counties. The seventy-one-bed hospital offers direct access to a comprehensive array of quality medical and surgical services including pediatrics, OB/GYN, skilled nursing, a geropsychiatric unit, emergency department, cardiac and intensive care, as well as outpatient diagnostic and surgical services. The three rural hospitals located in Alice, Beeville and Kingsville offer the finest radiological and MRI imaging systems for diagnostic services.

CHRISTUS Spohn Health System has grown far beyond the imagination of our founders. Just as they could not have predicted the world today, the future will change in ways unimaginable to us. But our mission—to extend the healing ministry of Jesus Christ—and our core values of dignity, integrity, compassion, excellence, and stewardship will always remain a constant.

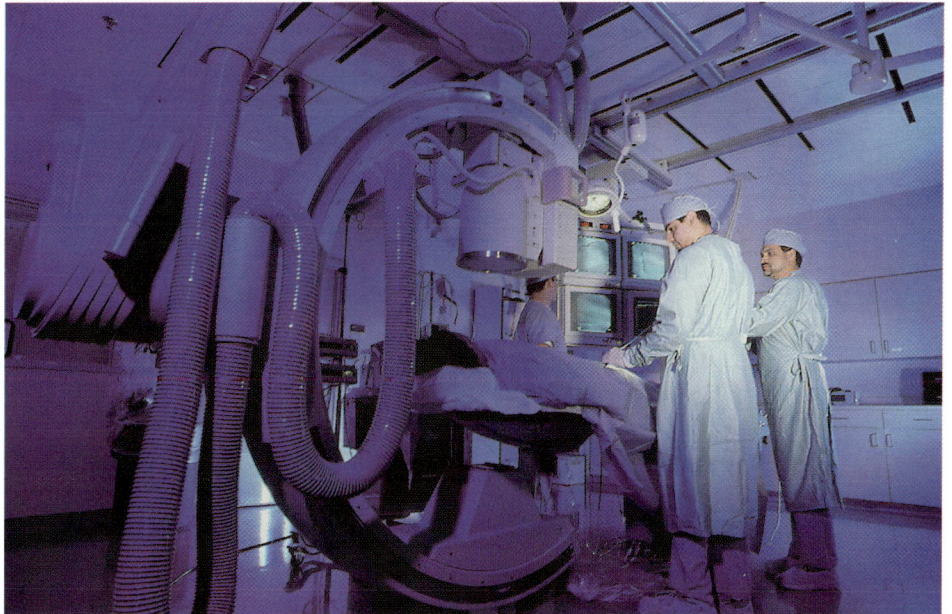

RAMADA INN BAYFRONT

One of Corpus Christi's premier, landmark hotels sits on ground that has both an intriguing and violent history.

The city's original Salt Mill was located at 601 North Water Street in 1850 erected by Captain John Anderson, a Swedish-born seafarer who brought his family to Texas in 1852. The wind-powered mill supplied the many packing plants along the Texas coast, shipped to distant markets, and provided products and employment for the citizens of Corpus Christi.

In 1900 the Anderson family demolished the windmill and built a two-story residence. The structure was sold in 1911 to become a part of the Nueces Hotel, completed in 1913. The Nueces occupied the land when Hurricane Celia wrought her catastrophic destruction in 1969, obliterating that well-respected enterprise.

Since 1971 the Ramada Bayfront has been on the land at North Water, and has received acclaim as a "home away from home" to legions of business people, vacation travelers, and numerous others with a reason to visit the Corpus Christi area.

This full service hotel has 200 guest rooms and 16,000 square feet of meeting and convention space. There are seventy-five full time employees as well as additional seasonal

workers. Ralph Ehrlich, a past president of the Texas Hotel and Motel Association, is the general manager of the Ramada Inn Bayfront.

According to Ehrlich, "Our mission at Ramada Inn Bayfront is to provide each guest with an exemplary stay in a high quality, professionally run hotel. Through our unique "Personal Best" commitment, each guest should feel special." Ehrlich goes on to say, "We strive to provide this level of service by applying the T.E.A.M. rule: Together everyone achieves more if there is a total effort from all members."

"To fulfill our mission," Ehrlich states, "all of us at the Ramada Bayfront commit ourselves to employee training and development, rewarding employee achievement, respect for each member of the Bayfront family, quality service which leads to guest enjoyment, and profitability."

The Ramada Bayfront is heavily involved in civic and charitable associations and endeavors, and provides meeting space and banquet facilities for, among others, the Chamber of Commerce, Hispanic Chamber of Commerce, the Rotary Club, and the Corpus Christi Mustangs.

The hotel and the site it occupies, have a long, colorful, and successful place in the history of Corpus Christi. According to Ehrlich, he and his staff are dedicated to many more years of the same.

❖

Above: Ramada Inn Bayfront is located at 601 North Water Street, one block from Corpus Christi Bay.

COURTESY OF BRIAN TUMLINSON.

Below: Relax in the lobby area while enjoying live music and complimentary hors d'oeuvres.

COURTESY OF BRIAN TUMLINSON.

Vann M. Kennedy and Mary Louise (Wittliff) Kennedy are pioneers in South Texas broadcasting. Both successful print journalists, the Kennedys founded and operated radio and television stations in Corpus Christi and Laredo.

Vann Kennedy, a decorated World War II veteran and licensed attorney, founded Corpus Christi's KSIX-AM radio in 1946 and 10 years later, KZTV-Channel 10, known as the "clear channel" for its clear signal. Prior to that, Kennedy founded the *State Observer* (now called the *Texas Observer*) and launched the Austin Bureau of the International News Service, which later merged with United Press.

Kennedy served as bureau manager at the state capitol, where he hired a University of Texas student named Walter Cronkite to work for him. Cronkite, who eventually rose to iconic status as anchorman for the *CBS Evening News*, describes Kennedy as his mentor.

As an infantry colonel in the U.S. Army Reserve, Vann served as personal advisor to many state and national political figures, including Vice President John Nance Garner and Presidents John F. Kennedy and Lyndon B. Johnson.

Vann and Mary Kennedy met in Austin while he was working as the Austin bureau manager for the International News Service. Mary Kennedy, employed as the editor of the *Texas Hotel Review* in San Antonio, looked up her future husband based on the advice of a Victoria Chamber of Commerce official, who described Vann as one of the best newspaper men and finest gentlemen in Texas.

They married in 1940. Mary played a central role in the family's business operations, beginning in World War II when Vann volunteered for military duty.

While he was away, Mary kept their many Austin enterprises afloat, which included the International News Service bureau, a print shop, the *State Observer*, and an oil and gas newsletter.

When he returned from the war, Vann and other investors formed a company called Corpus Christi Broadcasting Company, which launched KSIX-AM and KZTV-TV, Channel 10. The Kennedy's ran the stations, including KVTV in Laredo, for decades before selling the businesses in 2001.

VANN AND MARY KENNEDY

❖

Above: Vann Kennedy.
COURTESY OF RANDOLF PHOTOGRAPHY.

Left: Mary Kennedy.
COURTESY OF RANDOLF PHOTOGRAPHY.

Padre Isles Country Club

✧

Above: The clubhouse includes a dining room and lounge overlooking the 6,700-yard, par 72 links-style course.

Below: The Club features a junior Olympic-size pool and shallow wading pool.

Padre Isles Country Club is home to Texas' most recognized barrier island golf course, a links-style course described as the St. Andrews of Padre Island, decorated with sand dunes, thick natural grasses and water on 15 of the 18 strategically placed holes.

This country club located on Padre Island was created in the early 1970s by Bruce Littrel as an incentive by the original developer, Great Western Corporation to convince people to purchase lots and homes on the then undeveloped Padre Island.

They started with nine holes and promised to build the second nine once they reached their goal of of one hundred members, a promise kept when club membership surpassed the one-hundred-member mark in March 1972.

Club membership and Padre Island development have grown considerably through the years, with homes and businesses covering much of the island and Padre Isles membership topping the five-hundred mark.

Throughout the history of Padre Island, the country club has been a major selling point in convincing people to live or conduct business on the island, and serves as the focal point for community meetings and special events, including several not related to country club membership.

The golf course is the centerpiece of the club, with flat fairways lined with dangerously thick native grasses that club members refer to as "heather," making for one of the most challenging courses in South Texas. But, unlike other South Texas courses, this 6,700-yard, par 72 course enjoys steady, cooling breezes that make even summertime play fun.

The course is a recognized Audubon Sanctuary site, the third in Texas, a designation given to sites that demonstrate a commitment

to preserving and protecting the environment. Bird watchers and other naturalists will enjoy the wide variety of bird and plant life found along the course.

Six lighted tennis courts, a full-service pro shop, clinics and private lessons are available to tennis players, who enjoy active league and tournament play under the supervision of a United States Professional Tennis Association-certified director.

Many find the Padre Isles clubhouse the main attraction. The clubhouse, eclectic in design and motif, combines tradition with casual informality, accommodating both the social and formal needs of members.

Dining areas include the main dining room and lounge overlooking the course, locker rooms for men and women, an exercise room, personal trainers, board room and a patio that provides a perfect place for cookouts, picnics, tournaments, reunions, wedding receptions and other outdoor functions.

Take a refreshing dip in the club's swimming pool. The junior Olympic-size pool and shallow wading pool for small children is surrounded by fabulous island foliage, making for a relaxing and romantic setting.

The club's dining room and lounge offer a great place for everything from family casual to upscale dining. Thursday Night Family Nights are a tradition at Padre Isles, with a weekly special designed to accommodate busy family schedules. Saturdays are set-aside for Prime & Wine Dinners consisting of delicious smoked ribs with complimentary wine.

The club is situated just a few minutes from several beaches, fishing spots, Padre Island

National Seashore (the largest undeveloped barrier island in the world) and Corpus Christi's main shopping and dining areas.

General manager and owner, Charles Eskridge, purchased the club shortly before plans to dredge a pass through the island finally received approval. The dredging of Packery Channel between the Gulf of Mexico and the Laguna Madre is expected to trigger a $1 billion boon in development up and down the island.

That, along with plans to raise the flood-prone causeway linking the island with mainland, is expected to help the island and the club fulfill the vision of several prominent Corpus Christi businessmen, who years ago planted the seeds for what is now one of the most affordable and desirable coastal destinations and country clubs in the nation.

✧

Above: Waterfowl feed on one of the many wetland areas on the course, which features water on 15 of the 18 holes.

Below: Padre Isles Country Club is recognized Audubon Sanctuary site, the third in Texas.

CITY OF CORPUS CHRISTI STORM WATER DEPARTMENT

The City of Corpus Christi Storm Water Department strives to operate and maintain a drainage system that provides safe, dependable surface drainage throughout the city.

This vast system of ditches, underground drainage pipes and inlets protect the city from flood damage, while the Department's environmental service initiatives reduce the introduction of trash and pollutants into storm water runoff.

The City's drainage system is designed to remove storm water runoff from neighborhood streets throughout the city and carry it to natural drainage courses and receiving waters such as streams, bays and the Gulf of Mexico. The Storm Water Department maintains approximately 100 miles of major drainage ditches, 650 miles of minor roadside drainage ditches, 600 miles of underground storm drainage pipe, 18,000 inlets, two pump stations, and 23 storm drainage gates.

The Department cleans, grades and performs erosion repairs on ditches; maintains, repairs and cleans storm drainage pipes; and vacuums approximately 18,000 inlets throughout the city.

✧

Above: Storm Water Power Street Pump Station.

Below: Louisiana Parkway Outfall at Cole Park.

Storm Water mows and removes litter from approximately twenty-five hundred acres of roadside ditches, drainage right-of-ways and guardrails.

The Department also repairs and builds head walls, storm drain inlets, manholes and riprap sections. It performs minor repairs to more than 100 concrete bridges and is responsible for repair or replacement of approximately eighteen hundred miles of minor curb and gutter.

The Storm Water Department is also responsible for administering the City's National Pollutant Discharge Elimination System (NPDES) Municipal Separate Storm Sewer System (MS4) permit, which allows the City's storm water to discharge to U.S. waters.

As part of the Storm Water Quality Management Program, Storm Water staff performs inspections of construction sites and industrial facilities.

The Department also maintains and operates five storm water quality-monitoring stations. Staff collects data and grab samples to monitor dry and wet weather flows.

Through its outreach and educational programs, the Storm Water Department educates the public on the importance of proper disposal and handling of trash and pollutants that eventually find their way into the drainage system and ultimately the Corpus Christi Bay.

The Department funds the City's Household Hazardous Waste Program promoting the importance of reducing, reusing and recycling household products. Storm Water maintains a list of recyclers where residents can dispose of oil, antifreeze, tires, batteries, and household waste such as paint and cleaning supplies.

The Storm Water Department utilizes proactive planning to help ensure that new development does not negatively impact existing neighborhoods. Working with developers and city residents alike, the City of Corpus Christi Storm Water Department strives to keep the city safe and clean, contributing to the City's reputation as a great place to live and work.

CITY OF CORPUS CHRISTI WASTEWATER DEPARTMENT

The mission of the City of Corpus Christi Wastewater Department is to protect and improve the health, welfare and quality of life for the citizens of Corpus Christi by providing environmental protection through collection, treatment, and disposal of wastewater.

It collects and treats approximately 10 billion gallons of wastewater per year in the most cost-effective manner possible in accordance with federal, state and local regulations. Its service area is primarily within the Corpus Christi city limits and consists of more than 1,200 miles of gravity mains interwoven with approximately 58 miles of force mains and 94 lift stations.

The collection system serves more than 76,000 customers in a 137-square-mile area. The department is responsible for the maintenance, repair and rehabilitation of the wastewater system, including six treatment plants, other than those portions on private property.

The Broadway plant, which became operational in 1936, is the city's oldest treatment plant, and serves the downtown and Corpus Christi Beach areas. The city completed major additions to the plant in 1940, 1950, 1954, and 1980. The facility received the Platinum Award from the Association of Metropolitan Sewerage Agencies (AMSA) in 2002 with no NPDES permit violations for five consecutive years.

The Whitecap plant, the smallest of the six plants, also received the Platinum Award in 2002. The plant, which serves the North Padre Island area, was built in 1974 and underwent an expansion in 1991.

The Laguna Madre plant received the AMSA's Gold Award in 2001. Built in 1971 and expanded in 1986, the small plant serves the Flour Bluff area, and plans call for expansion and improvements in the near future.

The Oso plant, which received the AMSA's Silver Award in 2001, is the largest of the six plants and serves the Southside of Corpus Christi, where more than fifty percent of the population lives. Completed in 1941, the Oso plant has been expanded several times, most recently in 1982.

Another AMSA Silver Award winner in 2001, the Greenwood plant, was completed in 1959 and expanded in 1991 and 2001. It serves the Corpus Christi International Airport and approximately six thousand acres of the City's Westside.

The Allison plant, located close to the Nueces River, began treating wastewater in 1966 and was expanded in 1985, and serves the Northwest portion of the city, covering a fifty-six-hundred-acre area.

❖

Above: Broadway Wastewater Treatment Plant, #3936.

Below: Greenwood Wastewater Treatment Plant, 2001.

DRISCOLL
CHILDREN'S
HOSPITAL

✧

Above: Clara Driscoll.

Driscoll Children's Hospital believes all children deserve the highest possible healthcare. And the fourteen hundred professionals at this tertiary care regional referral center share that philosophy, first espoused by the hospital's namesake, Clara Driscoll.

Driscoll, who bequeathed her family's fortune toward the goal of building the hospital, and Dr. McIver Furman worked to turn an empty farm lot into a charitable children's hospital.

As one of only 38 freestanding children's hospitals in the nation, Driscoll Children's Hospital, which opened its doors in 1953, takes pride in its reputation for providing state-of-the-art healthcare to children in a 31,000-square-mile area. The hospital is continually expanding its services throughout this enormous region, with plans to build state-of-the-art medical clinics in the Rio Grande Valley cities of McAllen and Brownsville, not far from the border with Mexico.

Driscoll Children's Hospital, a 200-licensed-bed facility serving more than 150,000 pediatric patients per year, spares no expense in providing the most advanced technology available. In recent years, Driscoll has purchased and implemented the Picture Archiving and Communication System (PACS) for radiology, which provides the best and fastest imaging for diagnostics available.

PACS has revolutionized the way radiology images such as X-rays, CTs and MRIs are managed. It combines an automated computerized database with networking technologies to digitally produce and archive images and share them with other hospital healthcare workers. This sharing of information, accomplished through networked personal computers by staff members with established accounts on a secured system, can take place between people in adjoining rooms or between people hundreds of miles apart.

Another example of Driscoll's commitment to investing in new technology is its "Pharmacy Robot," a computer-controlled robotic system that dispenses medications with unprecedented accuracy. Systems similar to the one Driscoll

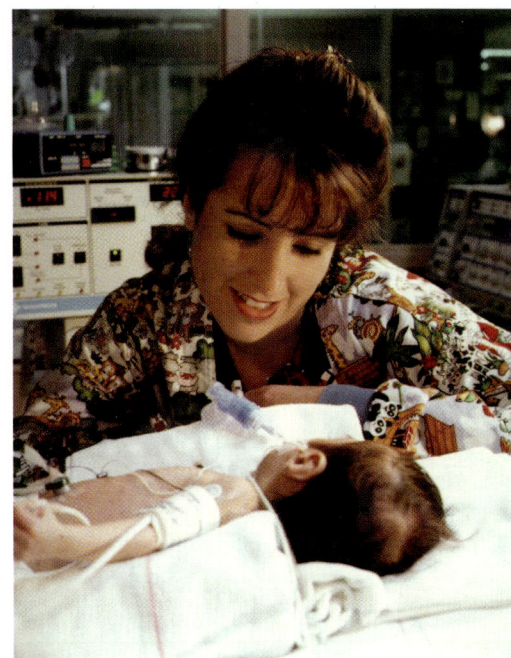

purchased have dispensed more than 365 million drugs without error, freeing pharmacists to spend more time counseling patients and family members.

Patients benefit in numerous ways from Driscoll Children's Hospital's reputation for providing state-of-the-art healthcare. The U.S. Food and Drug Administration chose the hospital's neonatal intensive care unit to conduct a trial for nitric oxide, and the hospital later received permission to administer the drug.

Providing additional nitric oxide to sick newborns through breathing tubes increases oxygenation and improves the survival rate for infants with pulmonary hypertension and severe infection. Nitric oxide and Driscoll's intensive multidisciplinary team efforts have saved infants who might have died at other hospitals.

Another addition, Driscoll's Transport Team, has also saved lives. The hospital developed this ground-and-air team in response to increased requests for specialized pediatric and neonatal transportation to Driscoll Children's Hospital from hospitals in the Rio Grande Valley. Some young patients have "earned their wings" in medical flights taken in an airplane or helicopter operated by Driscoll Children's Hospital. Emergency medical technicians, paramedics, respiratory therapists, and nurses receive training in all aspects of pediatric and neonatal patient care,

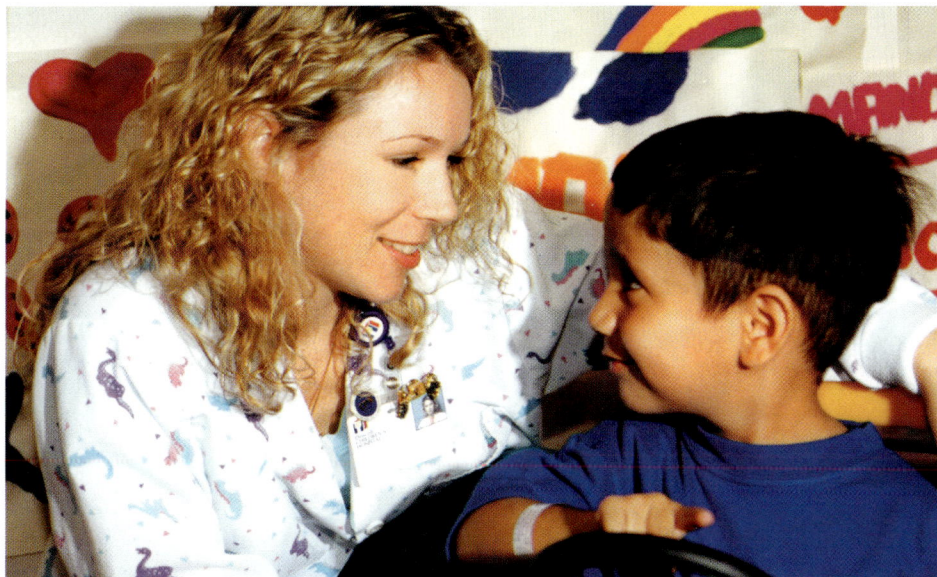

enabling critical emergency care to begin before patients arrive at the hospital.

Many patients end up in Driscoll's 20-bed pediatric intensive care unit or its 40-bed neonatal intensive care unit. The hospital emergency room receives 40,000 visitors each year and hospital physicians perform 6,000 surgical procedures annually. Driscoll provides comprehensive medical and surgical services in eight surgical suites and has staff working in 34 pediatric subspecialties.

The hospital, accredited with the Joint Commission on the Accreditation of Healthcare Organizations, handles more than 150,000 outpatient visits each year and operates the Driscoll Children's Hospital Child Abuse Resource and Evaluation Team, an inpatient consultation service to help patients with confirmed or suspected physical abuse, sexual abuse or neglect.

New technology and expansion efforts promise to extend Driscoll's mission. The hospital now operates 21 cardiology clinics and 5 subspecialty clinics throughout South Texas. It also provides healthcare services through a neonatal intensive care unit at Christus Spohn South in Corpus Christi and a children's clinic in nearby Robstown.

In coming years, Driscoll will continue to expand its services and state-of-the-art technology, while holding true to its commitment to relieve the suffering and meet the needs of children, regardless of their ability to pay.

TEXAS-MEXICAN RAILWAY COMPANY

The idea of the Texas Mexican Railway, Tex-Mex, began as early as 1856 when some Corpus Christi investors organized themselves to start a railroad line from Corpus Christi to a point somewhere along the U.S.-Mexico border. Several "paper railroads" were started in an effort to construct a rail line to compete with the wagon trains of the time, which were transporting passengers, wool, and skins, coffee and lumber in large quantities from northern Mexico and inland ranches. At the time this was considered a long and dangerous trip. In 1866 the Texas Legislature granted a charter to construct a rail line under the name of the Corpus Christi and Rio Grande Rail Road Company. Several financial set backs prevented the construction of such a line until the group appointed Corpus Christi businessman Uriah Lott as president of the company.

✧

Texas Mexican Railway Locomotive No. 11 built by the Baldwin Locomotive Works and purchased by Tex-Mex in 1921.

COURTESY OF ARTURO J. DOMINGUEZ COLLECTION.

Lott calculated that if the line was a narrow gauge they could almost double the distance of the line for the same cost as a standard gauge line. In 1875 the Texas Legislature granted the group a new charter under the name of the Corpus Christi, San Diego, Rio Grande Narrow Gauge Railroad. Certainly a long name for such a short line. In 1877 twenty-five miles of track had been laid from Corpus Christi to Banquette and in 1879 they reached San Diego. Soon after construction was started in Realitos, Lott heard about Mexican President Porfirio Diaz' efforts to construct a line from Mexico City to Laredo, Texas. Realizing an opportunity, Lott met with the Mexican government and sold the narrow gauge line. In 1881 the Mexican government acting through a promoter took over the operation under the name of The Texas Mexican Railway Company and continued the construction towards the City of Laredo.

By 1881, Tex-Mex had become the first U.S. railroad to arrive at this important gateway to Mexico. Two years later, a permanent bridge linked Laredo and Nuevo Laredo, Mexico. This occurred at an important point for rail development in South Texas because rail construction in Northeast Mexico had reached its height.

The National Railways of Mexico began building machine shops across the U.S.-Mexico border in Laredo, where as many as 200 mechanics worked. By 1889, U.S. railroads filled the last gaps between Mexico City and Canada. In 1902, Tex-Mex was converted to a standard gauge railroad. This meant that a train could travel from Mexico City, through the Laredo gateway, across the United States and into Canada without interruption.

The Mexican government held the Tex-Mex in trust until 1982, when it was sold to shipping conglomerate Transportacion Maritima Mexicana (TMM). In 1995, TMM sold forty-nine percent of the rail line to the Kansas City Southern Railroad (KCS), striking up a strategic alliance for the opening of a key railroad corridor for the North American Free Trade Agreement (NAFTA).

This joint venture further produced the birth of another railroad, Transportes Ferroviarios Mexicanos (TFM) when the Mexican Government privatized its northern rail line in 1997 and in 2002, Tex-Mex became a subsidiary of TFM.

The Tex-Mex network extends across 557 miles of rail in Texas. Tex-Mex owns 157 miles of main line between Laredo and Corpus Christi, and operates on 400 miles of Trackage Rights between Corpus Christi, Houston and Beaumont.

The connections with KCS and TFM gives Tex-Mex an extended rail network beginning in the southern most point at the Pacific Port of Lazaro Cardenas in the Mexican State of Michoacan to its northern most point in Chicago, Illinois and all other major railway connections in between. This network has positioned Tex-Mex to be a viable competitive alternative for business shipping between Mexico, the United States and Canada.

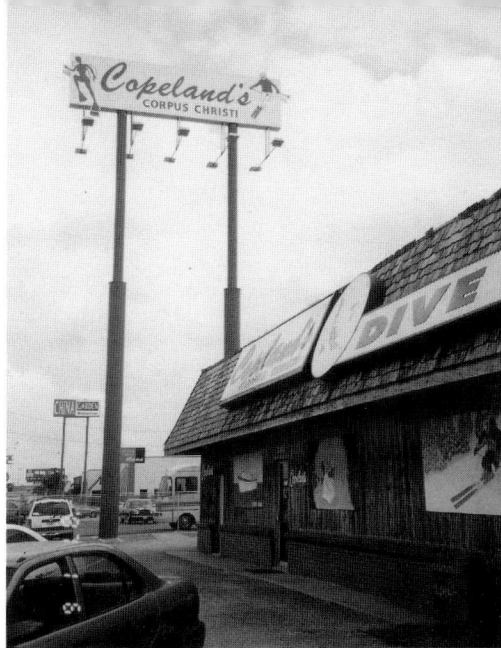

COPELAND'S INC.

Jim and Saundra Copeland of Copeland's Inc. are pioneers in the South Texas diving world. They helped introduce this exciting recreational activity to Corpus Christi in 1957 when they founded the Pescadores Dive Club.

At the time, Texas had only two dive shops—one in Houston and one in Dallas—and the only way to get a scuba tank filled in Corpus Christi was to take it to a local construction company and wait two hours. Jim Copeland set up a scuba-training program before certification agencies had been established, issuing his own card known as the "Coastal School of Scuba Diving" card.

In 1958 the Copelands purchased a high-pressure compressor, built a portable air station and began selling air and diving equipment from their home. In 1961 when the house got too crowded, they opened a store in the Six Points area of Corpus Christi, adding surfboards to become the first surf shop in South Texas.

Saundra ran the store while her husband worked full time for the Texas Highway Department and taught scuba lessons on the side. Jim eventually left the highway department to concentrate on his growing retail business.

Copeland's Inc. moved to its current location on Padre Island Drive on July 28, 1970, just days before Hurricane Celia hit. Although Celia spared the Copelands' new facility, it destroyed their factory that manufactured surfboards, which contributed to their decision to phase out that product line.

That was the same year Copeland's introduced snow-skiing equipment to Corpus Christi, providing the company with a winter income to complement their summer diving-related sales.

In 1992, the Copelands purchased an 85-foot diesel-powered dive boat, *The Adventurer*, to replace their original 22-foot dive boat, *Wet & Wild*, to take divers on excursions to the Gulf of Mexico. *The Adventurer* was sold in the summer of 2000.

Copeland's continues to be the South Texas leader in the sale of scuba and snow-skiing equipment. They also give scuba lessons and snow-skiing lessons. Jim and Saundra, along with two of their four children—Denise Copeland and Debbie Pennington—operate the Corpus Christi store.

The Copelands were there for the birth of scuba diving and introduced snow-skiing to South Texas, and you can be sure that residents will continue to benefit from their experience and knowledge for years to come.

✧

Above: Copeland's Dive Shop in Corpus Christi, Texas.

Bottom, left: Saundra Copeland, 1960.

Bottom, right: Jim Copeland with 52.8-pound Jew Fish, 1965.

CORPUS CHRISTI REGIONAL ECONOMIC DEVELOPMENT CORPORATION

❖

Above: One Shoreline Plaza, home of the Corpus Christi Regional Economic Development Corporation, overlooks tranquil Corpus Christi Bay.

Below: Ocean-going vessels like this are common sites at the Port of Corpus Christi, the fifth-largest port in the nation.

Corpus Christi's tropical climate and its location on a protected bay near a source of fresh water made it an ideal site for the trading post that Henry L. Kinney started in 1853. And the addition of a deep-water port in the early twentieth century guaranteed that the city would become the Coastal Bend's economic hub, a position it holds to this day.

Long considered a great place to work and live, Corpus Christi residents have taken steps in recent years to enhance that perception by supporting economic development projects designed to grow the economy and improve what is already an ideal lifestyle.

The Corpus Christi Regional Economic Development Corporation contributes to this effort by working to retain jobs, expand existing businesses, recruit new industries and promote entrepreneurial growth.

As the city celebrates its 150th birthday, $1.6 billion in construction projects are under way, while another $1 billion in projects is already in the planning stages.

Recent construction projects include the $18-million Harte Research Institute for Gulf of Mexico Studies, a premier marine science institute on the Texas A&M University-Corpus Christi campus. The institute, funded by a $46-million endowment by Edward H. Harte. This is the second-largest endowment among the nation's marine science institutes.

Another major development at the fast-growing university is the O'Connor School of Business, funded by an $18 million gift from Michael O'Connor, a local businessman and chairman of the board of the Hanover Compressor Company.

Other projects in the works include a $30-million multipurpose arena, expansion of the city's convention center, airport and freeway system, and maintenance of the city's historical seawall.

Existing industries also plan increased development in the Corpus Christi area. The petrochemical industry is projecting nearly $1 billion in new investment, including $500 million by Valero Energy and $145 million by Flint Hills Resources.

City officials are studying ways to enhance its beautiful bay front, marina and historic downtown areas, and construction to raise the John F. Kennedy Causeway is expected to expedite hurricane evacuation from Mustang and Padre Islands.

Padre Island, one of the most affordable coastal communities in the nation, is poised

for major change. Plans call for a pass to be dredged between the Gulf of Mexico and the Laguna Madre, a long-sought dream expected to trigger $1 billion or more in island development.

With help from the Corpus Christi Regional Economic Development Corporation and others, the oil-and-gas economy, which for decades determined the city's fortunes, has given way to a more diversified economic base led by tourism, oil refining, chemical manufacturing, military, healthcare and academia. Economic diversification has paid off for the city in the form of low unemployment and one of the fastest-growing economies in the nation in terms of job creation.

Corpus Christi is home to the Corpus Christi Army Depot, the world's largest helicopter-maintenance facility, and serves as a healthcare hub for South Texas that includes Driscoll Children's Hospital, one of the best children's hospitals in the nation.

The Coastal Bend is known throughout Texas and the nation as an ideal place to vacation and commune with nature. Shopping, restaurants, beaches, tourist attractions and nature preserves attract visitors and new residents to the region.

Attractions include the Texas State Aquarium, one of the ten best aquaria in the nation, and Padre Island National Seashore, the largest undeveloped barrier island in the

world and home to the endangered Kemps Ridley sea turtle.

Despite all the changes, Corpus Christi hasn't turned its back on Mother Nature.

The city that refines five percent of the nation's gasoline (much of it in the form of clean-burning fuels) is also the largest industrial-based city in the country to maintain federal clean-air standards.

And the Port of Corpus Christi, the fifth largest in the nation in terms of tonnage, maintains both "fishable" and "swimable" federal water quality in its inner harbor. This "Gateway to the Americas" is centrally located between North and South America and offers access to markets in the Caribbean and, via rail links to Los Angeles, the Far East.

Corpus Christi has changed dramatically since Henry L. Kinney started his little trading post next to Corpus Christi Bay. And although he might not recognize the city that has grown up around it, he would immediately recognize the atmosphere of free enterprise and a quality lifestyle that attracted him to the area in the first place.

The Corpus Christi Regional Economic Development Corporation is a major reason this pro-business atmosphere lives on in Corpus Christi. Regardless of whether it's an existing business looking to expand or a new company considering a move to Corpus Christi, the Corpus Christi Regional Economic Development Corporation can help.

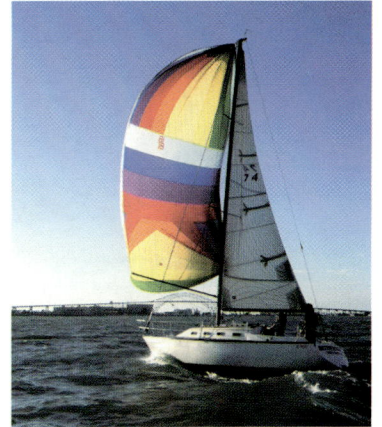

❖

Above: Warm weather, sunny skies and quick access to Corpus Christi Bay and the Gulf of Mexico make Corpus Christi a favorite spot for sailing and other recreational activities.

Below: Navy pilots earn their wings at the Naval Air Station-Corpus Christi and Naval Air Station-Kingsville.
The area is also home to the Corpus Christi Army Depot and Naval Station-Ingleside.

CORPUS CHRISTI BEACH BUSINESSES

Corpus Christi is working hard to recapture the glory days of Corpus Christi Beach. During its heyday in the 1930s, the beach, known then as North Beach, served as a playground for residents and tourists, who came to enjoy the carnival, salt-water swimming pool, boardwalk and shops.

Today, Corpus Christi is home to the Texas State Aquarium, the U.S.S. *Lexington Museum*, Blackbeard's on the Beach, Pier 99, Radisson Beach Hotel, and the Villa del Sol Resort Condominium.

Blackbeard's on the Beach, Pier 99, Radisson Beach Hotel and the Villa del Sol Resort Condominium are all members of "Bring Back the Boardwalk," a committee of the Corpus Christi Beach Association, which was established to rebuild the historical boardwalk that once ran along the beach. Add benches, foliage, shops, restaurants and places to stay and you have an attractive beachfront destination where the past and present meet.

By rebuilding the boardwalk, Corpus Christi will join a prestigious list of accessible beaches throughout the world. Four Corpus Christi Beach properties have been instrumental in efforts to revive the beach. They are:

- Blackbeard's on the Beach: One of Corpus Christi's most popular restaurants offering indoor patio dining. The menu includes fresh seafood such as the catch of the day and shrimp tacos, along with South Texas favorites like chicken fried steak and enchiladas. Patrons also enjoy a full bar and live entertainment.
- Pier 99: Just right…on the water, this seafood restaurant on Corpus Christi Beach offers indoor and outdoor dining with a scenic view overlooking Corpus Christi Bay, the U.S.S. *Lexington* and downtown Corpus Christi. The menu here includes seafood, steaks and burgers, too. You'll also find fresh-catch specials; pasta dishes, snow crab, and all-you-can eat fish and family platters.
- Radisson Beach Hotel: This quality accommodation offers guests a unique selection of elegantly decorated rooms with balconies overlooking Corpus Christi Bay. Guests enjoy a full-service restaurant, lounge, swim-up cabana pool and hot tub. Discounts tickets are available for the Texas State Aquarium, U.S.S. *Lexington*, and other nearby attractions.
- Villa del Sol Resort Condominium: Enjoy gorgeous bay views at Villa del Sol located on Corpus Christi Beach with the water at your doorstep and breathtaking views to delight you each day! This resort community offers all the amenities you need to feel like you're on vacation every time you visit. You may visit us on the Internet at www.villa-delsol.com.

❖

From top to bottom:

Pier 99.

Radisson Beach Hotel.

Villa del Sol Resort Condominium.

Blackbeard's on the Beach.

MOORHOUSE
CONSTRUCTION

Moorhouse Construction owes its success to its founder, B. L. Moorhouse, his family and the hard work and dedication of a number of long-time employees. The company began as an outgrowth of B. L. Moorhouse Company, a wholesale building materials dealer founded in Corpus Christi in 1947.

B. L. Moorhouse, who serves as chairman of Moorhouse Construction, started the company in 1975 as a general contractor specializing in remodeling and small construction projects.

Five years later his son, Burt Moorhouse, who earned a mechanical engineering degree from Trinity University and now serves as president, joined the company. Their first job as father and son general contractors, a $45,000 renovation at Memorial Medical Center, led years later to construction projects valued as high as $20 million.

Throughout its history, the company has built several Corpus Christi landmarks. Major construction projects include Luther Jones Elementary School, Mary Grett School, Congressman Solomon P. Ortiz International Center, International Bank of Commerce in Brownsville and the Early Childhood Development Center at Texas A&M University-Corpus Christi.

Along with B.L. and Burt Moorhouse, Maggie Moorhouse, treasurer and president of Moorhouse Associates, a consulting firm specializing in integrated resource planning, assists the company.

Other long-time employees critical to the company's success include Gary Willard, operations manager, joined the company in 1985; Ray Kiesel, superintendent, joined the company in 1995 at age seventy after closing his own construction company; Don Yates, superintendent, brought vast experience to the company in 1987; Kim Newton, receptionist, joined the company in 1989; Matt de la Garza, project superintendent, began as a truck driver in 1983; Mike Wiley, superintendent, joined the company in 1983; and James Croley, vice president-Houston operations, oversees chemical and industrial plant projects for Moorhouse since 1989.

The company also operates an office in the Rio Grande Valley, specializing in regional work that requires high-quality construction techniques. And, with help from its talented and dedicated staff, Moorhouse Construction plans to continue to provide top-quality construction services to the growing South Texas area.

RE/MAX METRO PROPERTIES

When Tim Teas opened Metro Properties in 1991 he was intrigued by the idea of offering a full line of services to real estate clients. Corpus Christi real estate until then had gone untouched by the one-stop shopping phenomenon.

So it's no surprise that in October 2001 Teas, thirty-five, broker/owner of RE/MAX Metro Properties in Corpus Christi, pulled it all together in two side-by-side locations at 5242 Holly Road.

Teas, who purchased the local RE/MAX franchise in 1995, noticed his clients didn't want to spend all day driving all over town dealing with several institutions, unexpected fees and a multitude of paperwork. Relocating from California, Houston and other areas, Teas said, his clients didn't have time to waste.

✧

Above: Tim Teas, broker/owner.

Below: The Re/Max racing truck.

"They have only a couple of days to find a house and they don't have time to get all of the things done they really need to and buy a house," Teas said. "I thought it would be a good idea for everything to be done in our office, so they could go out and get a house that they like and spend more time on that part. Homebuyers can get everything done quickly."

While Teas saw this approach as the future of residential real estate, he lacked the financing in 1995 to pursue his vision of a real estate complex where mortgage companies, title companies, insurance companies, inspectors and a home designer co-exist.

In 1991 he had just purchased the RE/MAX franchise and was losing about $14,000 a month trying to support a large office with only six agents. "I had to take time to get out of the hole before I could implement this," he said. "To do this I had to recruit and retain the very best real estate agents in Corpus Christi."

The only way to do that was to offer the experienced professionals 100 percent commission compared with 60 percent offered by other real estate companies. He charges a small flat fee per month, which means the agent nets more money as they become more productive.

"To do this we worked off of the concept that these agents are in business for themselves, but not by themselves" Teas explains. "I am still the broker and I'm responsible for all of the agents just as in a traditional real estate office. However, I allow the agents maximum freedom to run their businesses the way they see fit. I only hire the most professional, ethical agents. It would be ridiculous for me to hire an agent that causes problems or is unprofessional."

Today, RE/MAX Metro Properties has seventy-five agents. Teas spent $140,000 on just less than an acre to build his new 11,400-square-foot, million-dollar building, which accommodates all the agents and businesses has brought together. Teas opened RE/MAX on Padre Island July 1, 2002. The second location, 14225 South Padre Island Drive, will specialize in waterfront and island properties.

The real estate office, mortgage and title company are independent of each other, but together provide the ultimate service to clients. Champion Mortgage has an office in the building, and Teas has partnered with

Cathy Escovedo, an experienced loan officer with more than ten years experience, to head the mortgage brokerage company.

"The advantage to a mortgage broker over a traditional mortgage lender is that Cathy is able to shop with 15 or 20 different lenders and provide the purchaser with the best loan package for them."

Included in the RE/MAX advertising mix are the RE/MAX racing truck and The Hummer. Teas says he could not have been as successful if it were not for Greg Meza, RE/MAX manager, and Kathy Beaber, bookkeeper. These two are the best in the business, explains Teas, and have helped us achieve "Number One" status in Corpus Christi with more than 140 closings per month.

Clients are free to use any amount of services at RE/MAX Metro Properties. But most find the quality, convenience and prices so attractive they see no reason to go anywhere else. For more information, please call 361-994-9393.

DEL MAR COLLEGE SMALL BUSINESS DEVELOPMENT CENTER

The Del Mar College Small Business Development Center (SBDC) has promoted growth, expansion, innovation, increased productivity, and improved management for small businesses in the Coastal Bend since 1989.

The SBDC has done this through counseling, technical assistance, training seminars, workshops, advocacy, research studies, resource information, and coordination with the U.S. Small Business Administration and community business support services.

The SBDC's free, confidential services help start-up and small businesses improve performance, enhance economic growth, and increase success rates. Businesses owned by women, minorities, and veterans are the SBDC's primary constituency, along with owners of rural businesses and businesses that are active exporters.

The SBDC, funded by Del Mar College and the U.S. Small Business Administration, helps businesses grow and compete in today's global economy by providing assistance from counselors and trainers skilled in management and technical issues.

The resulting improvement in their business performance leads to job creation, investments, and economic growth for communities across the Coastal Bend. The program's success has been well documented, with a return of $7.66 in local tax revenues for every $1 invested.

The Del Mar College SBDC, a branch of a regional SBDC in San Antonio, provides services from its Del Mar College east campus headquarters, as well as satellite offices at the Corpus Christi and Alice Chambers of Commerce.

During fiscal year 2001, the Del Mar College SBDC provided more than 3,491 hours of professional consulting assistance to 620 clients. It also held 67 workshops attended by 1,555 small business entrepreneurs.

Services include accounting and bookkeeping, business planning, capital acquisition, cash flow, financial analysis, financing and loan packaging, and marketing and advertising.

Other services include market research, minority business development, public relations, regulatory assistance, strategic planning, and SBA loan guarantee assistance. Two critical SBDC programs are the Small Business Administration's MicroLoan Program and the Procurement Technical Assistance Center.

❖

An SBDC consulting session.

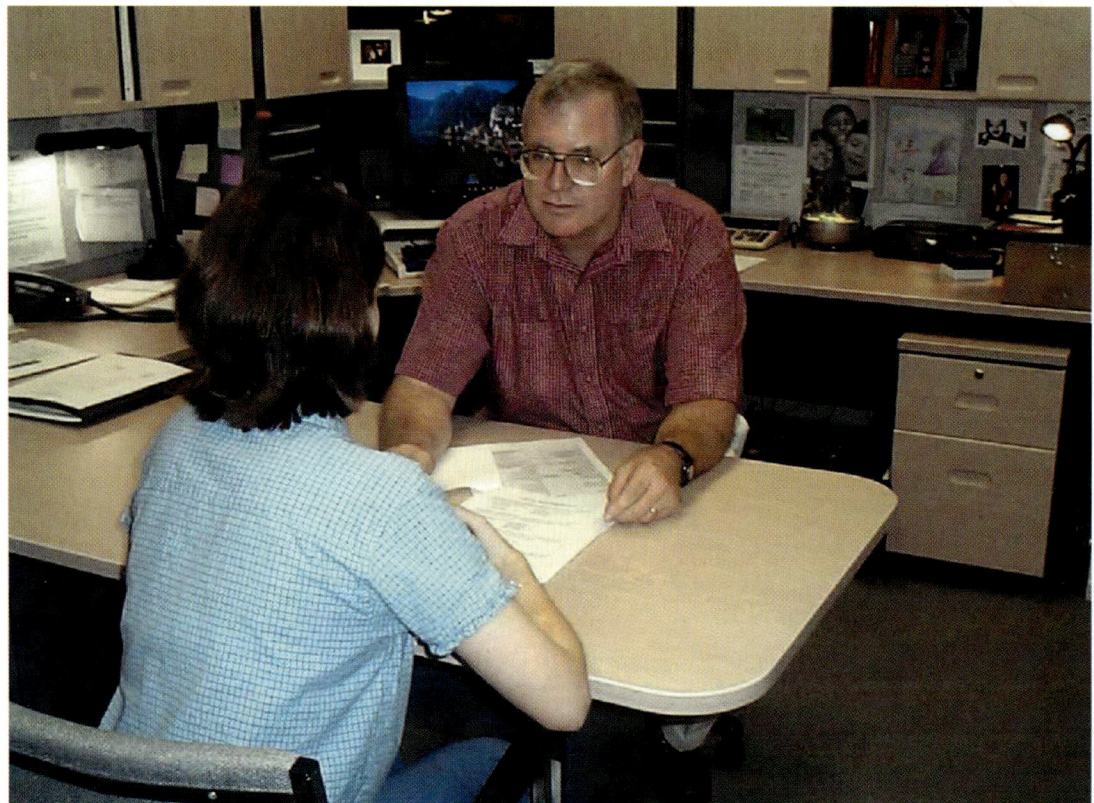

The MicroLoan Program offers non-lending technical assistance and training to micro-borrowers, who often must fulfill training and/or planning requirements before a loan application is considered.

The MicroLoan Program provides very small loans to start-up, newly established, or growing small business concerns. The SBA makes funds available to nonprofit community based lenders, who loan as much as $35,000 to eligible borrowers.

The SBDC can help businesses find a micro-lender in the immediate area. In one recent year, the MicroLoan office gave 285 clients 1,185 hours of free counseling.

The Procurement Technical Assistance Center is partially funded by the Department of Defense. It is designed to increase the number and type of businesses selling products and services to government agencies.

The PTAC serves some 160 clients by providing free procurement counseling, electronic bid match services, assistance with certification packages (8(a), SDB and HUBZONE), networking and training opportunities, and other government-related procurement opportunities.

Success stories abound at the SBDC. Island Marine is one such success story. With help from the SBDC—and three loans—Island Marine has grown from a home-based business working on boats to a stand-alone business that sells and services new and pre-owned boats.

Another success story, Diversified Consulting & Packaging, began when owner Laurie Keyes decided to go into business for herself after working for another company selling diesel engine parts to the federal government.

She started her business with a partner before converting to a sole proprietorship. With help from the SBDC, her business has grown and expanded into a new service area, providing packaging for people who sell products to the government.

Sandra Velasquez used the SBDC's MicroLoan Program to fund her business. Velasquez invented a masa spreader that makes tamale making quicker and easier.

Velasquez, who holds a patent on her invention, sells to customers all over the world.

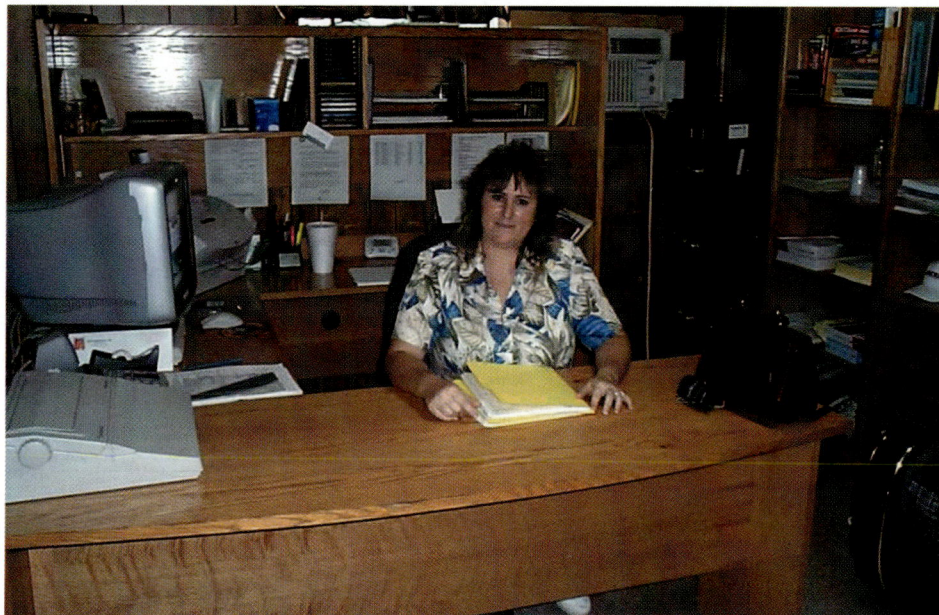

The SBDC helped her find a manufacturer, set up her books, and obtain a loan for research and development.

Thanks to the Del Mar College Small Business Development Center and its MicroLoan Program, people like Velasquez, often ignored by conventional lenders, receive the financing and consulting needed to become successful business owners and valuable contributors to the local economy.

The SBDC office is positioned as the focal point for small business development activities in the community by acting as leaders in economic development planning and delivery of highly effective counseling and training services.

❖

Two of SBDC's success stories: Diversified Consulting & Packaging (top) and Island Marine (above).

WATER STREET, INC.

✧

Above and below: Water Street Oyster Bar.

Brad Lomax, owner of Water Street, Inc., defied the skeptics when he opened a fresh seafood restaurant concept in downtown Corpus Christi more than two decades ago.

Critics scoffed at the idea of opening a full-service eatery in an area populated by prostitutes and panhandlers, but Lomax saw the potential in downtown Corpus Christi, located adjacent to the city's beautiful bayfront.

The San Antonio native began his restaurant career as a waiter while earning a business degree from St. Mary's University in San Antonio. After a brief stint in the financial world, he returned to his passion—the restaurant business—working for 1776, Inc. in San Antonio, starting as a waiter and working his way into management during his four years there. Then, having learned the restaurant business from the ground up, Lomax decided to strike out on his own.

He convinced a group of investors to stake his business venture. The Water Street Oyster Bar opened on December 12, 1983. The 140-seat restaurant opened in a refurbished transmission shop bounded on two sides by former topless bars. He received help from an accommodating landlord, who improved the surrounding landscape in the hopes that a successful eatery would spawn investors to open restaurants and shops in nearby buildings that he owned.

Lomax, meanwhile, quickly proved his skeptics wrong. By the second month, the restaurant was exceeding all projections and diners waited a half hour to be seated at lunch and an hour or more at dinner.

Flush with success, Lomax gambled on opening another restaurant within the same retail complex. This upscale Mexican Restaurant, called Otra Vez, fared poorly in a town packed with Mexican food restaurants, and tourists

craving fresh seafood and faced with a wait of an hour or more at Water Street Oyster Bar preferred to drive to another seafood restaurant rather than walk a few feet to eat Mexican food.

So Lomax decided to convert the restaurant into Water Street Seafood Co. to handle the overflow from Water Street Oyster Bar. Water Street Seafood Co. offers the same menu in a quieter, more family-oriented atmosphere.

The success of the two restaurants spurred downtown development in the center where the two restaurants are located and in downtown Corpus Christi in general. Topless bars gave way to more restaurants and shops, and an area once written off by locals is now among its greatest sources of pride.

The success of the two Corpus Christi restaurants spawned two more successful Water Street, Inc. restaurants. The San Antonio Water Street Oyster Bar debuted on Broadway in the Alamo Heights area of San Antonio in 1988, and the Executive Surf Club opened next door to the Corpus Christi originals in 1990.

Named for a group of local white-collar wave riders approaching middle age, the Executive Surf Club opened in 1990, and in the process became one of the first live music venues in downtown Corpus Christi. The Executive Surf Club, which offers more casual fare—hamburgers, nachos, and salads—contributed to the rebirth of downtown as an entertainment district. Following the Executive Surf Club's lead,

several more nightclubs and music spots have opened in the downtown area in recent years.

The success of Water Street, Inc. restaurants can be attributed to a consistent commitment to the company's core values of honesty, dignity of work, quality and service to community, as well as the efforts of committed employees.

For two decades, Lomax and Water Street, Inc. have anchored the revitalization of downtown Corpus Christi, and his recent purchase of the block that houses his three Corpus Christi restaurants assures his continued commitment to the neighborhood and to the city. Recent ventures include the opening of Agua Java, serving coffee and baked goods, and Surf Club Records, a music store featuring CDs from artists appearing at the Executive Surf Club. Both retail ventures are housed in the retail center anchored by the Water Street, Inc. restaurants.

❖

Texas A&M University Agricultural Research & Extension Center

The Texas A&M University (TAMU) Agricultural Research & Extension Center in Corpus Christi was established in 1974 to address major issues in agriculture; marine and seafood; natural resources and environment; and quality of life in the community.

The Center formally began in that year with the completion and staffing of its permanent headquarters building and supporting facilities between Clarkwood and Violet in Nueces County. Through the years, satellite research units including the TAMU Agricultural Research Station at Beeville, the TAMU Mariculture Research Laboratories at Port Aransas and Flour Bluff, and the TAMU Plant Disease Research Station at Yoakum were brought under the Center's administrative supervision.

The Beeville Station enjoys a rich historical legacy all its own. It became the first regional station of the Texas Agricultural Experiment Station in 1894, known as the Texas Agricultural Experiment Station Substation No. 1 at Beeville.

The Station helped advance the settlement of South Texas through research that translated into practical knowledge for farmers and ranchers. The Station added to the long history of efforts to improve crop and livestock yields and reduce the labor devoted to food production.

The mission of the Center is to serve the citizens of the Coastal Bend Region, Texas, the nation and the world through research, extension, graduate education and service that creates vital economic, environmental and societal benefits.

Agriculture profitability and sustainability were major issues in 1974 and are among the primary concerns of its current clientele. Dryland and more recently irrigated production systems for cotton, corn, grain sorghum and specialty field crops (soybean, sunflower, sesame) have been and remain focal points for research and extension activities.

Ranching under South Texas' semi-arid environment has always been a challenge. Faculty work on procedures to enhance reproductive efficiency of beef cows, meat goats and mares; enhance and maintain wildlife habitat; improve management of wildlife populations; promote ecotourism; develop integrated management systems for sustainable use of natural resources; develop environmentally safe bioremediation systems for improvement and sustainability of rangeland resources; and elucidate mechanisms for establishment, persistence and seasonal forage production for livestock and wildlife.

Research in shrimp mariculture has focused on developing cost-effective biosecure shrimp farming technology. The research includes basic studies on all aspects of shrimp biology, ecology, reproduction and growout; environmentally safe semi-intensive recirculating raceway and pond production systems; and improved utilization and marketing of table and bait farm-raised shrimp.

Changes in the external environment have substantially influenced the Center's program focus. A growing urban population investing non-agriculture dollars in land resources has separated land values and agricultural production. Fragmentation of sustainable land units for farming and ranching and the growing number of recreational landowners increasingly require answers and technical help on land use options.

Changing demographics and rapid advance in biotechnology and computer capabilities have limited the time available to adjust to these changes in the external environment. New technology such as genetically engineered foods, plants, animals, etc., presents the Center's faculty with a new set of social issues and challenges related to food safety and bio-ethics.

Environmental concerns have necessitated development of novel agricultural practices and made risk management a primary issue in agricultural production. The interrelationship between upland land use and estuary coastal wetland health has been of increasing concern in recent years. Issues of runoff from farm and ranch land and associated questions of impact on marine life have been and are currently being addressed by the Center's faculty.

The Center also addresses issues of international concerns. International cooperative efforts in grain sorghum research, shrimp mariculture, economic and environmental impact assessment of farm production technology and policy, and cooperative projects with Mexico on rangeland issues are but a few of the responses in this arena.

The Corpus Christi Center faculty and support personnel have had an impact in addressing these issues for the past three decades and undoubtedly will continue to have an impact into the future.

✧

Production systems for cotton, grain sorghum and other field crops are developed through the research at the headquarters location.

CITGO REFINING AND CHEMICALS

The CITGO refinery in Corpus Christi broke ground in 1935 and began operating as the Pontiac Refining Company on Thanksgiving Day 1937 when Saul Singer, the plant's owner and operator, gave the word to start up the new four-thousand-barrel-a-day facility located on the Corpus Christi Ship Channel and Nueces Bay Boulevard.

✦

Above: East Plant II was built in 1974.

Right: A heavy oil exchanger installed in 1991.

In the intervening years, CITGO has matured into one of the most sophisticated and efficient fuel and petrochemical refineries in the nation, refining 225,000 barrels of oil and feed stock a day and with an annual payroll of more than $70 million.

But for the first few years the company was a family affair. Saul Singer convinced his son, Edwin, to join the company as secretary and assistant manager in late 1937 to supervise, staff, and operate the plant. And, for the next twenty-three years, the little refinery cranked out products as periodic additions expanded the capacity of the facility.

In April 1960 Gulf Oil Foundation, a charitable institution founded by the Gulf Oil Corporation, purchased the Pontiac Refinery, and eventually expanded its capacity to 54,000 barrels per day. In 1967 Celanese Corporation, the parent company of Champlin Petroleum Company, bought the refinery, and three years later sold it to Union Pacific Corporation, heralding a period of unprecedented growth.

By 1972 the refinery had boosted its production by an additional 12,000 barrels per

day and a year later a $250 million expansion program raised the plant's capacity to 125,000 barrels per day by 1976. Modification of older units raised output capacity an additional 30,000 barrels a day 18 months later.

Champlin then moved the company into the petrochemical division with a $27-million cumene unit in1980, which was capable of meeting ten percent of the nation's demand for cumene. Derivatives of cumene are used in building materials, plastics, laminates and other products.

That same year marked the completion of the $700 million joint venture Corpus Christi Petrochemical Company ethylene complex. With Champlin's nearby refinery providing raw materials, the ethylene complex, in which Champlin had a 37.5 percent stake, produced 1.2 billion pounds per year. In 1983 a $260 million expansion created the West Plant, allowing the facility to refine less expensive heavy crude oil like that supplied by Venezuela into premium-grade fuels and petrochemicals.

In 1987 Union Pacific Corporation signed a contract with Petroleos de Venezuela, South America (the national oil company of Venezuela) to purchase crude oil over a long-term period. Two years later, Petroleos de Venezuela acquired full ownership of

Champlin's Corpus Christi Refinery, changing the name to Champlin Refining and Chemicals.

In 1991 Petroleos de Venezuela merged Champlin into CITGO Petroleum Corporation and a year later changed Champlin's Corpus Christi Refinery to CITGO Corpus Christi Refinery.

Along with a new name, the 1990s brought many new changes to CITGO Corpus Christi Refinery. A 20,000-barrel-a-day reformulated gasoline facility in 1993-94 helped the nation meet the requirements of the 1995 Clean Air Act, and in 1995 a Xylene Fractionation project allowed fractionation of high-value petrochemical used as feedstock for para-xylene.

In the same year, CITGO Refining and Chemicals, Inc., became CITGO Refining and Chemicals Co., L.P. The company now has 600 employees and works with 800 contractors to produce a high-quality fuel while placing paramount importance on keeping the environment clean. CITGO Corpus Christi Refinery supplies high-octane gasoline for automobiles and the basic ingredients that other industries need to make a wide assortment of products from CDs to carpets and aircraft windows to hosiery.

Today's CITGO Corpus Christi Refinery has been designed to refine heavy crude oil supplied by Venezuela into high-quality finished petroleum products. This assured supply of less-expensive primary raw material, together with a high-efficiency refining facility, positions CITGO's Corpus Christi Refinery as a strong competitor in the global marketplace and as a stable long-term contributor to the Corpus Christi economy.

And, answering the call of our nation's leaders, CITGO employees will continue to be active in the community as they strive to improve the area's quality of life through their volunteer efforts.

✧

Above: A ship loading gasoline at the CITGO dock.

Below: A ship unloading Venezuelan crude at the CITGO dock.

INTERNATIONAL DIVERS COMPANY, INC. AND BEST BET LINE HANDLERS

✦

Above: Peter S. MacCallum, Jr. (center), with his sons, Peter MacCallum III (right) and Luke MacCallum (left).

Below: M/V Bellagio, a crew boat operating out of Port Aransas.

Peter S. MacCallum, Jr., began his business career with a two-man diving team in 1963, and through the next four decades expanded his business ventures into five companies with 150 full-time employees and 50 part-time workers.

MacCallum's interest in maritime matters began as a child. His father, a physician and rancher in Webb County, brought the family to Port Aransas on a regular basis for vacations. He eventually learned to dive and discovered his love for working on the water. One summer, MacCallum decided not to return to the ranch and started work as an underwater welder for the Arco Company at Harbor Island.

This newfound passion for diving led to MacCallum spending most of his waking hours on or under the water. MacCallum developed and trained an excellent crew made up of other tenders and divers. With such a high demand for underwater work, MacCallum saw an opportunity to create a business.

International Divers Company was born. With such an efficient and recommended team, the company thrived. Their motto was "If you can do it on land, we can do it under water." International Divers Company never turned down a job, even if it consisted of something they had never attempted before.

This brought the company into every aspect of underwater work. Work at International Divers included general construction, such as the pouring of concrete, welding and burning.

The company also salvaged vessels in the Gulf of Mexico and Caribbean. In addition, they inspected and repaired underwater pipelines and assisted in laying pipe underwater.

Other services included intakes/discharge, inspection and cleaning, alloy welding, grouting, video and still photography. Back then, MacCallum's team worked out of one warehouse and operated two crew trucks. Most of the diving was done dockside or from small aluminum boats. The tools had to be custom designed and the equipment would be considered obsolete by today's standards. Diver and tender would communicate by quick tugs on the rope that was tethered to the diver. This elementary code was their only way of communicating underwater.

Today, the work is much safer and much more advanced. Diving helmets have built-in radio communications and are outfitted with underwater cameras. Forty years later, the company still offers the same services as before, as well as operations in Remotely Operated Vehicles (ROVs), bridge inspection and shoreline stabilization. International Divers today has yards in Aransas Pass and in Corpus Christi harbors and focuses on inshore work while catering to the shipping industry's needs.

International Divers has at its disposal everything it needs to sustain a major salvage operation. Equipment includes cranes, barges, heavy lift equipment, and an eighty-foot, Breaux-Built dive boat. International Divers works with classification societies such as ABS, Lloyds of London, and DNV to inspect every condition of a ship to ensure all the working parts meet the industry's strict safety standards.

Another MacCallum-owned business, Best Bet Line Handlers, evolved in 1997 out of the desire from Corpus Christi customers for competition in the line-handling business. MacCallum's design background and knowledge helped him to quickly start a business that has steadily grown and already has been called the best in the world. MacCallum spent three years working with a naval architect to design and engineer a 26-foot aluminum line-handling boat that combines both power and speed. The boats are truly state-of-the-art and outshine many like them in every aspect. His company now operates four line-handling boats in the Port of Corpus Christi. Each of MacCallum's companies operates 24 hours a day, 365 days a year and has evolved into a one-stop shop for any and all marine needs.

MacCallum has started other businesses through the years. MacCallum Marine is an offshore transportation company that delivers private industry and inspectors to offshore ships and oilrigs. The company handles crew changes as well as fuel and water delivery and carries cargo to ships and oilrigs. Another company, Chubasco Marine Services, is a shore-side company that repairs tugboats, barges, and ships.

The MacCallum Ranch is still in operation in Webb County, and although it is a working ranch, it provides an excellent retreat for the family when they need to get away. MacCallum is assisted by his two sons, Peter MacCallum III, who works in diving and transportation, and Luke MacCallum, who works for Best Bet Line Handlers.

❖

Above: Line boats used in the Port of Corpus Christi.

Below: Best Bet Line Handlers crew in Corpus Christi Harbor.

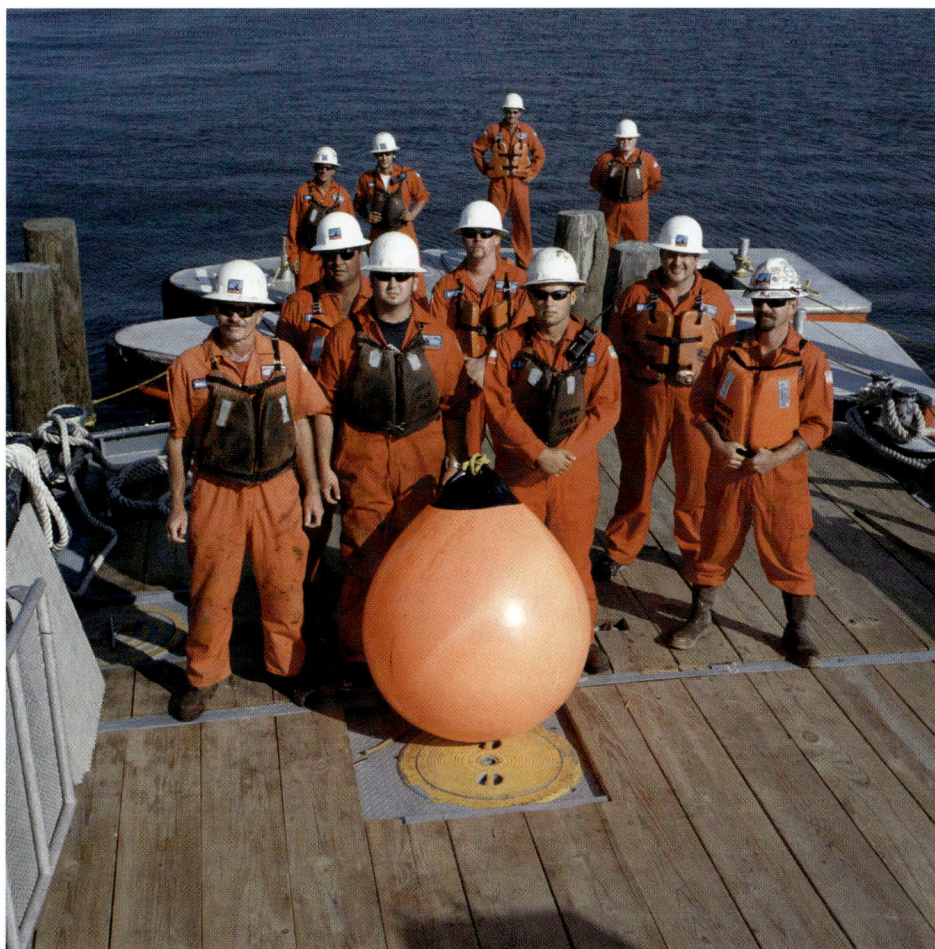

OCEAN HOUSE BED AND BREAKFAST

✧

Above: Celebrity guests at the Ocean House include Robert Wagner and Jill St. John. Dr. Stan Shoemaker (center) created Ocean House. Chef Steve Suarez prepares meals for the guests.

Below: Ocean House Bed and Breakfast at 3275 Ocean Drive, Corpus Christi, Texas, in 1938 (below) and 2000 (bottom).

The Ocean House Bed and Breakfast offers visitors a secluded, luxurious retreat minutes from downtown Corpus Christi and area tourist attractions. Located on Corpus Christi's scenic Ocean Drive, Ocean House Bed and Breakfast is the number one destination for those who value privacy, luxury and convenience.

Owner Stan Shoemaker, a successful Corpus Christi gynecologist, purchased this circa 1936 one-story home at 3275 Ocean Drive in 1977. Then, over a fifteen-year period, Dr. Shoemaker added onto the house, creating a three-story mansion on almost one acre with a wine cellar, swimming pool, pool house and tropical garden.

Ocean House Bed and Breakfast offers five fully furnished suites with private entrances that can turn each into a private bungalow. The main house, pool house and pool/patio areas make Ocean House the perfect choice for parties, wedding receptions, baptisms and family reunions.

The Marquesa Suite, located in the pool house on the lower level, features a king-size bed and is a few steps away from the pool and spa. Upstairs, the Key West Room features two queen-size beds and plenty of Hemingway books and Jimmy Buffett tunes.

The Caribbean Suite, upstairs in the main house, features a king-size bed, oversized tub, a balcony overlooking the yard and pool area and a separate den. The western-themed Lone Star Suite, on the ground floor of the main house, features a king-size, four-poster bed and opens onto a large deck.

The Capetown Suite is the largest in the Ocean House Bed and Breakfast. Decorated with trophies and art, it features a king-size bed, pool-size Jacuzzi, conference/board room and rooftop observatory with a commanding view of downtown and Corpus Christi Bay.

Each suite features a discreet, private entrance, full baths, televisions, VCRs and fax and modem hookups. The main floor of the house includes a living room, dining room, kitchen and big-screen television.

A full breakfast is served on weekends and guests enjoy an upscale Continental breakfast during the week. The wine cellar is a popular spot for romantic dinners that begin with champagne and hors d'oeuvres and end with dessert in the guest's private suite.

The large, sparkling pool, relaxing sauna, and tropical garden are never far away. The garden is awash in color and decorated with yucca, oleander, hibiscus, palm, and other warm-weather plants.

For more information on Ocean House Bed and Breakfast, call 361-882-9500 or visit www.oceansuites.com.

TRIGEANT PETROLEUM

TRIGEANT Petroleum, one of the largest asphalt manufacturers in Texas and one of the top twelve in the nation, has provided jobs and made important contributions to the Corpus Christi's economy since it began on September 13, 1983. On that day, Bay, Inc. contracted with Harbor Refining, Inc. to build a new refinery unit and signed an agreement with Petroserve, Ltd. to build a tank farm and offsite facility.

Sentry Refining sold its refinery equipment to Bay, Inc. to build the new refinery, and on February 10, 1984, Bay, Inc., formed a company called Trifinery to run the refinery unit, tank farm, and offsite facility.

Through the years, the company has changed hands—and names—several times.

In the beginning, Trifinery was jointly owned by Sanford Brass, general partner of Petroserve, and Marvin Berry, owner of Harbor Refining. Berry sold his interest to Brass in 1989 and, in 1993, Neste Oy purchased a fifty percent interest in the company and renamed it Neste Trifinery.

Five years later, Oy sold his interest in Trifinery and the name changed to Trifinery Petroleum Services. Then, in June 2001, TRIGEANT Holdings, comprised of Harry Sargeant, Sr., Harry Sargeant, Jr., Dan Sargeant, James Sargeant, and Arthur J. Brass, bought controlling interest in the company and changed the name again.

TRIGEANT Petroleum, which is located on the Corpus Christi Ship Channel, processes more than twenty-five thousand barrels per day of extra heavy crude oil. Its diverse product lines include all paving grades, roofing asphalts, and base stocks ideally suited to polymer modifications, emulsion, recycled tire rubber and other specialty applications. The company imports special crude oils that are processed to produce premium asphalt, vacuum gas oil, middle distillate oil, and pre-flash distillate.

The company's products are used to produce common, everyday items. Those include road construction products, shingles, wood treatment processes, mastics and as crack sealants in marine applications.

Its refinery operates 24 hours a day, 365 days a year, employs 50 people and operates a lab accredited by the American Association of State Highway and Transportation Officials.

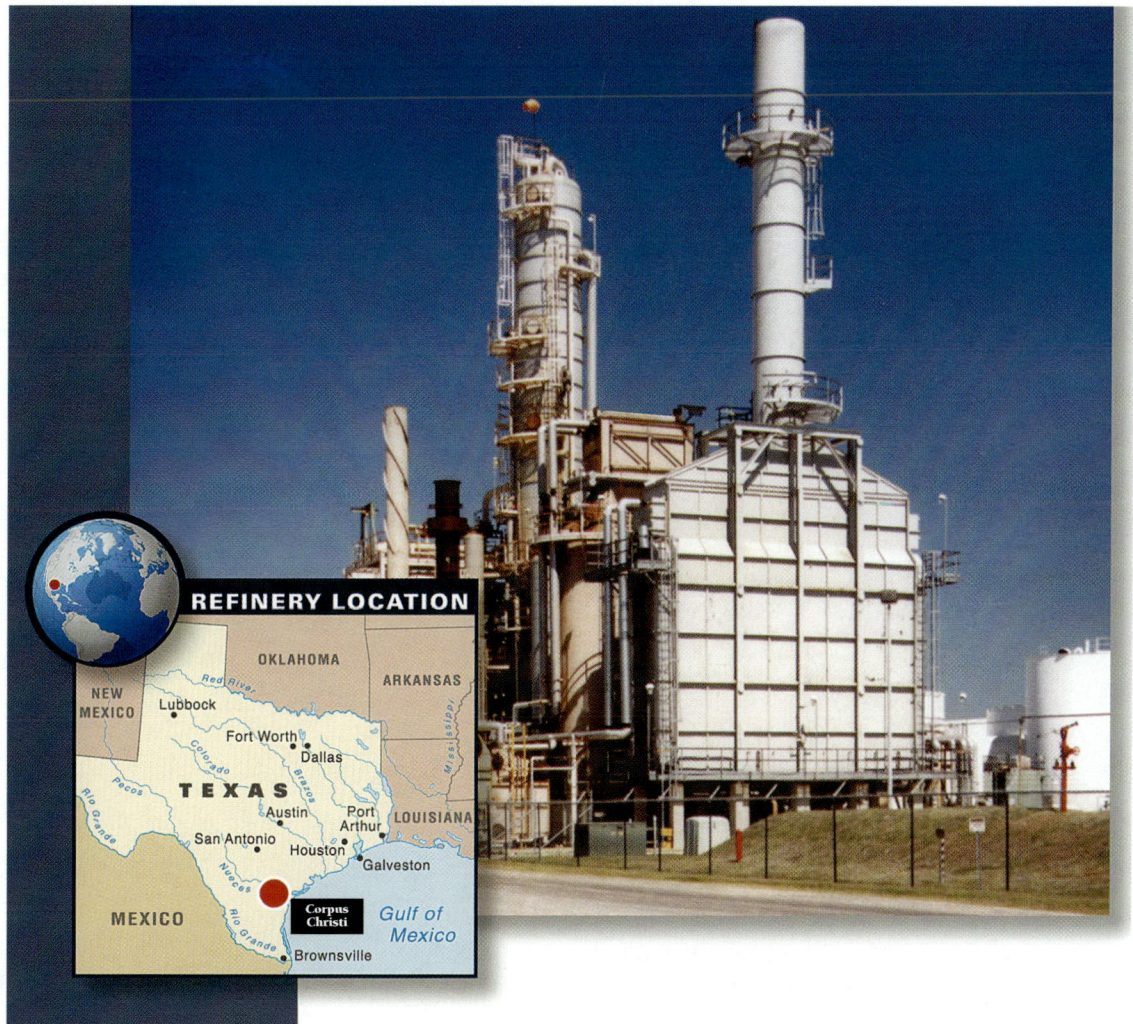

REFINERY LOCATION

TRIGEANT Petroleum receives and ships products by tanker, truck, rail, or barge throughout the United States, the Caribbean and South America. It is the primary supply source for distribution terminals along the Gulf Coast and throughout the central United States.

As for the future, TRIGEANT Petroleum plans to continue playing an important role in the Corpus Christi economy while manufacturing quality, environmentally friendly products that contribute to the fabric of our society.

HOLIDAY INN
AIRPORT

The Holiday Inn-Airport provides Corpus Christi travelers with the best value in town when it comes to service, cost and facilities. It's located less than five minutes from Corpus Christi International Airport and a short drive from downtown and area tourist attractions. The hotel was built as a prototype that is now used in Holiday Inns, Radissons and Marriotts throughout the United States.

Its ideal location makes it a good choice for both business and leisure travelers, who enjoy easy access to every part of the city. This 249-room hotel is conveniently located at Padre Island Drive and Leopard Street, close to Corpus Christi's main freeways.

Park. It is also a short drive from the scenic Corpus Christi bayfront and area museums, theaters and music venues.

Amenities at this six-floor hotel include four suites, a cocktail lounge, restaurant, dry cleaning, laundry, safe deposit box, wake-up calls, free parking and Jacuzzi tubs in some rooms. Each guestroom features two-phone lines with data ports, coffee makers, working desks or tables, free newspapers, free incoming faxes and in-room movies.

The hotel began renovation for its twentieth birthday and Holiday Inn's fiftieth birthday in 2002. Former guests included Martha Stewart, Chuck Norris and numerous musical entertainers.

As is policy at all Holiday Inns, "Kids Eat and Stay Free" at the Holiday Inn-Airport. Small pets are welcome.

Relax and rejuvenate in the hotel's modern exercise facility, indoor pool and whirlpool. Enjoy breakfast, lunch or dinner in the Atrium Café or drinks in the popular Sparky's lounge. Room service is also available from 6 a.m. to 11 p.m. daily.

The hotel's modern meeting facilities can accommodate conferences of 5 to 500 people. The executive boardrooms seat as many as twelve people, providing the perfect setting for small meetings.

The hotel participates in the "We Promise" program, providing presenters with complimentary meeting supplies and a guarantee that you will be satisfied with timely delivery of services, product quality and professionalism.

Video conferencing also is available. The hotel's on-site audiovisual specialists will be available to handle your audiovisual requirements, providing everything from flip charts to satellite links.

Holiday Inn-Airport can meet all your business or leisure-travel needs professionally and economically.

✧

The full-service Atrium has both meeting space and a business center available.

This full-service atrium hotel offers eleven thousand square feet of flexible meeting space and a full business center. It has been the annual site of numerous local functions such as the Coalition for the Advancement of Women, Odyssey, the Coastal A's and Rod Show and the Texas Beefmasters.

The Holiday Inn-Airport is a few blocks from the Corpus Christi Greyhound Race Track and minutes away from the Texas State Aquarium, USS *Lexington*, Padre Island National Seashore, and Mustang Island State

NUECES COUNTY MEDICAL SOCIETY

The Nueces County Medical Society has led the way in improving area healthcare since it was formed in 1904 with Dr. A.E. Spohn as president.

The medical society, which began with seven members who paid $2 per year in dues, also promotes continuing medical education and supports or opposes legislation and other initiatives affecting physicians and the community's healthcare.

Throughout its long history, the Nueces County Medical Society, which incorporated on April 14, 1930, has been instrumental in safeguarding the community's health.

A city-county health department, well-baby clinics, venereal disease clinic, and a tuberculosis sanitarium are among the programs instituted under the medical society's visage. The medical society also played a role in helping Del Mar College organize nursing, physical therapy, X-ray technician and respiratory therapy schools.

The Nueces County Medical Society also was instrumental in forming the Community Blood Bank and a medical library now housed at CHRISTUS Spohn Memorial Hospital.

This voluntary society with approximately 800 members provides support services for physician members, who serve on local and state bodies that make healthcare decisions.

The medical society works with the Texas Medical Association and the American Medical Association in standing up for patient and physician rights. It also works to promote the views of physicians on legislation and crucial issues such as tort reform.

The Nueces County Medical Society and Alliance Health Fair, which began in 1964, provides a wide array of healthcare information and services to thousands of Coastal Bend residents.

The medical society executive board is composed of elected officers, five past presidents, six board of censors members, eight TMA delegates, eight TMA alternate delegates, and three ex-officio members. Elected officers include a president, president-elect, vice president, secretary, treasurer, and treasurer-elect.

Members meet monthly for social events, continuing medical education seminars and speakers. The medical society's board of censors recommends approval of new members and decides whether to discipline members accused of wrongdoing.

To become a member, a person must be a licensed physician (either a medical doctor or doctor of osteopathy) in good standing and practicing or residing in Nueces County. The Nueces County Medical Society will continue to play a leading role in protecting the community's health and looking out for the interests of doctors and patients.

❖

The Nueces County Medical Society offices located at 1000 Morgan in Corpus Christi.

CORPUS CHRISTI BATTERY COMPANY

You won't find a Corpus Christi business with deeper roots in the community than Corpus Christi Battery Company, which began operating in July of 1923 after the company's founder, C. G. Turner, decided to go into business in Corpus Christi.

Corpus Christi Battery Company, commonly referred to as "CC Battery," began as the South Texas distributor for Willard Batteries and as a service center for automobile electrical systems.

Turner opened a second station in 1927 at the corner of Agnes and Staples Streets before closing the original store one year later. By 1943 CC Battery had moved to its current location at 3513 Agnes Street, where its reach extends well beyond the company's Corpus Christi confines.

World War II led to the company's first major expansion. The military, as well as civilian clients, needed generators, starters and armatures, and CC Battery adjusted to meet the demand, phasing out its role as an automotive battery distributor in the process.

Like their father before them, Kenneth Turner Jr. and Ted Turner began working in

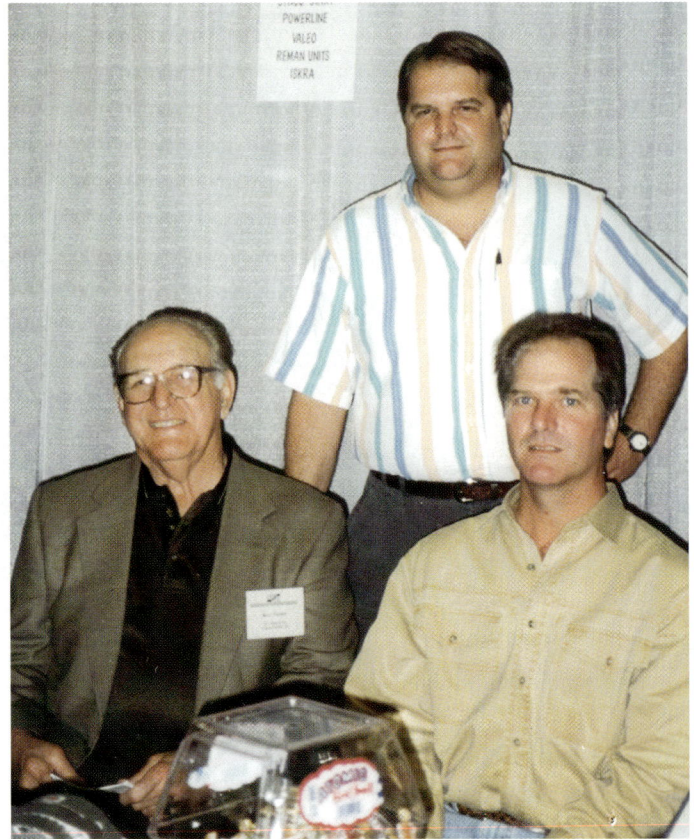

the family business as children, eventually joining the company full-time in the early 1980s after finishing college.

The company now serves the automotive electrical rebuilding industry and sells and services starters and alternators for the automobile, industrial, commercial, marine and agriculture sectors.

CC Battery carries all major lines, distributes new and remanufactured parts and, in recent years, has returned in a small way to its roots—selling automotive batteries to local customers.

As shipping methods have improved, CC Battery has expanded its service area even farther to Alaska, Canada, Hawaii, Mexico, Puerto Rico and South America, providing next-day delivery in most cases.

As the market changes, CC Battery will once again change with it, staying abreast of new developments, adding new lines to its inventory and anticipating customer needs. Corpus Christi Battery Company's ability to change with the times has ensured its continued presence in Corpus Christi, enabling the company to grow outward while simultaneously strengthening its roots in the community.

❖

Right: The descendants of Corpus Christi Battery Company founder C. G. Turner (from left to right): Kenneth Turner, Sr., Kenneth Turner, Jr., and Ted Turner.

Below: Corpus Christi Battery Company, founded in 1923 by C. G. Turner at the northwest corner of Agnes and Staples Streets, c. 1928. Note the 25¢ haircut sign. Standing by the company sign are (from left to right): C.G. Turner, Annie Lee Rule, Alford Sandlin and Alvin Marshall.

The newly remodeled Comfort Suites Corpus Christi at 3925 South Padre Island Drive provides guests with the amenities and services most desired when selecting a place to stay.

Its sixty-eight beautifully appointed suites provide the perfect combination of features to accommodate both business and leisure travelers, and the hotel's central location provides visitors with easy access to downtown, beaches and popular tourist attractions.

Nearby attractions include the Corpus Christi Greyhound Race Track, Texas State Aquarium and the USS *Lexington* aircraft carrier. The city's main shopping area is also a short distance away, as is downtown Corpus Christi, Corpus Christi Naval Air Station, Texas A&M University-Corpus Christi and Spohn Hospital.

The Comfort Suites Corpus Christi features speakerphones, free local calls, high-speed data ports, voice mail and oversized business desks. The hotel also features a business center with Internet access and copy service, providing guests with everything they need to conduct business away from the office.

All suites are equipped with coffee makers, microwaves, refrigerators, hair dryers, irons and ironing boards. Guests will also find AM-FM clock radios, message alert lights, non-smoking rooms, bus parking, smoke detectors, sofa beds and a sprinkler system. Other amenities include free TV movies and TV for the hearing impaired.

Comfort Suites guests receive both a complimentary deluxe Continental breakfast and a complimentary copy of *USA Today* and access to a safe deposit box in the lobby. Other amenities include computer hookups, lighted parking and free cocktails from 6 p.m. to 8 p.m. Monday through Thursday.

An outdoor swimming pool, hot tub and exercise room equipped with cardio-vascular equipment helps guests stay active. Banquet/meeting rooms, guest laundry, a newsstand, tennis and valet cleaning service also are available.

From the moment you step into the hotel's marble-tiled lobby with its crystal chandelier, you'll know that the Comfort Suites Corpus Christi is an exceptional hotel prepared to meet your every need at reasonable prices.

For more information, call 361-225-2500 or visit the website at www.comfortsuites.com.

COMFORT SUITES CORPUS CHRISTI

E.M. MARKETING COMPANY, INC.

✧

Above: Powerboat Shoot-Out.
COURTESY OF JAMIE RUSSELL.

Top, right: U.S. Open Windsurfing Regatta.
COURTESY OF MICHELLE WEEDON.

Below: The seventy-five-foot Tree of Lights at the Harbor Lights Festival.
COURTESY OF GENE CUTTER.

E.M. Marketing Company, Inc. is a professional events management company responsible for organizing several of Corpus Christi's most successful and popular events.

Founded in 1991 by Elaine Motl, E.M. Marketing plans and coordinates events from reunions and conventions to large festivals attracting tens of thousands of people.

Several major events like the Powerboat Shoot-Out, The Miss Texas USA Pageant, The Harbor Lights Festival, the U.S. Open Windsurfing Regatta and U.S. Open Kiteboarding Championships have attracted national attention. The events have been featured on CBS, NBC, ABC, and FOX television, Sports Channel America, Speedvision, ESPN 2, and Fox Speed Channel, as well as numerous national magazines and publications, putting Corpus Christi in the national spotlight and creating a $52-million economic and publicity value impact on the community.

Other public events include the Hobie 16 National Championships, Winner Speed Series, Prindle National Championships, CC Jet Ski Challenge, Cadillac Invitational Golf Tournaments, Waterstreet Market Days, Antiques by the Bay, Three Rivers Salsa Festival, and the Miss Corpus Christi USA Pageant.

Motl owns her own piece of history as the first female race producer in Offshore Powerboat Racing and has also owned INFINITY Models and Talent since 1996.

The Harbor Lights Festival, founded in 1980, is held each December and is the city's official kick off to the Holiday Season. Created by the Junior League, the event has been managed by several groups including the Downtown Business Association, E.M. Marketing, and a large volunteer committee involving hundreds of people over the years. Various cultures come together in celebration on Corpus Christi's Bayfront. The event features a children's parade, choirs and caroling, a lighting ceremony with a seventy-five-foot tree of lights, an illuminated boat parade, Santa's Motorcade, laser light show, and fireworks display. The festival has remained free to the public due to the generous sponsorships of area companies.

The Corpus Christi office of Hilb, Rogal and Hamilton Company, more commonly known as HRH Insurance, got its start as Wallace L. Dinn and Company Insurance in 1923.

Dinn, whose first job was riding the mail between the nearby towns of Mathis and Sandia, began selling life insurance to farmers and homeowners. Not only did Dinn start a successful company that he later passed on to his son, he also worked as an agent for Farm and Home Savings and developed property in the Del Mar College area. History regards him as one of a handful of people who made a significant difference in Corpus Christi before the Great Depression.

The insurance agency grew substantially under Dinn's leadership. His son, James Dinn, joined the company in the 1940s, and became one of the first in Texas to earn the Chartered Property and Casualty Underwriter designation. His leadership took the firm through the mid-1970s, managing the company as it and Corpus Christi grew. A third-generation family member, Alan Dinn, joined the firm in 1975 and retired on January 1, 2002.

In 1990, in an effort to provide customers with the best insurance protection, W. L. Dinn and Company merged with HRH, joining one of the largest insurance networks in the world. The local office, which celebrated its seventy-fifth anniversary in 1998, provides a wide variety of insurance services to many large industries and financial institutions in the area.

Through the years HRH, the oldest and one of the largest insurance firms in the city, has experienced the highs and lows of life in South Texas, from the opening of the Port of Corpus Christi in 1926 to Hurricane Celia in 1970.

With its nationwide resources, HRH acts as an intermediary between clients and insurance companies to provide insurance contracts to individuals and businesses seeking to identify and manage risk in their organizations and personal lives.

HRH is now one of the leading middle market intermediaries in the United States and the world, providing the Corpus Christi office access to insurance markets and expertise not available to other insurance agencies in the area. And that access bodes well for the Corpus Christi office, offering competitive advantages and opportunities for continued growth in the foreseeable future.

❖

Left: W. L. Dinn, seen here in 1975, started the Hilb, Rogal and Hamilton Company in 1923.

COURTESY OF PORTRAIT BY GOLD.

Below: President Dave Cavenah and Chairman Loyd Neal.

KORO-TV 28
UNIVISION

KORO-TV, Channel 28, became the first Hispanic-owned television station in the country when it went on the air in 1977. The station began as an affiliate of the Spanish International Network (SIN), which later changed its name to Univision.

The eight Corpus Christi investors who started KORO knew nothing about operating a TV station, which many in the community considered a novelty when it went on the air. KORO drew largely upon the programming of San Antonio station KWEX, which donated an old transmitter to the Corpus Christi station.

At first, KORO featured one hour of local programming, a 30-minute talk show followed by 30 minutes of local news, all done with one camera used for commercial production and in the studio.

The greatest challenge the station faced was convincing businesses to advertise. H-E-B Grocery Company became the station's first local advertiser and has continued ever since, while Colgate-Palmolive Company became the first national advertiser.

The station struggled financially in the early years, with the eight partners frequently loaning the station money to meet payroll. In 1998 KORO was sold to Entravision Communication, LLC, the largest Univision-affiliated television group in the United States.

Now under new management, KORO has become the leader in Spanish language television. The station, which began in a 1,000-square-foot office in the 600 Building, now employs more than 40 people and has plans for a larger facility in the near future.

It also operates a second television station, KCRP-TV, Channel 41, a Telefutura affiliate launched in January 2002. Telefutura represents the future of Spanish Language television with a twenty-four-hour lineup of exciting programs, nightly blockbuster Hollywood movies, news briefs and original Latin American talk shows. The network also entertains sports fans with sports briefs, prime time live boxing and extensive coverage of Mexican soccer.

In 2002 KORO-TV, Channel 28, celebrated its twenty-fifth anniversary of bringing Spanish-language programming to Corpus Christi viewers. Univision has become the network of choice among Hispanics, consistently outperforming any other network.

Although many advertisers were hesitant at first, more and more advertisers are using the power of Univision to reach the highly profitable market. The community continues to receive KORO-TV with open arms and gratitude for the station that brought Spanish-language television to the Coastal Bend.

CORPUS CHRISTI MEDICAL CENTER

Committed to the care and improvement of human life, Corpus Christi Medical Center has been a growing part of South Texas since 1962. What began as a 26-bed facility in the early 1960s has grown into a three-campus system with 494 beds offering a full range of healthcare services with outstanding clinical care, superior technological care, and comforting and reassuring personal care.

Corpus Christi Medical Center includes three campuses: Corpus Christi Medical Center-Doctors Regional, Corpus Christi Medical Center-Bay Area, and Corpus Christi Medical Center-The Heart Hospital. These three facilities merged under one license in June of 1998 to become what is now known as Corpus Christi Medical Center.

The Heart Hospital is the newest of the three Corpus Christi Medical Center facilities. Opening in 1998, The Heart Hospital broke new ground by becoming the first hospital in the area dedicated exclusively to cardiovascular procedures. The Heart Hospital offers cardiac catheterization laboratories, state-of-the-art operating rooms, coronary care and telemetry beds, non-invasive diagnostic facilities, and a fully equipped cardiac rehabilitation center.

Corpus Christi Medical Center-Bay Area, which opened in 1993, houses a medical education residency program, the Breast Center of South Texas, comprehensive nursing services, a twenty-four-hour emergency room, and a women's services department.

Corpus Christi Medical Center-Doctors Regional is a full service, acute care hospital offering a full range of inpatient and outpatient services, including a twenty-four-hour emergency room, state-of-the-art cardiac cath lab, neonatal intensive care unit, MRI diagnostic center, and sleep lab.

The Joint Commission on Accreditation of Healthcare Organizations has accredited Corpus Christi Medical Center.

This family of three hospitals has one purpose—life.

✧

Top, left: Corpus Christi Medical Center-The Heart Hospital.

Top, right: Corpus Christi Medical Center-Bay Area.

Below: Corpus Christi Medical Center-Doctors Regional.

Humpal Physical Therapy and Sports Medicine Centers

Humpal Physical Therapy and Sports Medicine Centers, P.C., is the largest outpatient physical therapy provider in the Coastal Bend. Humpal facilities in Corpus Christi, Alice, Aransas Pass, and Sinton are state-of-the-art and Humpal only allows "top notch" therapists to join his team. These therapists are held to extremely high standards when providing patient care.

All of the Humpal facilities feature large gyms with the latest in gym rehabilitation equipment. All of the facilities with the exception of Sinton have therapeutic pools on site and Humpal meets the ever-increasing

demand for aquatic therapy programs. These individualized programs are tailored to meet each patient's specific needs.

Humpal Physical Therapy and Sports Medicine Centers, P.C., and its owner, Scott A. Humpal, P.T., have long been involved with "giving back to the community." The company has sponsored numerous youth baseball and soccer teams, made contributions to high school athletic training facilities, and have devoted thousands of hours toward youth programs. Humpal feels that serving as a good role model is extremely important.

Humpal has also served on the board of the Corpus Christi Boys and Girls Club, Sinton Chamber of Commerce, and Corpus Christi Deaf Council, and supports many area charities on an annual basis.

The Corpus Christi facility at 5026 Deepwood Circle boasts 20,000 square feet and is enviously one of the most impressive privately owned outpatient physical therapy practices in the country. Humpal facilities treat more than four thousand new patients per year, assisting patients' doctors and area industry with high quality medical care.

All facilities have private treatment rooms and the Corpus Christi facility is a showcase for proper ergonomic design throughout. Humpal Physical Therapy has more than seventy-five employees to provide patients with a wide range of clinically proven treatment options to give each patient the best quality rehabilitation experience possible.

The volume of patients treated at Humpal facilities has grown each year, but personalized one-on-one care where each and every patient feels special has not been sacrificed by growth.

For more information about Humpal and its services, please call 361-854-2278 or visit www.humpalphysicaltherapy.com.

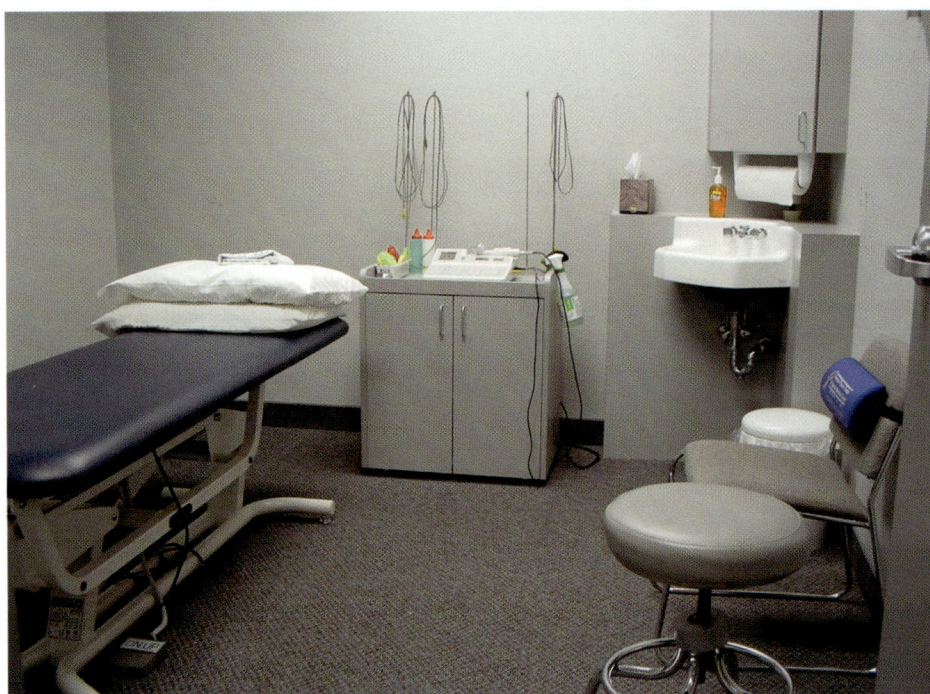

HOLIDAY INN EMERALD BEACH

The Holiday Inn Emerald Beach has operated under the same name since 1970, making it one of the longest continually owned hotels in Corpus Christi. It originally opened in 1965 as the Emerald Cove Hotel before joining the Holiday Inn family.

It opened with 216 rooms that rented for $8.50 a night. A 1978 expansion added 152 rooms and a 7,200-square-foot convention center. This family leisure hotel, with a mixture of business, convention, and tourist traffic, is the only downtown Corpus Christi hotel located on the beach.

With the six-hundred-foot-long beach right outside its back door and the hotel's location a half mile from downtown Corpus Christi allows the Holiday Inn Emerald Beach to provide the best in both leisure and business travel.

The hotel now offers 368 rooms, including several with private balconies overlooking Corpus Christi Bay, and 11,000 square feet of meeting space. Its indoor recreation facility includes a swimming pool, Jacuzzi, children's play area, and ping pong tables. With two onsite restaurants—the Sandpiper and Kokomo's Bar & Grille—Holiday Inn Emerald Beach offers casual dining in a relaxed atmosphere.

Holiday Inn Emerald Beach offers longevity and stability in an ever-changing industry. Many visitors stayed at the hotel 20 to 25 years ago and appreciate Holiday Inn's commitment to the property. America has grown up with Holiday Inn, which began in the 1950s as a place for families to stay while on vacation.

The Temple Inland Corporation, based in Diebold, Texas, purchased the hotel in 1969 and invited Holiday Inn to run it. The hotel is now independently owned by E.B. Holdings and operated by Talbert Hotel Corporation.

Holiday Inn Emerald Beach is close to business and leisure opportunities. It is a short drive to the Bayfront Plaza Convention Center, Texas State Aquarium, and U.S.S. *Lexington* Museum, while downtown shops, nightclubs, and restaurants are within walking distance.

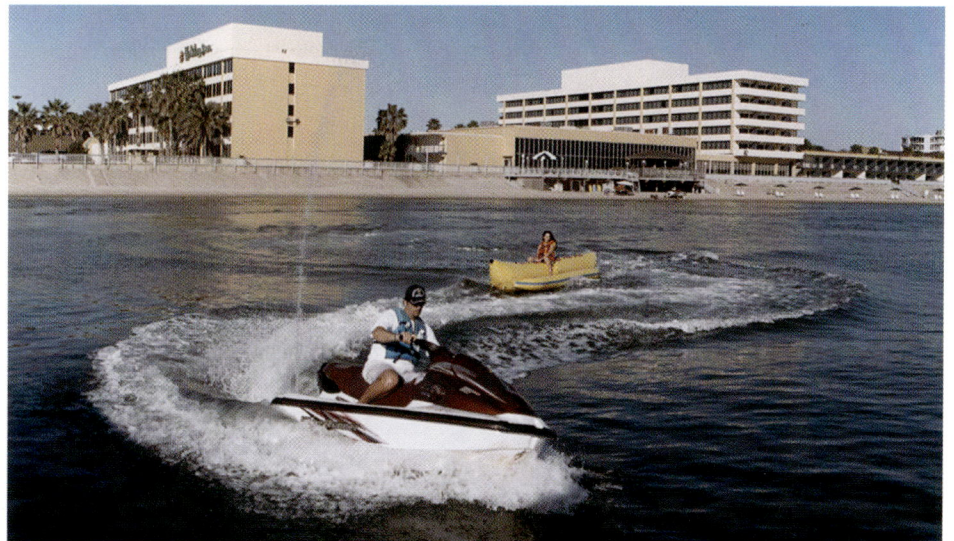

The Corpus Christi Marina is also a short walk away. There you can take a scenic harbor cruise or join a fishing party, and the historic Corpus Christi Seawall, adjacent to hotel property, is a popular place to walk, skate, or jog with the Corpus Christi Bay as a backdrop.

INMON
RESPIRATORY
SERVICES, INC.

INMON RESPIRATORY
SERVICES

❖

Above: Inmon Respiratory Services located at 4639 Corona, Suite 42 in Corpus Christi, Texas.

Below: Examples of medical equipment carried by Inmon Respiratory Services.

Coastal Bend residents in need of respiratory therapy and home medical equipment have come to rely on Inmon Respiratory Services. That's because this independently owned company, in business since 1997, offers the caring, personalized service that its corporate-owned competitors can't match.

Owners Gary Inmon, a registered respiratory therapist, and Stan Willson, a respiratory therapist and registered nurse, know how to meet the medical needs of clients and to operate the equipment their clients need to make their lives better.

Inmon, a registered respiratory therapist since 1986, has worked in both hospital and home care, while Willson, a respiratory therapist since 1995, has worked in hospital, home care and nursing homes. This experience in caring for clients has led to a compassionate, customer-centered business approach.

As a provider of Equipment Management Services, the company's primary objective is to promote, encourage, and support each patient's optimum use of prescribed home medical and respiratory therapy equipment and supplies. As a provider of Clinical Respiratory Services, the company's primary objective is to facilitate the movement of certain patients toward optimum self-management of their respective medical conditions through an established regimen of home respiratory care.

Clients, family members and primary caregivers receive the highest possible service as the company monitors, evaluates, and strives to improve performance in all aspects of its operation. Inmon Respiratory Services carries a wide array of home medical equipment, including hospital beds and wheelchairs, and provides oxygen, nebulizers, CPAP and BiPAP units and heavy-duty compressors to clients with breathing difficulties. Inmon Respiratory Services delivers equipment to many of its clients, and employs qualified technicians trained to set up and maintain equipment and to train clients in their use.

The company sells, rents, and services the latest in technologically advanced equipment. Inmon Respiratory Services focuses on providing top-notch service to its clients at the time it is needed. And because it's an independently owned business, the company isn't always driven by profit, allowing it to carry equipment and supplies that its competitors can't.

At Inmon Respiratory Services you'll get the caring, personalized service you deserve.

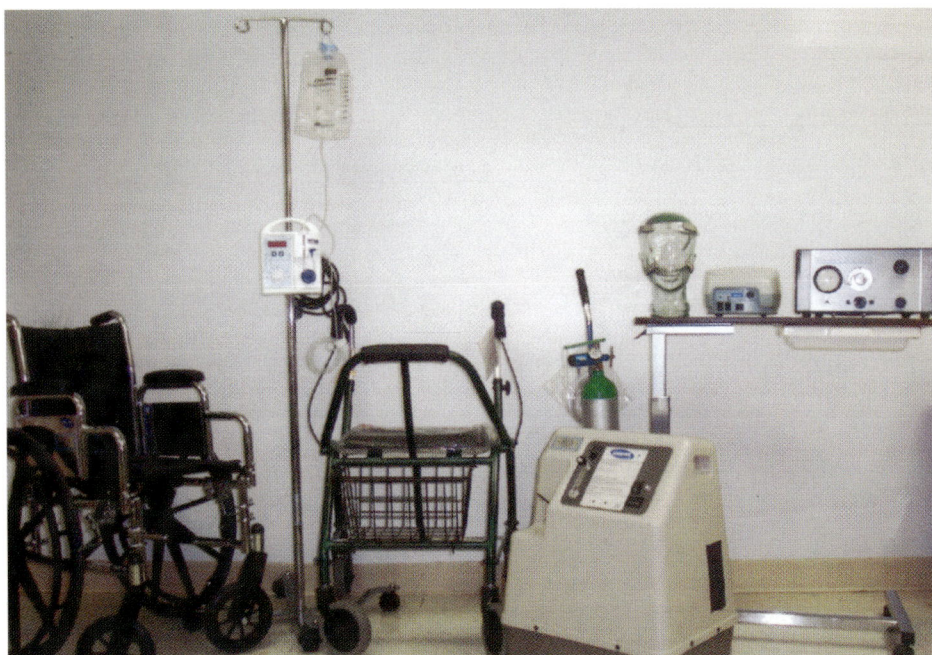

SONSHINE PHOTOS

January 1, 2000, heralded the arrival of the new millennium as well as the advent of Sonshine Photos, an inspirational photography business founded by longtime Corpus Christi resident Larry Weingartner.

It all began when Larry and his wife, Jane, went to Bob Hall Pier on Padre Island to watch the sun rise on the new millennium. There he took a series of five photographs with a thirty-five millimeter "Point-and-Shoot" Nikon camera.

Larry ordered an enlargement of the fifth photo as an anniversary present for his wife. Told of its significance, Larry took his photo to experts for appraisal.

His photo earned the copyright for the first sunrise of 2000 and first sunrise of the millennium, and Sonshine Photos was born.

Sonshine Photos is so-named because God's son, Jesus, shines in all our lives. God has given Larry an eye to see and photograph his creation in a way that inspires others.

God has also given Larry guidance and provided him with a peace that allows him to walk among deer and photograph them at close range. His skills in marketing have earned his photos placement in the Governor's Mansion, the White House, the Bush Presidential Library in College Station and the South Texas Institute for the Arts in Corpus Christi.

Corpus Christi Mayor Loyd Neal gave a framed print of the Millennium Sunrise to Barbara Bush to represent Corpus Christi and to thank her for her work with Driscoll Children's Hospital.

"Calming the Storm" hangs in the White House living quarters, and Larry's photo of the sun rising behind Kent Ullberg's sculpture "It is I" has represented Corpus Christi, Latin for "Body of Christ," in conventions from Florida to Canada.

"I am honored and blessed to take such a beautiful photo to represent the city I love," says Larry, who won his first camera in the second grade in a grand opening drawing.

His photos of the Christ statue, as well as photos of bluebonnets, butterflies, hummingbirds, shrimp boats, lighthouses and many others, can be found in gift shops and art shows throughout Texas.

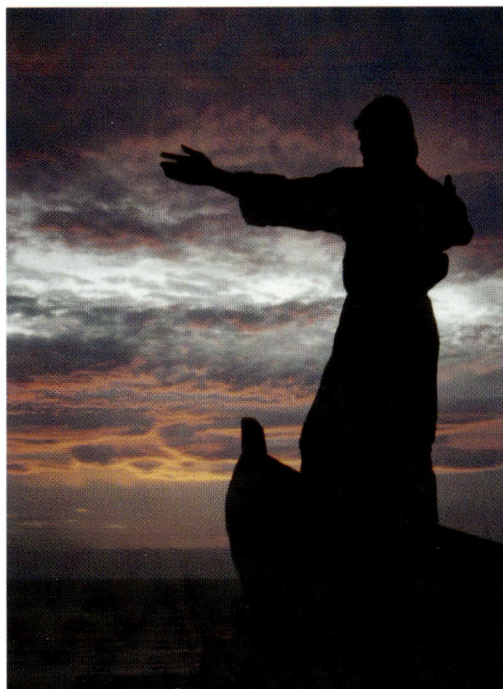

EDUCATION SERVICE CENTER, REGION 2

❖

Above: A view of ESC-2's facilities at 209 North Water Street.

Below: A view of the bayfront from ESC-2's third floor meeting facilities.

The Education Service Center, Region 2 (ESC-2) has provided quality services to school districts throughout 11 counties of the Texas Coastal Bend since 1967.

The organization's roots go back to 1965 when Congress passed Title III of the Elementary and Secondary Education Act, providing limited funding for instructional-related training and services for teachers. Two years later, the Texas Legislature established twenty centers, including ESC-2, to provide Title III funded services in Texas.

ESC-2 strives to be a catalyst for change resulting in student improvement and efficiency and economy of operation. It now serves 42 school districts, eight charter schools, about 108,000 students and 15,200 educators and staff in the Texas Coastal Bend.

In 1979 ESC-2 purchased the Fedway Department Store building and parking lot at 209 North Water Street, and recent renovations have expanded the center from 75,000 to 150,000 square feet. ESC-2 is organized around six departments designed to improve student achievement through relevant professional development for teachers, administrators, school board members, parents and other clientele.

The ESC-2 also helps schools implement state and regional initiatives, apply for grants, comply with federal programs and train district personnel in financial matters. It also provides data processing, Internet services and wide area network services, as well as support for data analysis, research development, evaluation and information dissemination to improve educational quality and effectiveness.

The ESC-2 offers more than eighty-five specific programs to assist school districts. These programs are highly specialized and relate to a full range of public education functions. The ESC-2 strives to help regional school districts obtain the best professional development opportunities and coordinated assistance in their quest for continued student and school improvement.

The ESC-2 seeks to proffer world-class services and products and envisions Region 2 schools achieving world-class status and comparability. The ESC-2 works with the Texas Education Agency and local education agencies, and has created partnerships with higher education institutions, educator organizations and government entities.

Associates at ESC-2 seek to live up to its vision: "World Class Service for World Class Schools."

Marion Luna Brem, president and chief executive officer founded Love Chrysler in Corpus Christi in August 1989, less than five years after she entered the auto profession as a salesperson.

Not only was Brem relatively new to the business, she also had been battling breast cancer while raising two sons on her own.

Love Chrysler opened with seven employees in a small facility in an out-of-the-way location. It didn't take long to outgrow its facilities by selling more vehicles than any previous Chrysler dealership in Corpus Christi.

By 1992 the dealership employed 60 people and had moved to larger, more accessible facilities on Staples Street. Love Chrysler has repeatedly received Chrysler's highest award known as the Five-Star Award for Excellence and has often occupied the number one spot in Texas by outselling every other Chrysler dealership in the state. In 1994, Love Chrysler Dodge Jeep was opened in Alice, Texas, and today, the two dealerships employ 120 people.

Love Chrysler, Inc. is ranked nationally in *Hispanic Business,* and in *Working Woman* magazine's top five hundred. Brem's inspirational story has been featured in the *Washington Post, Reader's Digest,* and *USA Today.* She has appeared on *The Oprah Winfrey Show,* Robert *Schuller's Hour of Power* and ABC's *Good Morning America.*

She is among forty women worldwide (ten from the United States) to be selected among the Leading Women Entrepreneurs of the World for 2001.

As one of the "100 Most Influential Hispanics in the United States" (according to Hispanic Business magazine's annual listing), Brem's philanthropic works include her fight against breast cancer and innovative programs to improve education.

With her two sons active in her business, she has started six additional companies, including an ad agency that produces Love's advertising and a real estate holding company. She is author of *The 7 Greatest Truths About Successful Women* (Penguin Putnam Publishers), ranked one of the top ten business books for 2001.

Love Chrysler in Corpus Christi and Love Chrysler Dodge Jeep in Alice under Brem's leadership operate under the winning philosophy that states: "Love keeps you going."

✧

Above: President/CEO and author Marion Luna Brem.

Below: Marion Luna Brem with her sons, Travis (right) and Brannon (left).

Aartron Communications, Inc.

Had it not been for the recession in the U.S. auto industry in the early 1980s, Aartron Communications, Inc. in Corpus Christi would never have been born.

Now more than twenty years old, Aartron Communications, which sells and services satellite systems for commercial and private clients, was created in the fall of 1982 by John Murphy and his sons, Terrance and Kelly.

John Murphy operated an air charter business in Pontiac, Michigan, that carried airfreight from all over the country back to the auto manufacturers. But the recession forced him to close down and move to Corpus Christi, where as a youngster, he had visited his uncle, Don Bibeau.

The Murphys began Aartron Communications, Inc., by selling and servicing two-way radios for the oil industry, then transitioned into satellite television systems when the Texas oil boom went bust.

Aartron Communications found a ready market for satellite television. People liked it because it was free and the broadcast was clear, features that eventually changed as broadcasters scrambled signals and charged fees.

As dish sales for the home market slowed, Aartron Communications broadened its base to include commercial systems for hotels, apartments, financial services companies and gas stations, which installed systems to speed credit card authorizations.

Over the past two decades, Aartron Communications has installed every type of satellite system; from the largest sixteen-foot satellite systems used by radio and television stations, to the eighteen-inch dishes seen on many homes today.

They also transmit and receive high-speed Internet service by satellite, a system that is ten times faster than conventional dial-up methods and doesn't tie up phone lines. The company has added satellite telephones to its list of products, a system that, for a small monthly fee, allows users with satellite Internet to call anywhere in the world.

Aartron Communications, Inc., has grown to own a Corpus Christi business and housing complex and works with customers nationwide that need satellite system installation and repair in South Texas.

As for the future of Aartron Communications, Inc., which can be seen at www.aartron.com the company will stay on top of technological developments, providing South Texans with the latest in high-tech products and service.

MENTAL
HEALTH &
MENTAL
RETARDATION
CENTER OF
NUECES
COUNTY

The Mental Health & Mental Retardation Center of Nueces County has provided treatment and support for children and adults with mental illness, mental retardation or developmental disabilities since 1969.

Its mission is to promote independence and inclusion in the community by providing responsive and supportive services, valuing individual strengths, and working with consumers for their greatest independence.

Authorized under state law in 1965, the Corpus Christi City Council and Nueces County Commissioners Court entered into a sponsoring agreement that established the MHMR Center of Nueces County in 1969.

The center began with two employees and a $229,000 budget, which grew to more than 300 people and more than $17 million in 2002.

Throughout its existence, the MHMR Center of Nueces County has adapted to changing treatment strategies and community needs. It serves Nueces County residents who are children under age 4 with developmental disabilities; youth ages 3 to 17 with severe emotional disturbance; individuals with mental retardation, autism, or pervasive developmental disorders; and adults with severe and persistent mental illness.

The MHMR Center of Nueces County provides an array of community-based services from 17 Corpus Christi locations. In fiscal year 2001, the center spent more than $16 million on services to 3,328 mental health consumers and 547 mental retardation consumers.

Services include screening and assessment, service coordination, residential living, respite, foster care, housing and employment assistance, skills training, medication management, counseling and vocational training. Services are provided at the center, at schools, in clients' homes and various places in the community.

Some sixty percent of its funding comes from the state, with the majority of the remaining balance drawn from Medicaid. All fees are charged on a sliding scale based upon family income and size. No eligible Nueces County resident is refused service due to an inability to pay.

The center is committed to continuous improvement, personal and professional integrity and public service. It is accredited by the Joint Commission on Accreditation of Healthcare Organizations and is governed by a nine-member board and three advisory committees made up of clients, family members, advocates, and community representatives.

The center is dedicated to developing an environment that inspires and promotes innovation, fosters dynamic leadership, and rewards creativity among its staff, volunteers, and the individuals it serves.

CITY OF CORPUS CHRISTI GAS DEPARTMENT

Above: Employees of Corpus Christi Gas Department in 1999.

Below: A work crew making a two-inch extension on the 900 block of Mohawk, Corpus Christi, Texas, c. 1950.

The City of Corpus Christi Gas Department has provided Corpus Christi and neighboring customers inexpensive, safe, and dependable natural gas since 1922.

On August 4, 1922, the City of Corpus Christi elected officials took steps to build a natural gas distribution system to provide natural gas at reasonable rates to attract people and businesses to the city.

This process included a $350,000 revenue bond issue approved by voters on March 9, 1923, allowing the city to purchase natural gas and provide service to residents through a variety of franchise agreements with various transmission companies.

Through the years, the City of Corpus Christi Gas Department has sought to acquire inexpensive, dependable supplies of natural gas from various providers through an array of negotiated contracts.

After major annexations in the early 1960s, the city purchased the Houston Natural Gas Corporation and Southern Community Gas Company, and formed the Corpus Christi Municipal Gas Corporation. Years later, the City of Corpus Christi Gas Department bought out the Corpus Christi Municipal Gas Corporation.

Today, the Gas Department serves the city, as well as a few areas immediately outside the city limits, in a 180-square-mile area. This area extends 40 miles from northwest Calallen to Padre Island, and includes 1,239 miles of service lines.

The gas system serves more than fifty-five thousand customers. Ninety four percent are residential and the rest are commercial and industrial accounts.

The gas system now receives all of its supply from National Energy and Trade, L.L.C., with approximately eighty-five percent delivered to the city through three principal city gate stations. The rest flows through four smaller purchase points to serve the Annaville/Calallen System, the Padre Island System and the Country Creek/King Estates System.

The gas system consists of around 1,125 miles of coated steel mains of various sizes up to 16 inches (all under cathodic protection) and 125 miles of polyethylene mains. The Gas Department normally installs 10 to 15 miles of main each year, including the replacement of 1 to 3 miles of main.

After more than eighty years of safe, dependable natural gas service, the City of Corpus Christi Gas Department continues to serve its customers with the same reliable source of energy that flows uninterrupted to its many destinations within the city.

In September of 1955, Woo Sung Lee left Korea for the United States. He arrived in Corpus Christi, Texas as a student sponsored by the late Dr. W. A. Miller, president of the University of Corpus Christi and received a tuition scholarship. The university was relatively new, built after World War II with Navy Surplus buildings.

Lee faced the problem of having only $506, which was the maximum amount allowed by the Korean government for airfare from Seoul to Los Angeles. He had to exchange some money in the black market at a higher rate for the flight from Los Angeles to Corpus Christi and to pay for his room and board at the university.

After he paid for his room and board, most of the money he brought was spent. He had to look for a job and walked the streets looking for employment for several months. His shoes had holes and he had no socks; he could not afford a haircut for three months; Christmas vacation that year was spent eating raw eggs in the dormitory.

Lee had to wait for the first semester to end before he could apply for the Korean government's permission to allow his parents to send him the permitted amount of money. Once he received permission, his parents sent him some money every month while he worked school days to help defray the cost of his room and board. During the summer vacation he would hitchhike from Corpus Christi to Oregon and Washington State to find employment.

Earning money was tough, but harder for him to bear was the statement, on the first day of registration, by the business manager at the university, who asked him, "With only this money are you going to graduate?" Since he had never had a financial problem in Korea, he cried for the first time in his life with the tears coming down like rain on his cheeks.

Lee, while a student, also faced another problem. He had to face discrimination. In Corpus Christ at that time, there were not many Asians, and it was more than 10 years before he met another Korean. He faced unfair treatment in several of his classes from his professors. To this day, he still feels badly about this treatment but is beginning to understand why this happened. In one example, he relates an anecdote in which the teacher told him he had a C+ in class while all

BOAT 'N NET, INC.

✧

Woo Sung Lee

the other students had A's. Lee had made 100% on all the weekly tests, completed his homework on time and solved all the problems correctly on the blackboard. The teacher advised Lee that he should not copy the other students' homework, while Lee could not believe what he was hearing. Lee earned his Bachelor of Science degree from the University of Corpus Christi.

He realized that the only way to succeed would be to open his own business. He began the first fast food restaurant in 1961 by renting an empty Tastee Freeze building on Port Avenue. He cleaned it for three months rent-free and bought a used fryer for $25.00. He paid $5.00 down, and $5.00 weekly to pay it off. On the first day of business at Boat 'N Net, he had less than $10.00 in sales, and the following Friday about $50.00. Customers had to wait nearly 30 minutes since he had to cook shrimp, fish, chicken, and French fries in one fryer.

He was not making any money at that time, only sustaining his living. Currently, he has 10 stores in Corpus Christi and the surrounding area. He is planning to begin new Boat 'N Nets in San Antonio, McAllen, Edinburg, Alice, Beeville, and two others in Corpus Christi. Because of the challenges throughout his life, he has a continuous drive to succeed in business and to expand future operations.

STRATEGIC MANAGEMENT SOLUTIONS, INC.

✧

Above: Jane Herring Stanford, Ph.D.

Jane Herring Stanford, Ph.D., a native South Texan and longtime educator, brings her lifelong passion for learning and teaching to her latest educational endeavor—Strategic Management Solutions, Inc.

Strategic Management Solutions is a management consulting firm specializing in strategic planning, organizational processes, and learning. Continual workforce education and organizational development are keys to organizational success. To help meet these needs, Strategic Management Solutions delivers customized learning services and tools to South Texas profit and nonprofit organizations.

An avid believer in education and a supporter of South Texas educational programs and institutions, Stanford is proof of the importance of continuing education as well as practical experience.

Following her graduation with a bachelor's degree, Stanford taught for several years at Miller High School in Corpus Christi. She returned to college to earn a master's degree in counseling, an M.B.A. in management and a doctorate in management from the University of North Texas in Denton. She also developed practical experience in the business world by starting and managing her own business and helping to manage her husband's oilfield service company.

She taught for many years as a tenured, full-time faculty member at Texas A&M University at Kingsville, and is an adjunct professor of management at Texas A&M University-Corpus Christi, College of Business, and a member of the graduate faculty. She is active in the community and a graduate of Leadership Corpus Christi Class XXX.

Now, as president and principal consultant of Strategic Management Solutions, also known by its website address of www.planyourbiz.com, Stanford provides a variety of services and products designed to improve your business or organization.

Strategic Management Solutions will:
- Develop processes that will become solid infrastructures for strategic-planning activities;
- Align organizational structures to these processes;
- Provide workshops tailored to particular organizational needs in strategic planning;
- Provide workshops on organizational structure, development, change and leadership from graduate level to basic;
- Provide free, email evaluation of the strategic planning process based on a questionnaire offered on the website.

The company also offers a newsletter and guidebooks and disks entitled "Key to Success Learning."

Stanford's long-range objectives include consulting on employee training and development needs, advising organizations on the best training sources and developing and initiating an assessment center.

The assessment center would help organizations identify employees' training and development needs and evaluate potential employees using work sampling and performance simulation tests.

The Strategic Management process Benefits Your Organization with:
- Visioning
- Objective Setting
- Planning Strategically
- Implementing
- Assessing Outcomes
- Then the dynamic cycle begins again......

The *future* of your organization depends on the decisions you make *now!*

PlanYourBiz.com®

Strategic Management
Planning Processes for the New Millennium

Jane Herring Stanford, Ph.D.
Member, Institute of Management Consultants (IMC)

In any organization, profit or not-for-profit, large or small- the act of planning "Strategically" is to:
- Collect data from internal & external
- Analyze and interpret this information
- Diagnose strengths and weaknesses
- Evaluate the current competitive position
- Decide on plans (strategies) that can:
  - achieve objectives
  - build competitiveness
- Implement these plans (strategies)